Hispanic Elderly
in
Transition

Hispanic Elderly in Transition

Theory, Research, Policy and Practice

EDITED BY
Steven R. Applewhite

CONTRIBUTIONS TO THE STUDY OF AGING,
NUMBER 9

GREENWOOD PRESS
NEW YORK • WESTPORT, CONNECTICUT • LONDON

To my parents, who taught me the meaning of caring:
Juanita Amparo Applewhite–Lozano
Jesse Edward Applewhite Jr. (November 16, 1902—April 19, 1976)

Library of Congress Cataloging-in-Publication Data

Hispanic elderly in transition : theory, research, policy, and
  practice / edited by Steven R. Applewhite.
      p.   cm.—(Contributions to the study of aging, ISSN
0732-085X ; no. 9)
    Bibliography: p.
    Includes index.
    ISBN 0-313-24478-2 (lib. bdg. : alk. paper)
    1. Hispanic American aged—Services for. 2. Hispanic American
aged—Social conditions. I. Applewhite, Steven R. II. Series.
  HV1461.H57   1988
  362.6'0896873—dc19   87-37563

British Library Cataloguing in Publication Data is available.

Library of Congress Catalog Card Number: 87-37563
ISBN: 0-313-24478-2
ISSN: 0732-085X

First published in 1988

Greenwood Press, Inc.
88 Post Road West, Westport, Connecticut 06881

Printed in the United States of America

The paper used in this book complies with the
Permanent Paper Standard issued by the National
Information Standards Organization (Z39.48-1984).

10 9 8 7 6 5 4 3 2 1

CONTENTS

TABLES AND FIGURES

TABLES

FIGURES

INTRODUCTION: ADDRESSING THE ISSUES

The focus of this book is on aging and the aged from the Hispanic elderly perspective. It takes as its point of departure the view that while the Hispanic elderly share common experiences with the total elderly population, life circumstances and opportunities are substantially different when mediated by social class and ethnicity.

The diversity in the Hispanic community is exhibited by the distinct communities of Mexican, Puerto Rican, Cuban, and other Spanish-origin groups. Further distinctions exist within these subgroups based on self-identification (e.g., Latinos, Mexicanos, etc.), region, language/dialect, origin or descent, and level of acculturation, to mention only a few. Therefore, the emphasis on diversity in this book also serves to distinguish degrees of difference between Hispanic and non-Hispanic elderly as well as to examine conditions specific to the Hispanic elderly.

The primary goal of this book is to offer a contextual overview of Hispanic aging—ranging from complex issues and questions to tentative answers. We shall examine health, economic, social, and cultural issues influencing the quality of life of older Hispanics in the United States. Above all else, the guiding assumption of this book is that Hispanic elderly are in transition—serving as links to the past, yet adapting to the present and shaping the future.

The idea for this volume originated primarily as a result of my constant search for a suitable book on Hispanic aging for graduate and undergraduate students and practitioners interested in learning more about ethnic variations in aging. More substantive motives were my introspection and dialogue with other gerontologists and practitioners over the years regarding Hispanic circumstances and quality-of-life issues. Each person stressed the need for a collection of original essays exploring a plethora of broadly defined issues, trends, and prospects facing the Hispanic elderly.

This book differs from others on minority aging in at least two important respects. First, the essays are integrated in such a fashion that each chapter builds on each other, chapters are bound by current themes and perspectives, and presented with options and recommendations. From each author the lessons gained from working with the elderly or conducting research serve to create a foundation and spirit for working with Hispanic elderly in various settings. For those pursuing careers in gerontology, or seeking to enhance their knowledge of different cultures, or simply coming to grips with issues in later life, this book may be of help.

Second, as the themes unfold the reader is challenged with essays covering various topics, ranging from comprehensive analyses of health and sociopolitical issues to brief descriptive accounts of community life experiences and case studies, and in three chapters, theoretical paradigms and practice models.

The Hispanic elderly are a diverse population experiencing rapid and widespread growth. In 1980 the Census Bureau estimated that there were slightly more than 14 million Hispanics in the United States. This population constitutes approximately 6.4 percent of the total population and has experienced a 61 percent increase since 1970. The bureau's population estimates in March 1983 were 15.9 million, representing an increase of 1.9 million. However, the figures in this section are based on the 1980 census rather than the provisional independent estimates provided by the bureau for 1983.

Since the Hispanic population is relatively young, there is a lower proportion in the older age groups. Of the total Hispanic population, 4.9 percent are 65 years old and over. Among Mexican elderly, 4.2 percent are over 65 compared to 3.6 percent for Puerto Ricans. Interestingly enough, the Cubans are the oldest group; for example, the median age is 38 years while 14.8 percent of all Cubans are over 65. These older Cubans are immigrants who left Cuba in the early 1960s to enter the United States. Only 1.8 percent of all Hispanics were 75 years old and over (U.S. Bureau of the Census, 1987).

Torres-Gil (1981) notes that from 1975 to 1980, the Hispanic elderly population 60 years and over experienced a dramatic growth—nearly 2.5 times that of the remaining Hispanic population (25 percent v. 9 percent), and twice the rate for non-Hispanics in the same age group (25 percent v. 10 percent). Even more impressive was the increase in the 65 and over age group, that grew by 34 percent during this period. Other significant issues remain to be addressed, such as educational characteristics, employment and occupations, health statistics, income and poverty status; however, major attention will be given to these areas in later chapters.

This volume consists of five parts. Part 1 introduces the reader to theoretical perspectives in gerontology, social work, and demography. Attention is given to defining culture, human behavior, and the social environment. Chapter 1 focuses on cross-cultural perspectives in social work practice with Hispanic elderly. Minority group membership is examined and a service perspective for practitioners is elaborated. Chapter 2 provides a historical and sociodemographic overview of elderly Puerto Ricans in the United States. An insightful discussion of the differences in conceptualization between elderly men and women and their effect on patterns of interaction provides the reader with different perspectives on the use of supportive networks and family expectation.

Part 2 (chapters 3 and 4) provides an extensive overview of the health status of the Hispanic elderly population of the southwestern United States. General mortality statistics for 1970 and 1980 are provided, followed by interview data on physical health. Also covered is the nature of the demand for health and human services, including determinant parameters of accessibility and utilization of services by Hispanic elderly.

Part 3 describes interest group politics, policy and income maintenance, and the Hispanic elderly. Chapter 5 begins with a comprehensive analysis of the role of older Hispanics as a developing interest group in the United States. The effects of empowerment of the elderly on the family, politics, and senior citizen interest groups is explored. In addition, evolutionary changes and transitional periods set the stage for viewing new roles in politics and their potential influence for change. Chapter 6 deals with social legislation and the impact of aging policies on the traditional support networks of the Hispanic elderly. The limits of social policy, eligibility barriers, and impacts of social policies are analyzed across various programs, such as the Old Age Assistance Program, the Older Americans Act, Social Security, and Medicare and Medicaid. Taking the analysis one step further, chapter 7 carefully examines the American stratification system and income adequacy as a variable inseparable from social class, power, and prestige. Differentials in labor force participation and analysis of income maintenance programs provide the framework for looking at future trends and income prospects for the Hispanic elderly.

Part 4 focuses on the family, the barrio, and natural support systems. Chapter 8 deals with the role of the elderly in Hispanic extended families and multigenerational family relationships. Intervention considerations with Hispanic elderly and their families is discussed in the context of a family model and case study. Chapter 9 introduces the reader to the complex phenomenon of the barrio. Four views of the barrio are presented that offer insight and make valuable contributions to a broader understanding of barrio life for the elderly. In chapter 10 the problems facing the Chicano rural elderly are examined in terms of their natural helping networks and their help-seeking behavior. Social systems theory is used to describe distinct force fields in the Hispanic elderly's environment and their positive impact.

Part 5 presents different research and marketing perspectives. Chapter 11 is based on a descriptive study of age- and gender-linked norms among Mexican,

Puerto Rican, and Cuban elderly women. Gender-linked sanctions, sex appropriate behavior, and the pursuit of realism constitute the major findings of this chapter. Chapter 12 details the ethnography of Hispanic aging and also provides the reader with a well-defined series of steps to guide ethnographic investigation. Chapter 13 presents a cultural analysis of death and dying in a selected Hispanic enclave in northern New Mexico. A cultural-historical perspective provides a naturalistic view of life and death in rural areas. Broader questions of attitudes toward life and death, familial and communal influences, and the impact of modernization are examined. For readers who view Hispanics and the elderly as the market of the future, the final chapter provides a provocative view of mass media, telecommunications, and the Hispanic elderly. Developments in the field of cable and telecommunications are presented as issues and opportunities for Hispanic elderly consumers of Spanish television.

Throughout this volume an attempt has been made to integrate critical concepts and valid statements without entering into polemics. One thing is certain: the Hispanic elderly population will continue to grow at a remarkable rate along with the general population. Within Hispanic communities major changes may occur as the elderly assume pivotal roles in all aspects of life. At the broader community and national level, others may benefit from the greater involvement of Hispanic elderly.

REFERENCES

U.S. Bureau of the Census (1987). The Hispanic Population in the United States: March 1986 and 1987 (Advance Report). *Current population reports* (Series P-20. no. 416). Superintendent of Documents, U.S. Government Printing Office, Washington, D.C.

Torres-Gil, F. (1981) Policy issues affecting older Hispanics: Implications for the 1981 White House Conference on Aging. In P. Vivo & C. D. Votaw (Eds.), *The Hispanic Elderly La Fuente de Nuestra Historia, Cultura y Carino* (pp. 3–14). Rockville, MD: Public Health Service, U.S. Department of Health and Human Services. pp. 3–14.

U.S. Department of Commerce, Bureau of the Census. (1983). *Conditions of Hispanics in America today.* Washington, DC: U.S. Government Printing Office.

U.S. Department of Health and Human Services, Human Development Services, Administration on Aging. (1981). Characteristics of the Hispanic elderly. *Statistical reports on older Americans.* Washington, DC: U.S. Government Printing Office.

Part I

CULTURAL, HISTORICAL AND SOCIODEMOGRAPHIC OVERVIEW

CROSS-CULTURAL UNDERSTANDING FOR SOCIAL WORK PRACTICE WITH THE HISPANIC ELDERLY

Steven R. Applewhite and John M. Daley

INTRODUCTION

Historically social work has recognized and served the needs of disenfranchised segments of society. Since the turn of the century, social work has developed into a specialized profession with humanistic values, a knowledge base focusing on the interaction of the individual with the social environment, a set of methods, and specific social functions. These functions include the restoration of impaired social functioning, provision of social and individual resources, and prevention of social dysfunction. Skidmore and Thackery define social work as "an art, a science, a profession which helps people to solve personal, group (especially family), and community problems. . . . Social work not only helps people to solve problems, but also assists them to prevent problems and enrich daily living" (1964, p. 8).

Social work practice incorporates into its mission the needs of the elderly in America. The elderly, perhaps more than any other segment of society, have drawn increasing attention due to the size of this group and its immense problems, most notably economic vulnerability and chronic illness. A host of other problems such as poor housing, limited social resources, alienation, and the multiple discriminatory effects of ageism also impact heavily on the elderly. These circumstances are compounded for those aged who are members of ethnic and racial minority groups. The minority aging experience thus represents the cumulative effects of problems facing all aged in America compounded by problems experienced by ethnic group members, including markedly lower income levels, lower life expectancies, language barriers, and the harmful residual effects of a lifetime of institutional victimization and discrimination.

Social work and other helping professions have evolved in response to emerging human needs. In order to address the needs of minority elderly, practitioners must know about the people who are to be served, their social conditions, needs, and problems in a cross-cultural environment, and the various methods of intervention that are applicable to the minority elderly. (For a discussion of culturally sensitive practice, see Miranda & Kitano, 1986; Lum, 1986; Devore & Schlesinger, 1981.)

To work effectively with the Hispanic elderly, helping professionals must appreciate cultural influences at two levels: the client's culturally defined behavior in specific environmental contexts (e.g., the family, the workplace, the church, the neighborhood); and the client's culturally defined behavior within the professional intervention process (Olmstead, 1983; Newton & Arciniega, 1983). The helping professional needs to understand how these aged order and give meaning to their life experiences, including their interactions with helping professionals and human service systems.

This chapter briefly describes selected characteristics of the Hispanic elderly, discusses the influences of cultural factors on their life conditions, and suggests a few practical considerations for professionals seeking to work with the Hispanic aged. Although a thorough review of the emerging literature on the Hispanic elderly is beyond the scope of this chapter, the reader will find recommended literature that promises to inform effective interventions. Despite impressive efforts by an expanding group of scholars who seek to enhance professionals' understanding of the Hispanic elderly, contemporary literature may be characterized as being at an early stage of development, with broad gaps in the knowledge base.

THE RICH DIVERSITY
AMONG THE HISPANIC ELDERLY

The study of aging has traditionally been viewed in terms of universal concepts and their applications for minority elderly. Historically the assumptions have been that most elderly experience similar aging processes and problems. Neither race, ethnicity, nor social class were given great importance (Bengtson, 1977). Today, however, it is recognized that social, economic, and cultural group status affects actual life conditions, behavior, expectations, and goals. Within this context, the traditions, life conditions, needs, and aspirations of an extremely diverse group, the Hispanic elderly, must be incorporated into the corpus of gerontological theory and practice.

Human service professionals need to be aware of the rich diversity of peoples within this group. Further, professionals need to locate or position individuals and groups they seek to serve within this broad Hispanic elderly population. Specific individuals and groups may to a large degree share many characteristics, life experiences, needs, and aspirations with other Hispanic elderly. At the same time, each individual and group will have unique "common sense knowledge" and distinct perspectives that must be considered if the professional is to understand fully the manner in which Hispanic elderly define, constitute, and order reality.

The authors of the various chapters in this book have taken great care to identify the specific subpopulations dealt with in their essays. The reader needs to be equally careful about generalizing from one subpopulation to another. In some instances, generalizations are valid. In other situations, the transferability of propositions about one group to another would have limited utility or might even be harmful. A key task in the development of a better knowledge base for understanding the Hispanic elderly will be to identify those propositions that are valid about a specific subpopulation under specific conditions and those that apply across subgroups—common traditions, life conditions, needs, life tasks and goals among the Hispanic elderly. A number of factors distinguish one subgroup of Hispanic elderly from other subgroups.

Ethnic Variations Among Hispanic Elderly

Hispanic elderly in the United States differ by country and region of origin, dialect, culture and degree of acculturation/assimilation, socioeconomic class, educational level, political ideology, and philosophical and sociohistorical perspectives, to mention only a few dimensions. The Hispanic elderly thus exemplify the diversity that exists among the total elderly population.

1. The Hispanic elderly have been identified and identify themselves as *Latinos*, Hispanic, Chicano, *Puerto Riquenos, Cubanos, Mexicanos, Nortenos, Mestizo*, Spanish, Latin American, or Spanish American. Identification (including self-identification) may change through time and often reflects geographical, historical and political influences.

2. The current Hispanic elderly cohort grew up during a pre-civil rights era that was characterized by overt institutional and systemic discrimination and prejudice, particularly in the Southwest. Yet people may hold political views ranging from conservative to liberal, with some individuals politically active and others inactive.

3. The Hispanic elderly share many cultural values and experiences, yet they differ in degree of acculturation, assimilation, and cultural awareness. Many elderly reflect Mexican, Cuban, or Puerto Rican traditional attitudes, others dominant culture (U.S.) attitudes.

4. The Hispanic elderly have developed varying resources and other coping skills both individually and as members of groups and communities.

5. The Hispanic elderly vary in language proficiency, ranging from either Spanish or English dominance to bilingualism.

6. Individuals migrated from specific regions or states of Mexico, Cuba, Puerto Rico, and South and Central America at various periods in history for reasons including economic, sociopolitical, and ideological differences.

7. The Hispanic elderly include the affluent and the impoverished; the highly educated and the illiterate; the young/active elderly and the older frail elderly.

Professionals working with members of this group need to appreciate this diversity and locate individuals within this complex, psycho-socio-cultural-historical-political-economic map. This map is composed of a number of overlaying maps. To serve effectively, the professional must learn how to read the multiple map overlays with sensitivity to both common elements within the group and individual variations that characterize the human spirit.

GROUP CHARACTERISTICS
OF THE HISPANIC ELDERLY

Demographics

The Current Population Survey (CPS) of the U.S. Bureau of the Census (1987) provides data for the total Spanish-origin population and its subcategories: Mexican, Puerto Rican, Cuban, Central or South American, and other Spanish origin. There are an estimated 18.8 million Hispanics in the United States, with 11.8 million of Mexican origin, 2.3 million of Puerto Rican origin, and 1.0 million of Cuban origin, with the balance comprised of Central, South American, or other Hispanic origin.[1] The elderly (those 65 years of age and older) represent approximately 5 percent, nearly 921,200 of the total Hispanic population in the United States (U.S. Bureau of the Census, 1987).

In the United States, Mexican-American elderly live primarily in five southwestern states (California, Texas, New Mexico, Arizona, and Colorado). The majority of Puerto Rican elderly live in New York, the eastern seaboard, or the Commonwealth of Puerto Rico. Cubans reside primarily in Dade County, Florida (U.S. Bureau of the Census, 1985).

Economic and Educational Status

Poverty is common among the Hispanic elderly. Twenty-six percent of elderly Hispanics live below the poverty level, twice the rate of poverty experienced by elderly whites. Median personal income for Hispanic men over 65 years of age is $4592 compared to $7408 for white males, and $2873 for Hispanic elderly women compared to $3894 for white elderly women (American Association of Retired Persons, n.d.). Lacayo (1981) adds that low income levels are attributed largely to the markedly low educational attainment for aged Hispanics: nearly 45 percent of all elderly Hispanics are functionally illiterate. The proportion with no formal schooling is eight times as great as for whites.

Of Hispanics 65 years and older, 16 percent have had no education and 64 percent have less than a fifth grade education (American Association of Retired Persons, n.d.; Lacayo, 1981). Addressing the members of the House Select Committee on Aging, Lacayo (1981) concluded:

Some people say that the 1980's will be "the decade of the Hispanics" because we may become the second largest minority group in the United States by 1995.

This positive and upbeat theme, however, seems cruel and ironic when we examine closely the life of a Spanish-origin person in the United States today. This is certainly true for the aged Hispanic population, which includes some of the most economically and educationally deprived persons in the United States. (p. 64)

History

Spicer's (1971) analysis of ethnic terminology and its meaning notes that historical experiences are vital elements of an ethnic group's identity system. Distinctive historical experiences, whether positive or negative, serve as focal points for understanding ethnic group membership. Within this context, Korte (1981) aptly states:

Distinct histories, such as those of Spanish speaking people who lived for more than 400 years in the upper Rio Grande drainage in Northern New Mexico and Southern Colorado, or histories of those people who settled the lower Rio Grande Valley in Texas or for those who migrated to California and Arizona during and after the Mexican Revolution, have had their influence on these generations now considered elderly. (p. 7)

In a similar vein, Cuellar's (1977) concept of aging along three dimensions (maturational aging, historical aging, and generational cohort aging) emphasizes the significance of sociohistorical events and shared experiences for explaining the Hispanic elderly's perceptual framework.

A discussion of history must also take into account the Hispanic elderly's patterns of interaction within the larger social environment. Such concepts as manifest destiny, the Protestant work ethic, Social Darwinism, and rugged individualism are historical-philosophical views that greatly affected both the larger society's perceptions of Hispanics and the Hispanic elderly's personal frame of reference and subjective perceptions of life in the United States. Individual life-styles of the Hispanic elderly were formed with constant adjustments to the dominant culture. The Hispanic elderly today represent a pre-civil rights population, who endured discrimination, alienation, cultural affronts, and social, cultural, or sociocultural dislocation (De Hoyos et al., 1986).[2]

Language and Support Systems

The Spanish language is the common thread that unites the national Hispanic community. A majority (58 percent) of Mexican-American elderly were born in Mexico and immigrated to the United States (Maldonado, 1979). Almost 60 percent of elderly Hispanics are either Spanish dominant or of limited English-speaking proficiency (Lacayo, 1980).

The language factor remains a bonding element within natural support systems. Yet language can be seen as a double-edged sword. The lack of English proficiency has posed a barrier in communicating in a larger social context as well as established distance between the older generation and the younger Hispanic cohort whose preference may be English.

The Spanish language has enabled the elderly to retain a sense of their past and maintain a "persistent identity system" (Spicer, 1971). The dominant language shapes in significant ways the structure of how the person conceptualizes; language reflects culture and influences personal interaction.

Language is a critical factor in the maintenance and transmission of culture. The elderly thus represent the bond across several generations. The Hispanic elderly are repositories of history, tradition, and values. They generally occupy a highly respected and secure role within Hispanic family support systems. However, Maldonado (1979) and Mirande (1977) and other investigators suggest that the automatic guarantees of emotional support in multigenerational households may be threatened as the matriarchal and patriarchal roles of the elderly in extended family structures are slowly abandoned. Barrera adds that readily accessible support systems of kin and kith relationships may not necessarily lead to "actual support or satisfaction with these social ties" (Barrera, 1980, p. 128).

According to Gratton (1987), more recent studies suggest that two major determinants have affected extended family support systems for Mexican-American elderly. First, the traditional extended family system has largely been impacted by industrialization, urbanization, and the welfare state (Gratton, 1987) leading investigators to believe that perhaps solidarity and reciprocity are a myth among Mexican-American families (Mindel, 1985). Second, increases in institutionalization and entitlement programs have resulted in decreases in extended family aid to Hispanic elderly (Mindel, 1985; Becerra, 1983).

These two factors are presumed to have impacted heavily on the elderly. Such new findings may be preliminary but critical. Therefore cautious and careful examination of the issues is necessary in order to reduce the risk of overgeneralizing or substituting one myth with another.

Culture, Norms, and Values

Perhaps the most common fault of the helping professions has been their failure to fully recognize and accept social behavior patterns that differ markedly from those of the dominant culture. This stems from the fact that society has established social norms that prescribe expected and acceptable behavior in socially defined positions. Departure from these norms often result in negative sanctions (Beaver, 1983).

To understand minority group status, one must first define culture, norms, and values. Linton (1945) defines culture as "the configuration of learned behavior and results of behavior whose components and elements are shared and transmitted by the members of the particular society" (Atkinson, Morten, & Sue, 1983, p. 5). Mehr (1986) defines norms as "standards of behavior that are maintained by individuals and groups . . . usually (some would say always) determined by the referent group to which one belongs and to which one is accepted" (p. 87). Values may be class and culture bound, stemming primarily from one's accumulated experience, and include attitudes, beliefs, and customs, constituting class and cultural differences or integral parts of the group's social structure (Padilla, Ruiz, & Alvarez, 1975; Mehr, 1986).

When norms and values of a subculture differ from the majority culture, social sanctions as well as labeling or coercive measures have often been imposed on the group or individual to bring about expected behavior (Beaver, 1983). In counseling, Sue and Sue (1977) state that helping relationships and therapy traditionally are viewed as attempting to change individuals whose ideas, beliefs, and behaviors differ from the majority group's. Thus cultural differences and the consequences of cultural dissonance demand of the professional cultural sensitivity, awareness, and cross-cultural affectivity (Montalvo, 1986).

For example, a caseworker working with an Hispanic elderly client may expect a high level of self-disclosure about a range of problems, attitudes, values, and feelings during the initial phases of the helping process. The elderly Hispanic may define a high degree of self-disclosure under these conditions as culturally unacceptable. The result may be confusion, alienation, and frustration on the elder's part and possibly lead to the caseworker labeling the client as uncooperative or resistant. While the middle class values verbal disclosure of emotionally loaded topics, this disclosure may be inappropriate for many minority individuals who come from a background that values restraint of strong feeling, low level of disclosure, or subtleness in approaching problems, especially with individuals who are relatively unknown (Sue & Sue, 1977). Padilla et al. (1975) add that language barriers, class and culture bound values, often differ between client and therapist and result in an "intrinsic culture conflict" ultimately leading to professional misjudgment.

Ethnic and Social Class Identity

For the elderly Hispanic, ethnic self-identity means an understanding of one's culture and the relationship one has with others within the culture and others from different cultures. Maldonado (1975a) states that as the individual relates to his or her own culture, and recognizes that differences exist between cultures, a more conscious understanding and acceptance of one's own culture, as well as other cultures, may develop.

In a similar vein, Devore and Schlesinger (1981, p. 6) add that "the intersect of ethnicity and social class, what Gordon (1973) has termed ethclass, converge to generate identifiable dispositions and the behaviors . . . the *ethnic reality* of ethclass in action." Thus for Hispanic elderly, the effects of ethnic and social class membership is particularly significant in describing relationships and the "sense of peoplehood" associated with it (Gordon, 1964, p. 28).

Self-Concept

Like the elderly in general, older Hispanics view themselves positively (Lacayo, 1980). However, self-concepts often relate to how one feels about old age, which in turn is influenced by one's health. According to a national study of Hispanic aged in America, many Hispanics report their health conditions as fair to poor (Lacayo, 1980). Their perceived health status is one factor that influences their self-image and presumably their subjective sense of well-being, which include such concepts as life satisfaction, happiness, mood, and morale (Horley, 1984; George, 1986). In addition, socioeconomic status may limit the individual's ability to utilize health and social services, thus potentially affecting an older Hispanic's health (for a detailed discussion see Markides et al., chapter 3) and self-concept.

ACCESS AND UTILIZATION OF SERVICES

Access to and utilization of services continue to be major issues in social service provision. Views regarding the Hispanic elderly vary from underutilization to overutilization of services (Newton Cota-Robles, 1980). In general the literature suggests underutilization, especially if socioeconomic status of the Hispanic elderly is considered. Moreover, affordability of care largely influences the elderly's ability to access the health and human care systems of the United States. For example, Villareal (1984, p.17) states that with regard to health care, access is a complex issue:

Access is determined by characteristics of the population, i.e., health status, age, education, employment, income, and insurance status. Access is multifactorial, dependent on indicators of process, such as personal source of health care and insurance status; utilization indicators demonstrating amount and kind of health care received; and satisfaction indicators, such as degree of courtesy shown by health care providers and cost of primary care visit to the client. (In Andersen et al., 1981)

Similarly, reasons for not using social services have been suggested in the literature. Johnson (1982) identifies barriers in terms of personal, social, economic, geographic, organizational, and suppositional (i.e., stereotype views and generalizations about the aged) factors. Cuellar and Weeks (1980) add that program characteristics often prevent older minorities from participating in public programs and services. Among the characteristics are income eligibility (i.e., means test), age requirements, lack of ethnic group members participating in the planning process, and a lack of facilities in the elderly's residential area. In a similar vein Guttmann (1980) notes that problems in applying for and receiving public benefits centered mainly on matters surrounding eligibility (e.g., age, income, residence, general) and procedures in obtaining benefits.

Barrera (1980) addresses the issue of service use among Mexican-Americans and the influence of service variables and personal variables on utilization. He opines:

Service characteristics, such as the availability of bilingual/bicultural therapists, is the factor most consistently identified as a chief influence on the utilization rates of Mexican Americans. To a lesser extent, reviewers cite the role of gatekeepers (such as physicians and priests) and informal support systems as keys to understanding Raza utilization of formal services. (p. 125)

The effects of ethnicity on service utilization may entail a lack of knowledge among the ethnic aged about other cultures and available services. Other significant factors influencing low utilization include an unwillingness or inability to travel beyond defined neighborhood (barrio) boundaries, lack of transportation, low expectation of services, and a strong preference to maintain the ethnic culture by utilizing local service providers or natural helpers rather than dominant culture institutional arrangements (Gelfand, 1982).

Combined, these factors influence utilization of services. This is particularly true of the many Hispanic elderly who first expect to be known as total persons *(personalismo)* before addressing personal matters or formal tasks. Thus it may be necessary to establish a working relationship reflecting a sense of *dignidad* (dignity and self-worth), *respeto* (respect between the interacting individuals), and *confianza* (trust) between the professional and the elderly Hispanic client. The elderly may also place high value on support from members in the extended family (including fictive kin), as well as natural support systems (Valle & Vega, 1980). Certainly, key elements of the culture, such as filial responsibility *(el deber de los hijos)*, are culturally imbedded rules of interaction among Hispanics and may be a predisposing factor influencing the elderly's use of services.

This brief discussion suggests that ethnicity may be a potential predictor in determining accessibility and utilization of services. Depending upon how services are designed and delivered, the Hispanic elderly experience varying degrees of comfort in identifying with a service program and may expect varying results from association with it. Thus Hispanic elderly may seek out folk healers *(curanderos)*, herbalists *(yerbistas)*, or indigenous counselors *(consejeros)* in health related matters or matters of the heart. Still others may adhere to the modern medical model of health care. Ostensibly there can be no preconceived notions or expectations of *all* Hispanic elderly. Customs, culture, language, personal experiences, barriers, and opportunities all serve to create the Hispanic elderly's rhythms and patterns of participation in community services and programs.

PRACTICE CONSIDERATIONS

Intervention

Professionals working with the Hispanic aged must address two clusters of practice variables: practitioner tasks and practitioner roles. For example, the professional's first task is to try to understand the elder as an individual within environmental systems, including barrio systems, family networks, natural support systems, and an array of other broader environmental influences. Professionals who practice at the family, group, organizational, or community level need to understand appropriate client and environmental systems. The professional can use a mixture of approaches to gain an appreciation of the Hispanic elderly, including reviewing published and unpublished reports, personal involvement, and using Hispanic elderly as mentors.

The second practitioner task is to establish a relationship with the client system and to penetrate the elderly's environments. For example, the worker may attend community functions where the elderly may be found or try to identify key individuals such as link persons *(conjuntadores)* in the community who may be helpful in orienting the worker to the elderly's environment.

The third task involves mobilizing and utilizing the elder's systems (individual, family, and community) to identify basic concerns, specific needs, and problems. Based on these identified needs, the professional can then delineate types of services and resources needed. The practitioner thus provides services and other resources not only within the confines of an office, but also within the elderly's environment; this may be a nutrition site, a church, the barrio, or the home. The practitioner encounters the elderly literally where the clients live, constantly observing and respecting the elderly's culture, position, needs, and preferences, and recognizing and using strengths/resources of the elderly and their environment. Ultimately, the helping relationship should be guided by the assumption that the elderly should be viewed as problem solvers, not problems to be solved.

The second cluster of intervention variables involves the identification of the practitioner's role(s). Consistent with the previous discussion, the practitioner is not strictly a "service provider." Instead, practitioner roles may include advocate, broker, link person, facilitator, consultant, and/or educator. Zane et al. (1980, p. 46) describe a "culture broker . . . a social scientist with expertise in the culture being served and in most cases of the same ethnicity . . . [able] to exert influence in both the community and the mental health network [or other networks] as well as on the relationship between these systems." The professional recognizes the limitations of his/her own role(s), yet capitalizes on the knowledge of "the system" and how to use that system for the benefit of the client. Borrowing a principle from community organization, the professional does not do anything for a client that the client can do for himself or herself. The idea is to help the client gain greater capacity to wield power over his or her own life (Alinsky, 1972).

To this end the practitioner soundly embraces the concepts of empowerment and conscientization. The former calls on the practitioner to assist the elderly "to manage emotions, skills, knowledge and/or material resources in a way that effective performance of valued social roles will lead to personal gratification" (Solomon, 1976, p. 16). The latter, based on Freire's model of critical consciousness, assumes that "the social environment does not represent a fixed reality to which people must accede or adjust. It represents, instead, a *problem* [emphasis added] to be worked on and solved through critical thinking and action" (Reisch, Wenocur, & Sherman, 1981, p. 114). Reflection and action thus provide the basis for what Freire refers to as "praxis," and perhaps the starting point for direct practice with Hispanic elderly.

This chapter has identified a number of factors that shape the life conditions, life chances, and opportunities instead of needs, problems, and aspirations of the Hispanic elderly. To be effective in serving the Hispanic elderly, the professional must develop an understanding of their culture, history, traditions, resources, and needs. The professional must locate each individual or group on the complex maps that identify common and unique aspects of the Hispanic elderly. Obviously, the understanding needed to work with Hispanic elderly is developed both during formal education/professional training and during the professional's practice. Finally, based on these understandings, client-specific interventions can be planned and implemented. Meeting the needs of this diverse group is a formidable challenge to the human services.

NOTES

1. According to the U.S. Bureau of the Census "Unless otherwise noted, persons reporting 'Other Hispanic' origin are those whose origins are from Spain, or they are Hispanic persons identifying themselves generally as Hispanic, Spanish, Spanish American, Hispano, Latino, etc."

2. The three types of dislocation refer to conditions in which majority groups deny minority group members access to opportunity structures and rewarding roles (social dislocation). This is followed by a loss of hope and ability to defer gratification (cultural dislocation). Ultimately, when the opportunity structure becomes accessible, minority group members are blocked, and unable to function in the mainstream of society (sociocultural dislocation). DeHoyos, G. D., DeHoyos, A., and Anderson, C. B., 1986, p. 64.

REFERENCES

Alinsky, S. D. (1972). *Rules for radicals*. New York: Vantage.
American Association of Retired Persons. (n.d.). A portrait of older minorities. Washington, DC.: Emily M. Agree.

Andersen, R., Lewis, S., & Giachello, A. L. (1981). Access to medical care among Hispanic population of the southwestern United States. *Journal of Health and Social Behavior, 22* 78–89.

Atkinson, D. R., Morten G., & Sue, D. W. (1983). *Counseling American minorities.* Dubuque, IA: William C. Brown.

Barrera, M. (1980). Raza populations. In L. Snowden, (Ed.), *Reaching the underserved: Mental health of neglected populations.* (pp. 119–142). Beverly Hills: Sage.

Beaver, M. L. (1983). *Human service practice with the elderly.* Englewood Cliffs, NJ: Prentice-Hall.

Bengston, V. L. (1979). Ethnicity and aging: Problems and issues in current social science inquiry. In D. E. Gelfand, & A. J. Kutzik, (Eds.), *Ethnicity and aging* (pp. 9–31). New York: Spring.

Cuellar, J. B. (1977). *El oro de maravilla: An ethnographic study of aging and age stratification in a urban Chicano community.* Unpublished doctoral dissertation, University of California, Los Angeles.

———. (1980). Understanding culture for the delivery of services to minority elders. In R. Wright, (Ed.), *Black/Chicano elderly: Service delivery within a cultural context* (pp. 13–18). Arlington: University of Texas at Arlington, Graduate School of Social Work.

Cuellar, J. B., & Weeks, J. R. (1980). *Minority elderly Americans assessment of needs and equitable receipt of public benefits as a prototype for area agencies on aging* (Final Report AoA, Contract No. 90-A-1667(01)). San Diego: Allied Home Health Association.

De Hoyos, G., De Hoyos, A., & Anderson, C. B. (1986, January–February). Sociocultural dislocation: Beyond the dual perspective. *Social Work, 61*–67.

Devore, W., & Schlesinger, E. G. (1981). *Ethnic-sensitive social work practice.* St. Louis: C. V. Mosby.

Gelfand, D. E. (1982). *Aging: The ethnic factor.* Boston: Little, Brown and Co.

George, L. K. (1986). Life satisfaction in later life. *Generations, 10*(3), 5–8.

Gordon, M. M. (1964). *Assimilation in American life.* New York: Oxford University Press.

———. (1973). *Human nature, class and ethnicity.* New York: Oxford University Press.

Guttmann, D. (1980). *Perspective on equitable share in public benefits by minority elderly: Executive summary* (Administration on Aging Grant No. 90-A-1671). Washington, DC: Catholic University of America.

Horley, J. (1984). Life satisfaction, happiness, and morale: Two problems with the use of subjective well-being indicators. *The Gerontologist, 24*(2), 124–127.

Johnston, H. (1982). Delivering human services to minority older persons: Policy issues. In D. Maldonado & J. McNeil (Eds.), *Service strategies in aging: Coping with the times* (pp. 44–58). Arlington: University of Texas at Arlington, Graduate School of Social Work.

Kimmel, D. C. (1974). *Adulthood and aging.* New York: Wiley.

Korte, A. (1981). Theoretical perspectives in mental health and the Mexicano elders. In M. Miranda & R. Ruiz (Eds.), *Chicano aging and mental health* (pp. 1–37). Rockville, MD: National Institute of Mental Health.

Lacayo C. G. (1980). *A national study to assess the service needs of the Hispanic elderly.* Los Angeles: National Association for Hispanic Elderly.

————. (1981). *The Older American Act reviewed in the context of federal fiscal restraint* (pp. 61–64). Select Committee on Aging, Washington, DC: U.S. Government Printing Office.

Linton, R. (1945). *The cultural background of personality*. New York: Appleton-Century-Crofts.

Lum, D. (1986). *Social work practice and people of color*. Monterey, CA: Brooks/ Cole.

Maldonado, D., Jr. (1975a).Ethnic self identity and self understanding. *Social Casework, 56* (10), 618–622.

————. (1975b). The Chicano aged. *Social Work, 20*, 213–216.

————. (1979). Aging in the Chicano context. In D. E. Gelfand & A. J. Kutzik (Eds.), *Ethnicity and aging: Theory, research and policy* (pp. 175–183) New York: Springer.

Mehr, J. (1986). *Human services: Concepts and intervention strategies*. Boston: Allyn & Bacon.

Miranda, M. R., & Kitano, H. H. L. (1986). *Mental health research and practice in minority communities*. Rockville, MD: National Institute of Mental Health.

Mirande, A. (1977, November). The Chicano family: A reanalysis of conflicting views. *Journal of Marriage and the Family*, 747–756.

Montalvo, F. F. (1983). The affective domain in cross-cultural social work education. *Journal of Education for Social Work, 19*(2), 48–53.

Newlon, B. J., & Arciniega, M. (1983). Respecting cultural uniqueness: An Adlerian approach. *Individual Psychology, 39*(2), 133–143.

Newton, Frank Cota-Robles (1980). Issues in research and service delivery among Mexican-American elderly: A concise statement with recommendations. *The Gerontologist, 20*(2), 208–212.

Olmstead, K. A. (1983, July–August). The influence of minority social work students on an agency's service methods. *Social Work*, 308–312.

Padilla, A., Ruiz, R., & Alvarez, R. (1975). Community mental health services for the Spanish-speaking surnamed population. *American Psychologist, 30*, 892–905.

Reisch, M., Wenocur, S., & Sherman, W. (1981, Summer–Fall). Empowerment, conscientization and animation as core social work skills. *Social Development Issues, 5*(2–3), 108–120.

Skidmore, R. C., & Thackery, M. G. (1964). *Introduction to social work practice*. New York: Meredith.

Solomon, Barbara B. (1976). *Black Empowerment: Social work in oppressed communities*. New York: Columbia University Press.

Spicer, E. (1971, November). Persistent cultural systems. *Science, 174*, 795–800.

Spicer, E., & Thompson, R. H. (Eds.) (1972). *Plural society in the Southwest*. New York: Interbook.

Sue, D. W., & Sue, D. (1977). Barriers to effective cross-cultural counseling. *Journal of Counseling Psychology, 24*, 420–429.

U. S. Bureau of the Census. (1987). The Hispanic population in the United States: March 1986 and 1987 (Advance Report). *Current population reports* (Series P-20, No. 416). Washington, DC: U.S. Government Printing Office.

U.S. Bureau of the Census. (1985). Persons of Spanish origin in the United States: March 1982. *Current population reports* (Series P-20, No. 396). Washington, DC: U.S. Government Printing Office.

U.S. Department of Commerce, Bureau of the Census. (1983). *Conditions of Hispanics in America today*. Washington, DC: U.S. Government Printing Office.

Valle, R., & Vega, W. (Eds.) (1980). *Hispanic natural support systems*. State of California, Department of Mental Health.

Villareal, S. F. (1984). Current issues on Hispanic health. In M. Sotomayor (Ed.), *Dialogue on health concerns for Hispanics* (pp. 17–52). Rockville, MD: National Institute of Health.

Wilson, W., & Calhoun J. F. (1974). Behavior therapy and the minority client. *Psychotherapy: Theory Research and Practice, 11*, 317–325.

Wright, R. (Ed.) (1980). *Black/Chicano elderly: Service delivery within a cultural context*. Arlington: University of Texas at Arlington, Graduate School of Social Work.

Zane, N., Sve, S., Castro F. G., & George, W. (1982). Service systems models for ethnic minorities. In L. Snowden (Ed.) *Reaching the underserved: Mental health of neglected populations*. (pp. 229–258) Beverly Hills: Sage.

2

ELDERLY PUERTO RICANS IN THE UNITED STATES

Melba Sánchez-Ayéndez

INTRODUCTION

During recent years, research focusing on the Hispanic elderly has stressed the need for more data regarding similarities and differences among and within various Hispanic groups. This chapter discusses some historical and demographic aspects of the Puerto Rican group while focusing on specific data and studies on its elderly members. Some suggestions for service delivery and future research on Puerto Rican older adults are also offered.

HISTORICAL AND SOCIODEMOGRAPHIC OVERVIEW OF THE PUERTO RICAN MIGRATION

The emigration of a large sector of the Puerto Rican working class to the United States must be viewed within a historical context and linked to the politicoeconomic relationship of the two countries. Since 1898, and as a result of the Spanish-American War, Puerto Rico has been a territory of the United States. The economic development of the island during the first four decades of the twentieth century was characterized by an emphasis on agricultural production of export crops, especially sugar cane. From 1948 to the mid-1960s, an intense industrialization program tried to transform the economy from an agrarian to an industrial one. Presently, the predominant economic sector is geared to services. Corporations from the United States have controlled the majority of the means of production throughout the various periods.

Relations between the island and the mainland served to facilitate the migration of Puerto Ricans. As United States citizens, Puerto Ricans were able to travel to the mainland without the restrictions imposed on other immigrant groups.[1] Migration patterns were also influenced by the relationship of the two countries. The numbers and types of skills of the migrant workers and the available occupations within the island's economy were interrelated to the necessities of the U.S. economy (History Task Force, 1979).

In 1920, around 12,000 Puerto Ricans were reported living and dispersed throughout the 48 states (History Task Force, 1979). During the years of the Depression the migration rate was reduced, and between 1930 and 1934 about 20 percent of the Puerto Rican population on the mainland returned to the island (Vázquez-Calzada, 1979). By 1944, the number of those who had left for the United States increased to 90,000 (López, 1974), and as a group they began to concentrate in New York (History Task Force, 1979). After World War II, during the early years of the industrialization period, a massive exodus of Puerto Ricans to the United States occurred. Factors such as rapid population growth on an island 3435 square miles in size, high rates of unemployment, the prospect of higher wages, and the demand of U.S. corporate interests for labor in the services, agriculture, and garment industries lie at the roots of the large numbers of Puerto Rican immigrants to the mainland (History Task Force, 1979; López, 1974).

Efforts were made by the insular and mainland governments to cooperate in the displacement of workers to the United States. For the Puerto Rican government, this was a way of dealing with a "surplus" unemployed population, particularly rural farm workers; for the United States, the displacement was a source of cheap, unskilled labor (Leavitt, 1974; López, 1974). As a result, reduced air fares, seasonal farm worker contracts between Puerto Rican government agencies and U.S. corporations, and a propaganda campaign about prospective jobs and higher wages ensued.

Statistics show that in the decade of the 1940s an average of 18,700 Puerto Ricans migrated to the United States annually (Lopez, 1974). During the 1950s, the average increased to 41,200 per year;[2] in the 1960s it decreased to about 14,500 annually.[3] At the beginning of the 1960s, approximately 90,000 Puerto Ricans were living in the United States (López, 1974); in 1970, the number[4] had increased to 1,429,396 (U.S. Bureau of the Census, 1980b). The 1980 census cites a total population of 2,013,945 Puerto Ricans in the United States.

Prior to World War II—the period of corporate agriculture on the island—the migrants tended to be skilled and semiskilled urban workers (Leavitt, 1974). A great majority of those who migrated after World War II, however, were unskilled farm workers who were not incorporated into the labor force during the early years of industrialization. Abroad, some were employed in unskilled farm labor, while the majority entered semiskilled blue-collar and service work

norm was that only large towns and cities had secondary schools. The majority of the Puerto Rican older adults residing in the United States were born and grew up in the rural areas of the island where agriculture was the prevailing industry.

Older Puerto Ricans tend to have large families (Carrasquillo, 1982; Lacayo, 1980; Sánchez-Ayéndez, 1984; Zalduondo, 1982). The average number of children among those who have participated in studies ranges from four to five.

The majority of the Puerto Rican elderly live in their own households with their spouses, with children, or alone, but not in the households of their adult children (Cantor, 1975; Carrasquillo, 1982; Lacayo, 1980; Sánchez-Ayéndez, 1984; Zalduondo, 1982). They are the most likely of all Hispanic aged adults to live alone (Lacayo, 1980), but they tend to live near their children, most likely in the same neighborhood as at least one of their offspring. As the majority of the Puerto Rican population on the mainland, the elderly live in ethnic enclaves in inner city areas.

The number of years spent in the United States by older Puerto Ricans varies. However, many of the older adults left their country of origin during the 1950s and 1960s. Age at the time of arrival in the United States shows a slight variation according to the area of residence, and a thorough analysis is needed before making a conclusive statement. Nonetheless, a study of Puerto Ricans over 55 years of age residing in various states found that 61 percent of those interviewed had lived in the United States between the ages of 26 and 50 (Lacayo, 1980). It is probable that a majority of those in New York and New Jersey arrived before the age of 50. This might not be the norm for those in other areas—for example, in Massachusetts, Connecticut, and Florida. Many of the elders in these states could have arrived when they were over 50 years of age, following their migrant children (Sánchez-Ayéndez, 1984).

As for all Hispanic groups, Social Security provides the main source of income for Puerto Rican elders. They are the Spanish-origin group with the highest participation in the program (Lacayo, 1980), a factor related to their U.S. citizenship. Supplementary Security Income (SSI) is their second most frequent source of income.

The various occupations in which Puerto Rican older men and women were engaged throughout their lives fall within the unskilled and semiskilled categories (Carrasquillo, 1982; Lacayo, 1980; Sánchez-Ayéndez, 1984; Zalduondo, 1982). Contrary to common belief, many Puerto Rican women participated in the wage labor force of the island during their early and middle adulthood (Carrasquillo, 1982; Sánchez-Ayéndez, 1984), particularly in domestic and personal services and the needlework and tobacco industries (Sánchez-Ayéndez, 1984). Even many of those who never worked outside the house performed wage-earning tasks such as needlework and laundering (Sánchez-Ayéndez, 1984). These women frequently received payments in the form of merchandise or barter services as well as in cash.

SUPPORT SYSTEMS OF ELDERLY PUERTO RICANS

Research on the aged Puerto Rican in the United States has focused on utilization of informal and formal support systems. Thus, needs assessments, examinations of the types of support and patterns of assistance that the elderly receive from familial and friendship networks, and use of health and social services have been the prevailing topics in the few studies currently available.

Puerto Rican elderly, like the majority of the aged population in the United States (Harris & Associates, 1981), perceive poor physical health and lack of adequate income as two of their major problems (Cruz, 1977; Lacayo, 1980; Sánchez-Ayéndez, 1984). Adjustment to the dominant culture, especially if the elders arrived in their middle or late adulthood, is another of the difficulties recognized by elderly Puerto Ricans (Cruz, 1977; Donaldson & Martínez, 1980; Lacayo, 1980; Sánchez-Ayéndez, 1984). Researchers and service providers explain that language difficulties lead to lack of knowledge and misuse or underutilization of existing health and social services.

Studies of Puerto Rican aged adults indicate that the family—particularly adult children—is still the predominant support network in everyday life and times of crisis. It provides instrumental (e.g., information, escort, shopping, chauffeuring, translation, errands, health assistance) and emotional (e.g., companionship, advice-giving, listening to problems) support. Financial help from the family is infrequent except in emergencies.

Almost daily contact with children living in the same city is the normal pattern for Puerto Rican elderly, whether in the form of visits or telephone calls. Contact with children is a source of emotional satisfaction. Studies indicate that what is important to Puerto Rican elders is that children and grandchildren be present, not so much that goods or services are provided (Carrasquillo, 1982; Sánchez-Ayéndez, 1984). Emotional support is considered more important than instrumental support.

Puerto Rican older adults have a place in the functional structure of the family, and play an important and active role in providing their families with assistance (Cantor, 1979; Carrasquillo, 1982; Delgado, 1981; Donaldson & Martínez, 1980; Sánchez-Ayéndez, 1984, 1986; Zambrana et al., 1979). The elders provide instrumental and emotional support to those in their immediate kinship group. Child care, cooking, listening to others, giving advice, and providing assistance during illnesses are among the supportive tasks frequently performed for adult children and grandchildren. A study found that one of the reasons offered for migration was to be near adult children in order to offer help when needed (Sánchez-Ayéndez, 1984). The aged sometimes assist their adult children in financial matters (Carrasquillo, 1982; Sánchez-Ayéndez, 1984). Direct monetary help and gift-giving are two of the most frequent patterns of financial supportive behavior.

Friends and neighbors are also part of the elders' network of assistance. Among the supportive tasks most often performed by friends are companionship and escort. Furthermore, neighbors and friends may provide daily care or check-ups during an illness. Neighbors, however, unlike kin and friends, do not play an essential role in providing emotional support (Sánchez-Ayéndez, 1984). They might become friends, but not necessarily. Nonetheless, relations with neighbors are deemed important since they are viewed as useful during emergencies and unexpected events. Contact with neighbors takes the form of greetings, occasional visits, and exchange of food. These exchanges help to strengthen and secure reciprocity when and if the opportunity arises.

Puerto Rican older adults are likely to use formal support services when they have knowledge of their existence (Donaldson & Martínez, 1980; Lacayo, 1980; Sánchez-Ayéndez, 1984; Zambrana et al., 1979). They are more apt to receive health care at government or other public health facilities than are their Cuban and Mexican-American counterparts (Lacayo, 1980). When they have knowledge and access to social services that take into consideration their cultural traditions—and where language is not a barrier—the trend is for the elderly to use the services provided and not to rely upon their families for assistance (Donaldson & Martínez, 1980; Sánchez-Ayéndez, 1984). However, they are somewhat reluctant to communicate directly with government agencies and prefer to use Hispanic community agencies as mediators. Cultural barriers, unpleasant past experiences, and/or discomfort with bureaucratic procedures are factors that cause this reluctance to communicate directly with certain agencies that provide formal sources of support.

VALUE ORIENTATIONS AND SOCIAL RELATIONSHIPS OF PUERTO RICAN ELDERLY ADULTS

A comprehensive understanding of Puerto Rican elders must consider the meanings that social relationships have for the aged—and others in their ethnic group—as well as the ways in which cultural ideals influence different forms of interaction. Social networks and the supportive relations that ensue from them have a sociocultural dimension that embodies a system of shared meanings. These meanings affect social interaction and the expectations that people have of their relationships with others.[8]

The Family

Despite social change and adaptation to life in a culturally different society, the Puerto Rican family continues to play a central and essential role in the support and governance of its members. The Puerto Rican family is characterized by strong norms of reciprocity that emphasize interdependence among the various family members, particularly those in the immediate kinship group. Interdependence within the Puerto Rican symbolic framework, as well as in other Hispanic groups, "fits an orientation to life that stresses that the individual is not capable of doing everything and doing it well. Therefore, he should

rely on others for assistance" (Bastida, 1979, pp. 70–71). Within this conceptualization, individualism and self-reliance assume a different connotation from
that prevailing in the dominant U.S. cultural tradition.

Family interdependence is a value to which Puerto Rican elders strongly
adhere. It influences patterns of mutual assistance with their children as well as
anticipations of support. Older Puerto Rican adults still expect to be taken care
of in old age by their adult children. The notion of filial duty ensues from the
value orientation of interdependence. Supportive behavior from children is addressed from the perspective of expected reciprocity from offspring. Adult children are perceived as having a responsibility toward their elderly parents in
exchange for the functions the parents fulfilled for them throughout their child-
hood.

Interdependence for the Puerto Rican older parent also means helping children and grandchildren. Many times elders provide help when it is not explicitly requested. They are happy when they can perform supportive tasks for their
children's families. Within the interdependence value orientation, this is viewed
from the context of parental obligations. The child who needs help, no matter
how old, is not judged as dependent or a failure.

Family interdependence is not necessarily based upon mutual giving or reciprocal exchange relationships. Due to the rapid pace of life and lack of financial
resources, adult children are not always able to provide the care the elder needs.
What is of utmost importance to older adults is not that their children be able
to help them all the time, but that they visit or call frequently. The aged place
more emphasis on emotional support from their offspring than on other forms
of assistance.

Frequent interaction with children is highly valued by older Puerto Rican
adults, although it is more important for women than for men (see Carrasquillo,
1982). Visits and telephone calls are interpreted as expressions of a caring
attitude from children and grandchildren and one that brings emotional satisfaction to the old person. Daily visits or telephone calls from children who live
nearby is the expected and prevailing pattern of interaction. This pattern is
expected more of daughters than of sons, as will be discussed later. Children
who cannot visit their parents during the week do so on weekends. Children
usually go to their parents' houses; rarely are visits made the other way around,
except during special occasions or holidays in which the family tends to be
reunited.

The importance attached to family interdependence does not imply that Puerto
Rican older adults are always requiring assistance from their children or that
they do not value their independence. They prefer to live in their own households than in those of their offspring, and, likewise, they try to solve as many
problems as possible by themselves. But, when support is needed, adult children are expected to assist their aged parents as much as possible.

Conceptualization of Men and Women

Elderly Puerto Ricans adhere to a double standard of conduct for men and women and a belief in the predominance of male authority. Women are conceptualized as patient and forebearing, particularly in relation to men. A woman's main role is motherhood. Despite the fact that many Puerto Rican women have joined the labor force, the house is the center around which the female world revolves. It is still considered a woman's domain. This is emphasized by the term *ama de casa* ("governess of the house"), which does not have the same connotation as "housewife." Decisions regarding household maintenance are generally made by women.

Men, on the other hand, belong "to the street" as breadwinners. Their main responsibility to the family is an economic one. Although fathers are expected to be affectionate toward their children, child care is not perceived as a man's responsibility. The ideal of maleness among Puerto Ricans in the United States, as well as in other Hispanic groups, is linked to the concept of *machismo*. *Machismo* refers to the need of the male to prove his virility by conquest of and dominance over women, a stronger sexual drive and a belligerent attitude when confronted by male peers. However, maleness involves more than sexual assertiveness and dominance over women; it also relates to being a good provider, a protector of the family—particularly of women and children—and, to a large degree, to being able to control emotions and be self-sufficient.

The difference in conceptualization between men and women affects the elders' patterns of interaction, use of supportive networks, and expectations of those in their familial group. The daily activities of Puerto Rican older women center around the family and the household. Among married couples, the woman is in charge of such tasks as cooking, cleaning the house, and doing the laundry, as well as of taking care of grandchildren and maintaining family relations. When telephones are present in the household, the older woman keeps in touch with those in her network through telephone conversations. She usually stays at home during most of the day. She goes out to shop for groceries, attend religious services, or keep doctors' appointments. Many times her husband accompanies her.

Elderly men, although in the house for long periods of the day, go out into the community more often. They usually go to the bank or the post office. Likewise, as part of their almost daily walks, they stop at the *bodegas* (grocery stores, generally owned by Puerto Ricans or other Hispanics, where native foods can be bought) to purchase staples needed in the house and newspapers from Puerto Rico. *Bodegas* also serve as places for socialization, exchange of information, and, oftentimes, as financial credit institutions (Delgado, 1981; Elman, 1983; Fitzpatrick, 1971).

The difference between elderly men and women in terms of patterns of daily activities is related to other variables such as health and marital status. When the wife is ill, the husband helps with household chores, but this is not the prevailing pattern. When the elderly woman lives alone, she goes out into the community more often; nonetheless, adult children perform tasks for their mothers or act as escorts for them, and sometimes elderly women accompany each other to medical appointments, banks, and religious services.

Friendship is determined along gender lines; few elderly women or men have friends of the opposite sex. Women tend to be careful about men. Mistrust of males is based upon the notion of *machismo;* since men are conceived as having stronger sexual desires, the possibility of advances from elderly males— whether physical or verbal—to prove their virility is a prevalent belief among elderly women. Therefore, relationships with males outside the immediate familial group are usually kept at a formal level.

The cultural definitions of male and female also affect the types of exchanges that occur within family networks in terms of support given and received. In relation to support received from offspring, Puerto Rican elders perceive their daughters as being more understanding and better able to comprehend their problems due to their womanly qualities. Daughters are also considered to be more reliable. Sons are not expected to help as much as daughters or in the same way. Complaints are more bitter when a daughter does not fulfill expected filial duties. Similarly, daughters are expected to visit and/or call more frequently than sons. As women, they are linked to the domestic domain and held responsible for the care of family members and the maintenance of family relations.

Elderly mothers tend to confide their problems more often to their daughters as well as to offer advice to their daughters on matters related to families and children. This does not mean that they do not discuss personal matters with sons or give them advice, but the approach is different. Elderly Puerto Rican mothers tend to be more direct with daughters than with sons when giving advice or inquiring about personal problems. Also, the standard pattern is to go first to a daughter when confronted by an emotional difficulty. Female offspring are perceived as being more patient and, since they are women like their mothers, better able to understand.

Motherhood is viewed as the link that creates a spiritual bond among women and separates them from men. After a daughter becomes a mother, a stronger tie with her own mother is expected. The basis for this tie are the sufferings experienced during childbirth and the hardships involved in child-rearing, which is considered to be the main responsibility of the woman.

Relations between elderly Puerto Rican men and their offspring are somewhat different. Fathers tend to keep their problems to themselves, particularly financial and emotional ones. This is related to the idea that a man is financially responsible for his family, more self-sufficient, and less emotional than a woman. Many times an older woman serves as a mediator in communicating her husband's problems to their adult children.

Many elderly fathers still play the role of protector by escorting their daughters (married or single) or granddaughters to various places. Relations with sons are more formal and exhibit less overt affectionate behavior. The father seems more distant and careful than the mother in his approach to adult male children. When a son has a problem, the father will not insist on finding out about it if the information is not offered willingly. Sons, as men, are perceived as able to take care of their own problems. Mothers, on the other hand, are more inquisitive than fathers. Advice to sons is given by both parents, although not as frequently as to daughters. Daughters are perceived by fathers as in need of more protection and support than sons. Mothers perceive an equal need of support for sons and daughters but differentiate in terms of need; daughters are viewed as facing additional problems due to their status as women in areas such as conjugal relations and sexual harassment.

Although most adult children give help during the illness of an elderly parent, daughters generally offer more help than sons. Quite often daughters take sick parents into their homes or stay overnight in parents' homes in order to provide better care. Although sons are part of the supportive network that provides health assistance, the general pattern is for the elderly to depend more on their daughters. Sons and daughters take aged parents to the hospital or to doctors' offices, buy medicines, and contribute money, if needed, but daughters check more often on their parents, provide care, and perform household chores during parents' illnesses.

Respeto

Puerto Rican elderly place a strong emphasis upon social relations and prefer to deal with others in terms of a network of personal relationships rather than through formal associations or groups. The basis of all proper relationships is *respeto* (respect). *Respeto* involves the notion of "generalized deference" in all social interactions as well as in a variety of deferential acts or rituals relevant to particular kinds of social relations (Lauria, 1964).

Respect has two connotations for the elderly Puerto Rican. One is related to age hierarchy. As an adult—one who is no longer a child and has assumed the responsibilities of a "grown-up"—the elder demands respect from his age cohorts and particularly from younger generations. Respect is related to increased status as one ages. Therefore, as older adults, the elderly expect the deference that their status grants them above other adults. The second connotation of respect involves the recognition of the elderly as persons, of their inherent value as singular human beings (*dignidad,* or dignity). As such, older Puerto Ricans demand respect from peers as well as those of higher social status.

Respeto is an essential component of parent-child relationships. One of the necessary qualities of a good child is to be respectful (*respetuoso*). Many Puerto Rican elderly parents believe that it is more important that children be respectful than affectionate. Adult children and other persons are not expected to talk back to or shout at the elderly. Other deferential acts involve asking for and listening to the advice that older individuals can offer as part of their life experiences, and standing up to greet them or to say farewell.

Older Puerto Ricans prefer to use of the terms *don* (for men) and *doña* (for women) before the first name or *señor* and *señora* before the last name as titles of respect. Likewise, the use of the pronoun *usted* instead of the informal *tú* (both meaning "you" in the singular form) is expected to accompany other deference terms. These ritual forms are common among peers, particularly between males and females. Younger generations (with the exception of persons in the immediate kinship group) and strangers are expected to use these forms when addressing the elderly.

Despite changes occurring in Puerto Rican families and communities, ritualized acts of deference are still bestowed upon Puerto Rican older adults. The pattern is more prevalent within family and friendship networks, and respect is more contingent upon the status of the elderly as older adults and parents than on their functions and power in familial and community structures.

CONCLUSIONS AND IMPLICATIONS

Amidst all the changes that Puerto Rican families have been undergoing in the process of adaptation to life in the United States, familial and community networks have remained functional sources of support for Puerto Rican older adults. It is also in the interaction with these in their natural support systems that older Puerto Ricans have been able to experience a sense of cultural continuity through the sharing of symbols and systems of meaning. These factors contribute to the adaptive process entailed in the aging process in a culturally different milieu from the one in which the elderly grew up.

More needs to be known about how variables such as income, education, gender, age at time of arrival in the United States, length of time on the mainland, area of residence, and generational differences affect the process of adaptation of aged Puerto Ricans to life in the United States. More information is also needed regarding how the interaction between these variables and community and familial networks can lead to better adjustment to old age. The fact that many of the Puerto Ricans returning to the island are adults 60 years of age and older cannot be overlooked. What factors are contributing to the dynamics of this migratory trend? What can it add to our knowledge of the processes of adaptation of Puerto Rican elders and of the Puerto Rican population in general?

To state that changes in family and community structures have drastically altered the functions and social position of the elderly is, to an extent, to oversimplify the present situation among Puerto Ricans and other Hispanic groups. Structural features and changes impinge upon certain aspects of life, but the dynamics of everyday existence are not contingent upon structural variables alone. Socially shared meanings affect individuals' attitudes, expectations, and relationships with others. Research on the various Hispanic groups cannot assume that Hispanic families and communities have remained unaltered throughout their experience in the United States, but neither can it assume that all value orientations have been completely transformed due to modifications in structural features. Cultural and structural changes do not necessarily go hand in hand.

Those involved in the planning and delivery of human services to Puerto Rican (and all Hispanic) elders need to be more aware of the influence of cultural traditions and value orientations on the aging process. The strengths inherent in the value of family interdependence and the dynamics involved in personal relationships must be considered by health and social service providers. Better coordination between formal support agencies and natural systems of support could be achieved if more attention were geared to understanding the social organization and value orientations of Puerto Ricans in the United States. This could help to ease the stress that many Puerto Rican families undergo when assisting their elderly members as well as to diminish the underutilization and misuse of existing services by Puerto Rican older adults.

NOTES

1. Puerto Ricans were granted U.S. citizenship in 1917 under the provisions of the Jones Law.

2. The year with the highest number of migrants—a total of 69,124—was 1953 (López, 1974).

3. The 1950s were the years of massive migration; migration during the 1960s was of an erratic nature (Vázquez-Calzada, 1978, p. 276)

4. First- and second-generation Puerto Ricans.

5. The percentage of Puerto Ricans 65 years of age and older residing on the island is 8 percent (Vázquez-Calzada & Carnivali, 1982). The difference in proportions between Puerto Rican older adults on the island and on the mainland could be linked to job availability in the United States for a young age group and the feasibility of returning to the homeland due to the nature of the political relationship between the two countries.

6. A total of 1804 Hispanic elderly from 14 states and the District of Columbia participated in the study. Puerto Ricans (N = 234) comprised 13 percent of the sample.

7. An analysis of 1980 census data shows that 43.4 percent of Puerto Ricans 65 years of age and older residing on the island were illiterate (Vázquez-Calzada & Carnivali, 1982). This study also indicates that the median completed years of schooling for elderly Puerto Ricans on the island was 2.5 and that 70.9 percent had 4 or fewer years of schooling. Data from the 1950s and the 1960 and 1970 censuses demonstrate that Puerto Rican migrants 25 years of age and older tended to have a higher level of education than those residing on the island (Vázquez-Calzada, 1979, pp. 229–230), but this was not the case among younger age groups.

8. This section is based on data from an ethnographic study of elderly Puerto Ricans in the city of Boston (Sánchez-Ayéndez, 1984). The research was supported by the Danforth Foundation, Sigma Xi, the Scientific Research Society, and the Delta Kappa Gamma Society International.

REFERENCES

Bastida, E. (1979). Family integration and adjustment to aging among Hispanic-American elderly. Unpublished doctoral dissertation, University of Kansas, Lawrence, KS.

Cantor, M. A. (1975). Life space and the social support system of the inner city elderly of New York. *The Gerontologist, 15*, 23–27.

———. (1979). The informal support system of New York's inner city elderly: Is ethnicity a factor? In D. E. Gelfand & A. J. Kutzik (Eds.), *Ethnicity and aging* (pp. 153–174). New York: Springer.

Carrasquillo, H. A. (1982). Perceived social reciprocity and self-esteem among elderly barrio Antillean Hispanics and their familial informal networks. Unpublished doctoral dissertation, Syracuse University, Syracuse, NY.

Cruz, H. (1977). *Advances for the Spanish-speaking elderly through advocacy programs*. Paper presented at the Texas State Department of Public Welfare Conference, Dallas, TX.

Delgado, M. (1981, November). Ethnic and cultural variations in the care of the aged: A special focus on Puerto Ricans. Paper presented at the Scientific Meeting of the Boston Society for Gerontologic Psychiatry, Boston.

Donaldson, E., & Martínez, E. (1980). The Hispanic elderly of East Harlem. *Aging,* 1–2, pp. 6–11.

Elman, R. M. (1973). A day at the bodega. In K. Wagenheim & O. Jimenez de Wagenheim (Eds.), *The Puerto Ricans* (pp. 42–69). New York: Anchor Books.

Estrada, L. (1977). Cultural and demographic characteristics of the Hispanic community. In C. Lacayo (Ed.), *Program planning and research for the Hispanic elderly: A call for action* (pp. 55–60). Los Angeles: Asociación Nacional pro Personas Mayores.

Fitzpatrick, J. (1971). *Puerto Rican-Americans: The meaning of migration to the mainland*. Englewood Cliffs, NJ: Prentice-Hall.

Harris, L., & Associates. (1981). *Aging in the eighties: America in transition*. Washington, DC: National Council on the Aging.

History Task Force. (1979). Capitalist development and migration. In History Task Force, Centro de Estudios Puertorriqueños (Ed.), *Migration under capitalism: The Puerto Rican experience* (pp. 67–193). New York: Monthly Review Press.

Lacayo, C. (1980). *A study to assess the service needs of the Hispanic elderly: Final report*. Los Angeles: Asociación Nacional pro Personas Mayores.

Lauria, A. (1964). "Respeto," "relajo," and interpersonal relations in Puerto Rico. *Anthropological Quarterly, 37*, 53–67.

Leavitt, R. R. (1974). *The Puerto Ricans: Culture change and language deviance*. Tucson: University of Arizona Press.

López, A. (1974). The Puerto Rican diaspora: A survey. In A. López & J. Petras (Eds.), *Puerto Rico and Puerto Ricans: Studies in history and society* (pp. 316–346). New York: Schenkman.

Ludwig, C. E. (1977). The social role of the grandmother among Puerto Ricans on the mainland. Unpublished master's thesis, Loyola University, Chicago, Illinois.

Sánchez-Ayéndez, M. (1984). Puerto Rican elderly women: Aging in an ethnic minority group in the United States. Unpublished doctoral dissertation, University of Massachusetts, Amherst.

————. (1986) Puerto Rican elderly women: Shared meanings and informal supportive networks. In G. B. Cole (Ed.), *All American Women* (pp. 172–186). New York: Free Press.

Sandis, E. E. (1970). Characteristics of Puerto Rican migrants to and from the United States. *Internal Migration Review, 4,* 22–42.

Torruellas, L. M., & Vázquez, J. L. (1982). *Los puertorriqueños que regresaron: Un análisis de su participación laboral.* Río Piedras, PR: Centro de Investigaciones Sociales, Universidad de Puerto Rico.

U. S. Bureau of the Census. (1980a). *Census of population: General population characteristics.* Washington, DC: U.S. Government Printing Office.

————. (1980b). *Persons of Spanish origin by state: Supplementary report.* Washington, DC: U.S. Government Printing Office.

————. (1981). *Persons of Spanish origin in the United States, March 1980: Advance report* (Current Population Reports, Series P-20, No. 361). Washington, DC: U.S. Government Printing Office.

Valle, R., & Mendoza, L. (1978). *The elder Latino.* San Diego: Campanile Press.

Vázquez-Calzada, J. L. (1978). *La población de Puerto Rico y su trayectoria histórica.* San Juan: Escuela Graduada de Salud Pública, Recinto de Ciencias Médicas, Universidad de Puerto Rico.

————. (1979). Demographic aspects of migration. In History Task Force, Centro de Estudios Puertorriqueños (Ed.), *Migration under capitalism: The Puerto Rican experience* (pp. 223–236). New York: Monthly Review Press.

————. (1983). *Estimaciones realizadas sobre migración, década 1970–1980.* San Juan: Programa Graduado de Demografía, Escuela Graduada de Salud Pública, Recinto de Ciencias Médicas, Universidad de Puerto Rico.

Vázquez-Calzada, J. L., & Carnivali, J. (1982). *Caracteristícas demográficas y socioeconomicas de la población de edad avanzada de Puerto Rico.* San Juan: Programa Graduado de Demografía, Escuela Graduada de Salud Pública, Recinto de Ciencias Médicas, Universidad de Puerto Rico.

Zalduondo, B. (1982). Assessment about the needs of the Hispanic aging: Sociocultural approach. Unpublished doctoral dissertation, University of Miami, Miami.

Zambrana, R., Merino, R., & Santana, S. (1979). Health services and the Puerto Rican elderly. In D. L. Gelfand & A. J. Kutzik (Eds.), *Ethnicity and aging* (pp. 308–319). New York: Springer.

Part II

HEALTH STATUS AND HEALTH SERVICE UTILIZATION

3

THE HEALTH STATUS OF HISPANIC ELDERLY IN THE SOUTHWEST

Kyriakos Markides and Jeannine Coreil

INTRODUCTION

Over the last few decades, scholars have shown a lively interest in the health care behavior of Hispanics in the Southwest. Weaver (1973) identifies three "generations" of related literature from the 1940s to 1970. The first generation, typified by the work of Saunders and his associates, emphasized "differences, not *within* the overall Mexican-American population but *between* it and the Anglo model, especially as revealed in what [Saunders] sees as the core of Mexican-American Health culture—folk medicine" (Weaver, 1973, p. 87). The second generation of research was largely in Saunders's tradition in that there was continued emphasis on the ubiquity of folk beliefs and practices (see, e.g., Clark, 1959; Madsen, 1964; Rubel, 1966), although there was some recognition of the influence of social class on folk beliefs and practices, particularly by Madsen (1964). The third generation of research, emerging in the 1960s, paid more attention to cultural variability within the Mexican-American community as exemplified by better sampling procedures and emphasis on such variables as place of residence, social class, and education (see, e.g., Karno & Edgerton, 1969; McLemore, 1963; Nall & Spielberg, 1967).

The third generation of research and later research conducted during the 1970s found little evidence of sole reliance on folk medicine and indicated that, where it existed, it complemented reliance on "scientific" medicine (e.g., Casas & Keefe, 1978). Moreover, low utilization of health services was more likely to be explained in terms of social and political factors that limit access to health care rather than in terms of a preference for folk medicine (e.g., Andersen et al., 1981; Bullough, 1972; Hoppe & Heller, 1975).

Although a great deal of interest has been shown regarding the health care behavior of southwestern Hispanics, little specific attention has been given to the health care behavior of older Hispanics. Much of the time this has been due to the few cases of elderly included in the samples. No special attention has typically been given to the elderly; it has usually been assumed that they are more traditional in their health care behavior.

The lively interest in the health care behavior of southwestern Hispanics has not been paralleled by an equal interest in their health status. Among other factors, defining "Hispanic" or "Mexican-American" has proven to be a difficult task. Moreover, health statistics have frequently not been recorded separately for persons of Mexican (or other Hispanic) origin because of the practice of classifying them as white by such agencies as the National Center for Health Statistics and the Bureau of the Census (see Roberts & Askew, 1972). Large-scale epidemiologic studies have been few, and, again, the elderly are often not included in them.

This chapter provides an overview of the evidence on the current health status of the Hispanic elderly population of the southwestern United States, most of whom are of Mexican origin. Because of this, we will refer to the population interchangeably as "southwestern Hispanics," "people of Spanish or Mexican origin," or "Mexican-Americans." We will, however, avoid using the terms *Mexican-American* or *Mexican origin* when referring specifically to the Spanish-origin population of New Mexico.

This overview of the health status of elderly southwestern Hispanics begins with an account of their general mortality in 1970 and in 1980. Subsequently, we review the evidence on cardiovascular disease, cancer, diabetes, and other less important causes of death. This is followed by a review of interview data on physical health.

GENERAL MORTALITY

Ellis's work with 1949–1951 data from San Antonio and Houston (Ellis, 1959, 1962) showed that Spanish-surname whites had considerably higher mortality rates and lower life expectancy than did Anglos (other whites), and this was particularly so for women (see Roberts, 1977, for more discussion). Roberts and Askew (1972), who studied 1949–1951 data from Houston, found that the mortality situation of Mexican-Americans at that time was even less favorable than that of blacks. However, their 1960 data showed marked improvements for Mexican-Americans, who by then were in an intermediate position between Anglos and blacks.

Not until 1978 did more recent mortality statistics for Mexican-Americans become available in published form. Bradshaw and Fonner (1978) computed

3.1

Age-Adjusted Mortality Rates per 100,000 Population for Selected Age Groups by Sex and Ethnicity: Texas, 1969–1971

Age	Spanish-Surname Whites		Non-Spanish-Surname Whites		Non-Whites	
	Males	Females	Males	Females	Males	Females
All ages	1,256	863	1,273	928	1,477	989
30-44	331	180	283	160	704	383
45-64	1,282	814	1,415	630	2,079	1,375
65 and over	6,941	5,154	7,338	4,516	6,579	4,708

Source: Adapted from Bradshaw and Fonner, 1978.

Note: Statistics are directly standardized on Texas non-Spanish-surname white female age distribution.

age-adjusted morality rates for 1969–1971 for Texas (table 3.1). They found that overall rates for Spanish-surname men were similar to rates for other white men. Spanish-surname women, however, had death rates approximately 19 percent above those for other white females. At age 65 and over, death rates for Spanish-surname males were slightly lower than those for other white males, while rates for Spanish-surname females were clearly higher than those for other white females. Rates for Spanish-surname whites and other whites were considerably lower than the rates for nonwhites, except in the case of black men age 65 and over.

Patterns similar to the ones described above are noted when we examine life expectancy figures for Texas circa 1970. Table 3.2 shows that the life expectancy at birth of Spanish-surname men was 67.2 years, compared to 68.1 for other white men. A larger gap is observed among females: Spanish-surname females had a life expectancy at birth of 73.4 years, compared to 76.5 for other white women. Blacks were clearly disadvantaged in both sexes with life expectancies of 61.7 and 69.5 years, respectively. At age 65, Spanish-surname men had a life expectancy slightly greater than that for other white men (15.3 v. 13.5 years) while the life expectancy of Spanish-surname women was slightly lower than that for other white women (16.4 v. 17.9 years).

Data from California for 1969–1971 show an even smaller gap in life expectancy between Spanish-surname persons and other whites. Spanish-surname men had a life expectancy at birth of 68.3 years, compared with 68.7 years for other white men and only 63.5 years for nonwhite men. Similarly, Spanish-surname

3.2
Life Expectancy at Selected Ages by Sex and Ethnicity: Texas and California, 1969–1971

State/Age	Spanish-Surname Whites		Non-Spanish-Surname Whites		Non-Whites[a]	
	Males	Females	Males	Females	Males	Females
Texas						
0	67.2	73.4	68.1	76.5	61.7	69.5
20	50.4	56.0	50.5	58.3	45.2	52.3
65	15.3	16.4	13.5	17.9	13.3	16.5
California						
0	68.3	75.2	68.7	76.0	63.5	71.5
15	55.4	62.1	55.5	62.4	51.3	58.9
40	33.4	38.3	32.5	38.6	30.5	36.3
65	14.1	17.4	13.6	17.7	14.5	17.7

Source: Adapted from Siegel and Passel, 1979 (Texas), and Schoen and Nelson, 1981 (California).

[a]Blacks only for California.

women had a life expectancy of 75.2 years, compared to 76.0 for other white women and 75.1 for nonwhite women. At ages 40 to 65, the male Spanish-surname life expectancy slightly exceeded the male other white life expectancy. The figures for females at these ages were virtually identical in the two ethnic groups. Nonwhites were, again, clearly disadvantaged relative to the other groups, except at age 65.

Data for 1980 have recently become available and show that Mexican-Americans may have narrowed the mortality gap even further. In fact, one set of estimates for Texas suggests that the life expectancy of Hispanics may be greater than that for all other groups combined (Gillespie & Sullivan, 1983). However, these figures are probably inflated since they are based on Spanish-surname numerators (deaths) and Spanish-origin denominators (population). It has been estimated that the Spanish origin classification tends to contain approximately 10 percent more people than the Spanish-surname classification (Gillespie & Sullivan, 1983). Even in view of this fact, however, the 1980 data do not

3.3

Ratios of Spanish-Surname Age-Specific Mortality Rates to Other-Surname Rates by Age and Sex: Texas, 1980

Age Group	Males	Females
Under 5	1.11	1.10
5-9	0.78	1.07
10-14	0.74	1.48
15-19	1.25	0.68
20-24	1.59	0.82
25-29	1.43	0.96
30-34	1.36	0.94
35-39	1.16	0.69
40-44	1.08	0.86
45-49	1.04	0.71
50-54	1.03	0.95
55-59	0.93	0.87
60-64	0.86	1.08
65-69	0.88	1.07
70-74	0.95	1.19
75 and over	0.92	1.04

Source: Adapted from Gillespie and Sullivan, 1983.

suggest that Hispanics in Texas have a significantly lower life expectancy than do Anglos.

Life expectancy figures for Hispanics at older ages are not yet available for 1980. However, age-specific death rates using Spanish-surname numerators and Spanish-surname denominators show that Spanish-surname males generally have slightly higher mortality than other-surname males until age 54 (table 3.3). At age 55 and later, their death rates are somewhat lower than those of others. Spanish-surname women, on the other hand, have lower death rates than other women from age 15 to 59. At age 60 and over, their rates become slightly higher than those of other women. When the overall mortality rates by sex were age-standardized relative to the age structure of "other" Texas males and females, Spanish-surname females had a total death rate of 7.5 per 1,000 compared with 7.0 per 1,000 for other females. Spanish-surname males, however, had a rate of 9.0, which is just below the 9.2 rate for other males.

MORTALITY BY CAUSE OF DEATH

Cardiovascular Diseases

The limited literature on Hispanic mortality by cause suggests that southwestern Hispanics have a lower prevalence of cardiovascular diseases than do Anglos or blacks. The literature also suggests that the Hispanic advantage exists only for males. In his San Antonio study, for example, Ellis (1962) found significantly lower mortality from heart disease among Spanish-surname men than among other white men in 1950. Spanish-surname women, on the other hand, had slightly higher rates than other white women. Similarly, Bradshaw and Fonner (1978) computed a lower age-adjusted death rate from ischemic heart diseases for Spanish-surname men in 1969–1971 in Texas than for other white men (table 3.4). The rate for Spanish-surname women, however, was higher than the rate for other white women, although the difference was very small (225.0 and 217.2 per 100,000).

Data for California for 1969–1971 presented by Schoen and Nelson (1981) show an overall male Spanish-surname advantage relative to other whites in total cardiovascular mortality. As in Texas, however, a female Spanish-surname advantage is not observed. Unfortunately, these data are not given separately for heart disease and cerebrovascular diseases. Age-adjusted death rates from cerebrovascular diseases in Texas for 1969–1971 were slightly lower for both male and female Spanish-surname persons and considerably lower than for nonwhites. Kautz (1982) suggests that, although the white/nonwhite differentials in total cardiovascular mortality are due to differences in cerebrovascular mortality, the Spanish-surname/other white differences can be attributed to differences in ischemic heart disease mortality, and this is totally due to differences among men.

Data from New Mexico also show that Hispanics may be advantaged in mortality from diseases of the heart. After excluding Indians with Spanish surnames, Buechley et al. (1979) found that Spanish-surname males had considerably lower age-adjusted death rates from ischemic heart disease than other white men during 1969–1975. Unfortunately, data for females were not given.

Although cardiovascular diseases are generally diseases of middle and old age, researchers rarely present their findings for different age groups. Bradshaw and Fonner (1978), however, have presented age-adjusted death rates from ischemic heart disease and cerebrovascular disease for broad age groups for 1969–1971 for Texas (table 3.4). The data show that the male Spanish-surname advantage relative to other white males in ischemic heart disease mortality is

3.4

Age-Adjusted Mortality Rates from Ischemic Heart Disease and Cerebrovascular Disease per 100,000 Population for Selected Age Groups by Sex and Ethnicity: Texas, 1969–1971

Disease/Age	Spanish-Surname Whites		Non-Spanish-Surname Whites		Non-Whites	
	Males	Females	Males	Females	Males	Females
Ischemic heart disease						
All ages	346.1	225.0	441.4	217.2	382.7	271.8
30-44	30.4	6.7	55.8	9.8	87.4	45.1
45-64	274.1	159.2	530.2	125.7	580.0	363.5
65 and over	2,283.1	1,663.1	2,789.6	1,652.7	2,129.2	1,627.9
Cerebrovascular disease						
All ages	123.9	99.9	130.4	107.7	165.6	159.4
30-44	10.6	10.3	8.1	7.5	33.4	35.1
45-64	95.4	62.5	65.3	46.0	195.2	194.0
65 and over	884.9	787.8	1,003.2	842.1	1,024.2	971.0

Source: Adapted from Bradshaw and Fonner, 1978.

Note. Statistics are directly standardized on Texas non-Spanish-surname white female age distribution.

present in each age group. Among people age 65 and over, Spanish-surname males had a death rate of 2,283.1 per 100,000 compared to a rate of 2,789.6 for other white men. Nonwhite men, on the other hand, who have the highest ischemic heart disease rate in younger age groups, have the lowest rate among men age 65 and over. This is consistent with the low overall death rate of older nonwhites, which may reflect the well-known racial mortality ''crossover'' phenomenon at advanced ages (see Manton et al., 1979; Markides, 1983). Among females, there is essentially no difference in ischemic heart disease mortality for the various age groups between Spanish-surname persons and other whites. Nonwhite women, like nonwhite men, have much higher death rates than the other two ethnic groups at younger ages but have slightly lower rates at age 65 and over, which suggests the existence of a racial mortality crossover among women.

Turning to cerebrovascular diseases, where the overall male Spanish-surname mortality rate is slightly lower than the rate for other whites, we note that Spanish-surname men are disadvantaged at younger ages relative to other whites. However, a crossover is observed in old age, where the Spanish-surname rate is lower than the other white rate (table 3.4). Nonwhite men are greatly disadvantaged at younger ages relative to Spanish-surname and other white men. At age 65 and over, however, their rate is only slightly higher than the rate for other whites. Like the men, Spanish-surname females have higher death rates from cerebrovascular diseases at younger ages but lower rates at age 65 and over. Black women have much higher rates than the other ethnic groups at younger ages. At age 65 and over their rate is slightly below that for other white women but higher than that for Spanish-surname women.

Data by age were recently presented by Friis et al. (1981) from their study in Orange County, California. They found that in 1978 mortality rates from diseases of the heart were considerably lower among Hispanics of both sexes than among non-Hispanics in all age groups. However, since Hispanic rates were computed using Spanish-surname data from death certificates (numerator) and Spanish-origin data for population estimates (denominator), the rate might underestimate Hispanic mortality from diseases of the heart, and this might be particularly so at the oldest ages (Gillespie & Sullivan, 1983).

Researchers have recently examined declines in cardiovascular mortality during the 1970s to investigate whether Hispanics have shared in those declines. Kautz et al. (1981) found that ischemic heart disease and acute myocardial infarction mortality rates showed smaller declines among Spanish-surname persons in Texas from 1970 to 1975 than among other whites and blacks of both sexes. On the other hand, chronic ischemic heart disease mortality increased in importance for all sex-ethnic groups except for Spanish-surname women. In addition, no significant declines in cerebrovascular disease mortality were observed for any of the groups. Stern and Gaskill (1978) observed somewhat similar trends in Bexar County (San Antonio), Texas from 1970 to 1976; ischemic heart disease mortality rates declined among Spanish-surname males and females and other white males. Acute myocardial infarction death rates declined in all sex-ethnic groups while chronic ischemic heart disease mortality declined only among Spanish-surname women. Finally, no significant declines were observed in cerebrovascular mortality in any of the sex-ethnic groups.

Kautz (1982) notes that the greater declines in overall cardiovascular mortality among blacks and the relatively smaller declines among Hispanics than among the other two ethnic groups are bringing the three ethnic groups closer to each other. However, Hispanic rates remain the lowest. Unfortunately, these data are limited to Texas and do not differentiate between the mortality rates of middle-aged and older people.

3.5

Systolic and Diastolic Blood Pressures (mmHg) in Persons 18 to 74 Years of Age by Ethnicity and Age: United States, 1971–1974

Pressure/Age	White	Spanish/ Mexican-American	Black
Systolic			
18-24	119.3 ± 13.6	114.8 ± 13.0	117.5 ± 15.2
25-34	120.4 ± 14.5	119.4 ± 14.0	125.2 ± 15.9
35-44	124.8 ± 17.0	123.3 ± 17.4	132.8 ± 20.7
45-54	132.8 ± 21.1	134.5 ± 17.2	146.4 ± 32.3
55-64	141.3 ± 23.1	142.4 ± 24.5	149.7 ± 26.1
65-74	149.2 ± 24.6	147.9 ± 20.4	159.3 ± 28.6
Diastolic			
18-24	73.8 ± 10.4	70.6 ± 8.9	74.2 ± 11.0
25-34	77.5 ± 10.6	76.7 ± 9.6	81.0 ± 12.9
35-44	81.7 ± 11.9	79.7 ± 11.2	88.5 ± 13.3
45-54	84.9 ± 13.1	85.0 ± 10.1	92.7 ± 16.2
55-64	86.3 ± 12.2	86.3 ± 8.7	91.7 ± 14.0
65-74	85.5 ± 12.7	82.0 ± 10.7	90.6 ± 15.1

Source: National Center for Health Statistics, 1977.

Note. Figures are means ± standard deviations.

The apparent advantage of Hispanics in cardiovascular mortality requires an explanation. National data show that Hispanics (Mexican-Americans) have the lowest systolic and diastolic blood pressures while blacks have the highest (table 3.5). The Hispanic advantage also exists among persons age 65 to 74, but it is slight. Moreover, it is not consistent for all age groups, as table 3.5 reveals. The study by Friis et al. (1981) in Orange County found no differences between Hispanics and non-Hispanics of either sex in systolic and diastolic blood pressure. Christensen et al. (1981) found no differences in either systolic or diastolic blood pressure levels between Mexican-American and other white women. Mexican-American women, however, had higher levels than other white women but lower levels than black women. These findings appeared in all adult age groups.

A California study found that Mexican-Americans had lower serum cholesterol than whites, but the difference was slight. Friis et al. (1981), on the other
hand, found higher serum cholesterol among Hispanic men than among non-
Hispanic men and slightly lower cholesterol among Hispanic women than among
non-Hispanic women. Christensen et al. (1981) found higher overall cholesterol
among Mexican-American men than other white men in Houston. Mexican-
American women, on the other hand, had lower total cholesterol than other
white women. National data show that Hispanics smoke and drink less than
other whites (National Center for Health Statistics, 1980a), findings that are
confirmed by the Orange County study (Friis et al., 1981). Finally, Hispanics
are more obese and less physically active than other whites (National Center
for Health Statistics, 1980a).

It should be obvious that the data are too sketchy and inconsistent to account
for the apparent Hispanic advantage in cardiovascular mortality. The answer
must be sought in factors other than primary prevention factors.

Cancer

Overall cancer mortality rates for Hispanics are similar to those of whites
and blacks; however, marked differences are seen across ethnic groups for specific sites (tables 3.6 and 3.7). The relative advantage for Hispanics is most
pronounced for cancers of the lung, breast, colon-rectum, prostate, and pan-
creas. Higher mortality rates among Hispanics, on the other hand, are found
for malignancies of the cervix, stomach, liver, and gall bladder. Cancer incidence data for Texas (McDonald & Heinze, 1978) and New Mexico (Young,
1982) confirm these ethnic mortality patterns. Examination of cancer rates by
sex and site points to possible etiological mechanisms.

Data for 1969–1971 for Texas show that, in contrast to males, Hispanic
females have a total cancer mortality rate that is slightly higher than that of
white females but lower than that of black females. This excess female cancer
mortality is present in the 45–64 age group as well as in the 65 and older group
(table 3.6). Spanish-surname men, on the other hand, have a lower cancer
death rate at every age, including 65 years and over. Blacks are clearly disadvantaged at younger ages, but in old age their cancer death rates are just below
the rates of other whites.

If we look at site-specific death rates, some interesting patterns emerge. For
cancers of the trachea and lung, Hispanic females again fare slightly worse
than the comparison groups, yet most of the excess deaths occur at older ages
(table 3.6). Hispanic males of all ages die of lung cancer at much lower rates
than other white males (see also Buechley et al., 1957; Lee et al., 1976; Menck
et al., 1975). The relative disadvantage of black men at younger ages becomes
an advantage at age 65 and over.

It is likely that ethnic differences in cigarette smoking account for part of
the lung cancer differential (Thomas, 1979). Hispanics of both sexes smoke

3.6

Age-Adjusted Cancer Mortality Rates per 100,000 Population for Selected Age Groups by Sex and Ethnicity: Texas, 1969–1971

Type of Cancer/Age	Spanish-Surname Whites		Non-Spanish-Surname Whites		Non-Whites	
	Males	Females	Males	Females	Males	Females
All neoplasms						
All ages	185.6	147.7	218.0	133.0	238.9	152.4
30-44	32.4	48.3	42.8	49.1	59.6	68.2
45-64	216.6	235.4	320.0	223.9	440.5	308.2
65 and over	1,136.7	748.5	1,211.4	640.7	1,151.5	621.4
Trachea and lung						
All ages	43.9	14.1	70.2	13.0	63.4	11.3
30-44	4.9	2.2	11.6	5.8	18.4	4.9
45-64	53.1	20.4	134.3	29.6	151.3	24.8
65 and over	277.9	82.3	346.6	49.5	243.1	
Breast						
All ages	-------	19.5	-------	24.5	-------	24.5
30-44	-------	13.2	-------	14.3	-------	18.5
45-64	-------	42.0	-------	55.9	-------	57.5
65 and over	-------	72.3	-------	87.3	-------	78.0
Cervix/uteri						
All ages	-------	12.6	-------	5.4	-------	15.2
30-44	-------	8.0	-------	5.0	-------	12.1
54-64	-------	28.1	-------	9.8	-------	37.5
65 and over	-------	42.3	-------	20.3	-------	42.4

Source: Adapted from Bradshaw and Fonner, 1978.

Note. Statistics are directly standardized on Texas non-Spanish-surname white female age distribution.

Health Status and Health Service

3.7
Colo-Rectal, Pancreatic, and Prostatic Cancer Mortality Rates per 100,000 Population for Selected Age Groups by Sex and Ethnicity: Texas, 1980

Type of Cancer/Age	Spanish-Surname Whites		Non-Spanish-Surname Whites		Non-Whites	
	Males	Females	Males	Females	Males	Females
Colo-rectal						
35-54	5	3	10	7	9	8
55-74	34	24	68	54	69	63
75 and over	98	85	244	215	195	295
Pancreatic						
35-54	5	4	5	3	14	2
55-74	28	30	37	23	57	40
75 and over	93	50	101	85	112	61
Prostatic						
35-54	1.2	--	0.6	---	1.3	---
55-74	39	--	52	---	87	---
75 and over	224	--	364	---	516	---

Source: Bureau of Vital Statistics, Texas Department of Health, 19 .

less than whites and blacks (National Center for Health Statistics, 1980a), yet data from New Mexico show that the smoking gap is much wider among males (Samet et al., 1980). Patterns of cigarette use might also explain the lower rates of chronic bronchitis and emphysema among Hispanic males, but lower rates of asthma persisted after controlling for smoking in the New Mexico study (Samet et al., 1982). Furthermore, cigarette habits cannot explain the higher lung cancer mortality rate among Hispanic females, especially the marked excess in older women. This excess mortality is particularly puzzling when one considers the evidence that lung cancer incidence is lower for Hispanic females in Texas (McDonald & Heinze, 1978). It is clear that factors other than smoking must underlie the ethnic cancer mortality differences.

Mortality differences by ethnicity for breast and cervical cancer suggest a possible association with reproductive behavior (Menck et al., 1975). Mexican-

American females have earlier and higher fertility than do women in other U.S. ethnic groups, a factor which may explain at least in part the lower risk for breast cancer and the elevated risk for cervical cancer found in this group (table 3.6). Early onset of sexual relations is associated with cervical cancer (Rotkin, 1973; Terris et al., 1967), and breast cancer has been linked to early child-bearing and high fertility (MacMahon et al., 1970; Research Group for Population-Based Cancer Registration, 1976).

A possible nutritional link is also suggested in the combination of lower risk for breast and colon cancer among Hispanics (tables 3.6 and 3.7). This trend appears to be consistent for both sexes across all age groups. Newell and Boutwell (1981) hypothesize that dietary patterns, perhaps involving levels of fat and fiber consumption, may explain the relative advantage for breast and colon cancer mortality among Mexican-Americans.

Finally, a possible genetic influence in ethnic cancer rates is suggested by the fact that populations with partial Indian ancestry, including Mexican-Americans, have rates for most cancers that are intermediate between those for Anglos and tribes with generally full Indian heritage (Sievers & Fisher, 1983). Data from New Mexico support the case for a proportionate genetic contribution to cancer mortality, with the strongest argument made in studies of gall bladder cancer among that state's tri-ethnic population (Devor & Buechley, 1980; Morris et al., 1978).

Diabetes

Prevalence rates for non-insulin-dependent diabetes are two to five times greater among Mexican-Americans than in the general U.S. population (Harris et al., 1983; Stern & Gaskill, 1978). Data for 1969–1971 for Texas show that mortality from diabetes was much higher among Spanish-surname persons than among other whites or blacks in both sexes and at every age. Elevated risk for diabetes is found among males and females at all ages; however, the largest is among older Hispanic women (table 3.8).

Obesity has been studied as a possible risk factor underlying these differences. High rates of diabetes and obesity are characteristic of economically disadvantaged groups in general, and Stern et al. (1981) found elevated rates of both obesity and diabetes among Mexican-Americans in Laredo, Texas. More recent findings from the San Antonio Heart Study (Stern et al., 1983), however, show that obesity alone cannot account for the high rate of diabetes. After controlling for social class and obesity, the risk for diabetes among Mexican-Americans of both sexes was even greater than without such controls.

As with cancer, it appears that genetic factors at least partially explain the prevalence of diabetes among Hispanics. High rates of diabetes are found among American Indians, and those tribes with close to 100 percent native genes, such as the Pima, have the highest rates of all. Moreover, a correspondence between genetic admixture and diabetes has been reported in studies comparing tribes

3.8

Age-Adjusted Mortality Rates from Diabetes Mellitus per 100,000 Population for Selected Age Groups by Sex and Ethnicity: Texas, 1969–1971

Age	Spanish-Surname Whites		Non-Spanish-Surname Whites		Non-Whites	
	Males	Females	Males	Females	Males	Females
All ages	34.3	53.0	15.7	16.2	22.5	36.9
30-44	9.0	4.4	3.7	3.2	10.5	9.7
45-64	59.1	77.3	15.1	13.8	36.4	72.0
65 and over	173.2	311.1	101.4	108.4	108.7	168.3

Source: Adapted from Bradshaw and Fonner, 1978.

Note. Statistics are directly standardized on Texas non-Spanish-surname white female age distribution.

of varying genetic makeup (Brosseau et al., 1979). Given the variable presence of Native American genes in the Hispanic population, one would expect genetic factors to influence diabetes in proportion to hereditary affinity. Research conducted in San Antonio has also uncovered that degree of Native American admixture is related to diabetes prevalence among Mexican-Americans even after other factors are taken into consideration (Gardner et al., 1984; Relethford et al., 1982; Stern et al., 1982).

Other Diseases

In addition to diabetes, Hispanics appear to be disadvantaged in other diseases. Data from Texas for 1969–1971 show that Spanish-surname whites were considerably more likely to die from infectious and parasitic diseases, influenza and pneumonia, and accidents and all violent deaths than were other whites. Their death rate from infectious and parasitic diseases was even higher than the rate for nonwhites, as was the female rate from influenza and pneumonia. The male Spanish-surname death rate from influenza and pneumonia was slightly lower than the nonwhite rate, and death rates from accidents and violence were considerably lower among Spanish-surname persons than among nonwhites.

Data from California for 1969–1971 are in general agreement with the data from Texas. Spanish-surname persons had higher age-adjusted death rates than other whites from infectious and parasitic diseases, from influenza and pneumonia, and from accidents and violence. Spanish-surname women, however,

3.9

Age-Adjusted Mortality Rates per 100,000 Population from Infectious and Parasitic Diseases, Influenza and Pneumonia, and Accidents and Violence for Selected Age Groups by Sex and Ethnicity: Texas, 1969–1971

Disease/Age	Spanish-Surname Whites		Non-Spanish-Surname Whites		Non-Whites	
	Males	Females	Males	Females	Males	Females
Infectious and parasitic diseases						
All ages	31.8	18.7	10.2	6.3	22.1	12.7
30-44	7.1	8.0	2.6	1.7	13.0	6.3
45-64	26.0	14.9	11.8	6.5	27.3	16.7
65 and over	150.9	73.1	46.6	25.6	74.0	30.3
Influenza and pneumonia						
All ages	49.3	36.8	41.6	25.6	54.0	30.7
30-44	4.1	7.3	4.1	4.0	20.8	10.4
45-64	27.9	17.4	26.0	13.4	55.6	27.9
65 and over	310.1	224.0	281.5	169.6	246.8	139.3
Accidents and violence						
All ages	123.8	37.6	108.6	47.6	183.6	56.8
30-44	157.5	30.9	111.7	43.0	315.1	66.2
45-64	142.9	32.9	138.8	51.3	245.5	55.8
65 and over	259.6	100.9	243.7	129.9	197.6	98.1

Source: Adapted from Bradshaw and Fonner, 1978.

Note. Statistics are directly standardized on Texas non-Spanish-surname white female age distribution.

had lower death rates than other white women from causes other than motor vehicle accidents and violence (Schoen & Nelson, 1981).

Table 3.9 shows ethnic differences in mortality from the diseases under discussion for broad age groups for Texas in 1969–1971. The Spanish-surname disadvantage in infectious and parasitic diseases relative to other whites is evident at every age, including persons 65 years old and over, where the death rate is approximately three times as great and holds for both sexes. The Spanish-surname disadvantage relative to nonwhites is also significant in old age, where the Spanish-surname death rate is twice as high as the nonwhite rate among men and two and a half times as high among women.

The Spanish-surname to other white disadvantage in mortality from influenza and pneumonia is slight among men, including those age 65 and over. Among women, however, the disadvantage is notable and exists at each age. The Spanish-surname death rate from influenza/pneumonia is considerably lower than the nonwhite rate at ages 30–64 but is higher at age 65 and over. This is observed in both sexes (table 3.9).

The Spanish-surname to other white disadvantage in male mortality from accidents and violence is notable at ages 30–44 but is only slight among persons age 45 and older. The female Spanish-surname disadvantage is marked among persons age 30 to 64 but reverses itself in old age. At ages 30–64, Spanish-surname mortality from accidents and violence is considerably lower than the rate for nonwhites. At age 65 and over, however, the Spanish-surname rate is higher than the nonwhite rate while no difference is noted among women (table 3.9).

Data from New Mexico for 1976–1978 are available for selected causes of death (State of New Mexico, 1980). They show that mortality from influenza and pneumonia is lower among Spanish-surname men aged 35 to 64 than among other whites of similar age. At ages 65–74, the rate is higher among Spanish-surname men but becomes lower again after age 75. Spanish-surname women also have lower death rates from influenza and pneumonia at ages 35 to 64 and slightly higher death rates at age 65 and over.

New Mexico data also show that Spanish-surname men have higher death rates than other whites from accidents and violence until age 54, and lower rates at age 55 and over. As in Texas and California, however, Spanish-surname women have lower death rates from accidents and violence than other white women.

FUNCTIONAL HEALTH INDICATORS

Most of the information presented thus far is based on relatively objective data obtained from death certificates and clinical assessments. Such data are useful in that they provide "disease" or "medical" models of the health of populations, but they say little about how populations perceive and cope with disease, illness, and disability. "Functional" models define health in terms of a person's ability to function. Such models have been particularly popular in gerontology. Their proponents believe that "the things that an old person can do, or thinks he can do, are useful indicators of both how healthy he is and the services he will require" (Shanas & Maddox, 1976, p. 597).

Shanas and Maddox (1976) suggest that the medical and functional models are not irreconcilable as evidenced by efforts to compare physical examination findings with self-reports by older people. Such efforts have shown moderate associations between physical examination findings or other objective health indicators and self-ratings (e.g., Fillenbaum, 1979; Maddox & Douglass, 1973), suggesting that the two represent different, albeit related, dimensions of health.

Elderly Hispanics have been found to rate their health as poorer than Anglos but as better than blacks. National data for 1976–1977, for example, show 24.4 percent of Spanish-origin elderly, compared with 30.9 percent of white and 20.3 percent of black elderly, rating their health as "excellent." Conversely, 11.4 percent of Spanish-origin, 7.4 percent of white, and 16.7 percent of black elderly rated their health as "poor" (National Center for Health Statistics, 1980, p. 42). Similar findings comparing elderly Mexican-Americans and Anglos in San Antonio were obtained by Markides and Martin (1983) (see also the review by Newton, 1980).

The extent to which the lower self-ratings of health by elderly Hispanics relative to elderly Anglos (as well as their better self-ratings relative to elderly blacks) reflect their more "objective" health status can be ascertained by examining data from the 1976 Health Interview Survey (Moy & Wilder, 1978). Table 3.10 shows that Spanish-origin persons reported lower age-adjusted limitation of activity due to chronic conditions and fewer days lost from work per currently employed person than the total and black populations.

On the other hand, persons of Spanish origin reported slightly greater restricted activity and bed disability days than the total but less than the black population. They also reported slightly fewer doctor visits and short-stay hospital episodes than the total population, although it is not clear whether the last two variables are indicators of health status or of health care utilization. Among persons age 65 and over, there is virtually no difference between Spanish-origin persons and the total population on activity limitation due to chronic conditions and doctor visits. Slightly fewer Spanish-origin elderly reported a short-stay hospital episode than all elderly. On the other hand, they reported more days of restricted activity and bed disability than the total population. Finally, Spanish-origin elderly reported fewer days lost from work, although this figure was based on too few cases to yield a reliable estimate.

The above figures on the functional health indicators of the Hispanic elderly are generally consistent with their lower self-ratings of health relative to elderly Anglos and higher self-ratings relative to elderly blacks. They are not, however, consistent with the lower prevalence of cancer and cardiovascular disease.

Percentage of Population with Selected Health Characteristics by National Origin or Race and Age: United States, 1976

Characteristic	Total Population	Spanish Origin[a]	Black[a]	Other
Limitation of activity due to chronic conditions				
All ages[b]	14.3	13.5	17.4	14.0
Under 17	3.7	2.8	3.7	3.9
17-44	8.9	7.7	10.5	8.7
45-64	24.3	23.5	32.3	23.4
65 and over	45.4	34.9	52.8	44.6
Doctor visit in past year				
All ages[b]	75.5	70.4	74.2	76.2
Under 17	74.2	67.6	67.6	76.2
17-44	75.4	69.8	76.9	75.6
45-64	75.2	71.2	76.1	75.2
65 and over	80.0	79.4	78.8	80.2
Short-stay hospital episode in past year				
All ages[b]	10.6	10.4	10.6	10.6
Under 17	5.5	5.4	4.7	5.7
17-44	11.4	12.0	13.5	11.0
45-64	12.5	10.8	12.0	12.6
65 and over	18.3	17.1	12.9	18.8
Days of restricted activity per person per year				
All ages[b]	18.2	20.3	23.3	17.6
Under 17	11.0	14.3	7.5	11.3
17-44	14.2	12.9	19.1	13.6
45-64	25.4	26.5	39.1	23.8
65 and over	40.0	53.1	52.5	38.4

3.10 (cont.)

Characteristic	Total Population	Spanish Origin[a]	Black[a]	Other
Days of bed disability per person per year				
All ages[b]	7.1	9.3	9.9	6.6
Under 17	5.1	7.8	3.9	5.0
17-44	5.6	7.0	8.5	5.1
45-64	8.9	10.5	16.9	8.0
65 and over	15.1	20.5	18.5	14.6
Days lost from work per currently employed person per year				
All ages under 17[b]	5.3	5.0	7.4	5.1
17-44	5.0	4.6	7.7	4.8
45-64	6.1	6.1	7.2	6.0
65 and over	4.0	3.7[c]	4.0[c]	4.0

Source: Moy and Wilder (1978).

[a]Persons reported as both Spanish origin and black are included in both categories.

[b]Figures for all ages were age-adjusted by the direct method to the age distribution of the civilian non-institutionalized population or that of the currently employed population.

[c]Figure does not meet standards of reliability and validity.

CONCLUSION

Little is known about the health status of Hispanics in the Southwest or elsewhere in the United States. Even less is known about the health status of older Hispanics, a small but rapidly growing component of the Hispanic population. The data presented here are largely from official records (vital statistics and census enumerations). Problems of linking the two for studying the health and demographic characteristics of Hispanics are numerous and well known (see, e.g., Hernandez et al., 1973; Trevino, 1982). Community surveys that avoid such issues are few, and they, too, have their problems in identifying Hispanic populations (Hayes-Bautista, 1980).

If anything can be deduced about the health status of Hispanics from the evidence presented here, it is that the health status of Hispanics in the Southwest falls between that of other whites and that of blacks. This is also true for older Hispanics. However, Hispanics appear to have lower death rates than other whites and blacks from heart disease and cancer. This advantage appears to be confined to men. Primary prevention factors might be involved, but they do not appear to explain this advantage. Why it occurs only among men remains a mystery at this time.

It should also be noted that the clear nonwhite disadvantage in overall mortality as well as in cardiovascular and cancer mortality disappears or even reverses itself in old age. Although poor quality data on older blacks might be a factor, scholars have speculated that high early mortality among blacks results in a kind of selective survival to advanced ages, particularly after age 75 (see Manton et al., 1979; Markides, 1983). The reversal of mortality differentials in old age has been referred to as the mortality crossover phenomenon. The absence of this kind of crossover in the mortality rates of Hispanics and other whites can perhaps be explained by the fact that Hispanic mortality rates are not markedly lower than those of other whites.

The data also make clear that Hispanics at all ages are disadvantaged relative to others in diabetes mortality (and also incidence) and in mortality from infectious and parasitic diseases and from influenza/pneumonia. Although their disadvantage in the latter two is probably related to their poorer socioeconomic conditions, their disadvantage in diabetes persists after socioeconomic factors are controlled. Here is, perhaps, a major disease that especially afflicts Hispanics in middle and old age and is related at least in part to the high degree of Native American admixture found in Hispanic populations, particularly in the Southwest.

Research thus far has not clearly demonstrated how socioeconomic and cultural factors affect the health status of older Hispanics. For example, little is known about how the Hispanic diet affects the incidence of certain diseases, whether positively or negatively. Data on such factors as smoking and alcohol consumption are too sketchy to indicate how they might affect health. There is often a great deal of discussion about how the Hispanic family might shield individuals from stress to a greater extent than families in other groups, but few systematic studies exist to support this notion.

As Hispanics are becoming more acculturated into the larger society, they appear to be adopting some of its values and practices that might affect their health. Alcohol consumption, for example, appears to increase with acculturation (Caetano, 1983). How these changes will affect the health status and health needs of older Hispanics in the years to come remains to be investigated. Fortunately, data from the recently completed Hispanic Health and Nutrition Examination Survey conducted by the National Center for Health Statistics will soon be available. These data covering approximately 12,000 Hispanics (including people to age 74) will present a challenge to investigators seeking a better understanding of the health of older Hispanics and of Hispanics in general.

NOTE

1. Although the Texas data in Table 3.1 do not show a racial crossover in total female mortality, a narrowing of differentials is observed. It should be noted that overall mortality crossovers are usually observed at around age 75 or later (Manton et al., 1979; Markides, 1983).

REFERENCES

Andersen, R., Lewis, S. Z., Giachello, A. L., Aday, L. A. & Chin, G. (1981). Access to medical care among the Hispanic population of the Southwestern United States. *Journal of Health and Social Behavior, 22,* 78–89.

Black, W. C., & Key, C. R. (1980). Epidemiologic pathology in New Mexico's tri-ethnic population. *Pathology Annual, 15,* 181–194.

Bradshaw, B. S., & Fonner, E., Jr. (1978). The mortality of Spanish-surnamed persons in Texas: 1969–1971. In F. D. Bean & W. P. Frisbie (Eds.), *The demography of racial and ethnic groups* (pp. 261–282). New York: Academic Press.

Brosseau, J. D., et al. (1979). Diabetes among the three affiliated tribes: Correlation with degree of Indian inheritance. *American Journal of Public Health, 69,* 1277–1278.

Buechley, R. W., Dunn, J. E., Jr., Linden, G., & Breslow, L. (1957). Excess lung cancer mortality rates among Mexican women in California. *Cancer, 10,* 63–66.

Buechley, R. W., Key, C. R., Morris, D. L., Morton, W. E., & Morgan, M. V. (1979). Altitude and ischemic heart disease in tricultural New Mexico: An example of confounding. *American Journal of Epidemiology, 109,* 663–666.

Bullough, B. (1972). Poverty, ethnic identity and preventive health care. *Journal of Health and Social Behavior, 13,* 347–359.

Bureau of Vital Statistics, Texas Department of Health. (1981). *Vital Statistics for Texas.* Austin, TX: Texas Department of Health.

Caetano, R. (1983). Drinking patterns and alcohol problems among Hispanics in the U.S.: A review. *Drug and Alcohol Dependence, 18,* 1–15.

Casas, J. M. & Keefe, S. E. (Eds.). (1978). *Family and mental health in the Mexican American community.* (No. 7). Los Angeles: Spanish-Speaking Mental Health Research Center, U.C.L.A.

Christensen, B. L. et al. (1981). Cardiovascular risk factors in a tri-ethnic population: Houston, Texas, 1972–1975. *Journal of Chronic Disease, 34,* 105–118.

Clark, M. (1959). *Health in the Mexican American culture.* Berkeley, CA: University of California Press.

Devor, E. J., & Buechley, R. W. (1980). Gallbladder cancer in Hispanic New Mexicans. *Cancer, 45,* 1705–1712.

Ellis, J. M. (1959). Mortality differentials for a Spanish-surname population group. *Southwestern Social Science Journal, 39,* 314–321.

———. (1962). Spanish-surname mortality differences in San Antonio, Texas. *Journal of Health and Human Behavior, 3,* 125–127.

Estrada, L. F., Hernandez, J., & Alvirez, D. (1977). Using census data to study the Spanish heritage population of the United States. In C. H. Teller, L. F. Estrada, J. Hernandez, & D. Alvirez (Eds.), *Cuantos somos: A demographic study of the Mexican-American population* (pp. 13–59). Austin: Center for Mexican-American Studies.

Fillenbaum, G. (1979). Social context and self-assessment of health among the elderly. *Journal of Health and Social Behavior, 20,* 45–51.

Friis, R., Nanjundappa, G., Pendergast, T. J. & Welsh, M. (September–October, 1981). Coronary heart disease mortality and risk among Hispanics and non-Hispanics in Orange County, California. *Public Health Reports, 96,* 418–422.

Gardner, L. I., Stern, M. P., Haffner, S. M., Gaskill, S. P., Hazuda, H. P., Relethford, J. H., & Eifler, C. W. (1984). Prevalence of diabetes in Mexican-Americans: Relationship to percent of gene pool derived from Native American sources. *Diabetes, 33,* 86–92.

Gillespie, F. P., & Sullivan, T. A. (1983, April). What do current estimates of Hispanic mortality really tell us? Paper presented at the annual meeting of the Population Association of America, Pittsburgh.

Hanis, C., Ferrell, R. E., Barton, S. A., Aguilar, L., Garza-Ibarra, A., Tulloch, B. R., Garcia, C. A., & Schull, W. J. (1983). Diabetes among Mexican-Americans in Star County, Texas. *American Journal of Epidemiology, 118,* 659–672.

Hays-Bautista, D. E. (1980). Identifying "Hispanic" populations: the influence of research methodology upon public policy. *American Journal of Public Health, 70,* 353–356.

Hernandez, J., Estrada, L., & Alvirez, D. (1973). Census data and the problem of conceptually defining the Mexican-American population. *Social Science Quarterly, 53,* 671–687.

Hoppe, S. K. & Heller, P. L. (1975). Alienation, familism and the utilization of health services by Mexican Americans. *Journal of Health and Social Behavior, 16,* 304–314.

Karno, M. & Edgerton, R. B. (1969). Perception of mental illness in a Mexican-American community. *Archives of General Psychiatry, 20,* 233–238.

Kautz, J. A. (1982). Ethnic diversity in cardiovascular mortality. *Arteriosclerosis Reviews, 9,* 85–108.

Kautz, J. A., Bradshaw, B. S., & Fonner, E. (1981). Trends in cardiovascular mortality in Spanish-surnamed, other white, and black persons in Texas, 1970–1975. *Circulation, 64,* 730–735.

Lee, E. S., Robert, R. E., & Labarthe, D. R. (1976). Excess and deficit lung cancer mortality in three ethnic groups in Texas. *Cancer, 38,* 2551–2556.

MacMahon, B., Cole, P., Lin, T. M., et al. (1970). Age at first birth and cancer of the breast: A summary of an international study. *WHO Bulletin, 43,* 209–221.

McDonald, E. J., & Heinze, E. B. (1978). *Epidemiology of cancer in Texas.* New York: Raven Press.

McLemore, S. D. (1963). Ethnic attitudes toward hospitalization. *Southwestern Social Science Quarterly, 43,* 341–346.

Maddox, G. L. & Douglass, E. B. (1973). Self-assessment of health: A longitudinal study of elderly subjects. *Journal of Health and Social Behavior, 14*, 87–93.

Madsen, W. (1964). *Mexican Americans of South Texas*. New York: Holt, Rinehart & Winston.

Manton, K. G., Poss, S. S. & Wing, S. (1979). The black/white crossover: Investigation from the perspective of the components of aging. *The Gerontologist, 19*, 291–300.

Markides, K. S. & Martin, H. W. (1979). Predicting self-rated health among the elderly. *Research on Aging, 1*, 97–112.

Markides, K. S. (1983). Minority aging. In M. W. Riley, B. B. Hess & K. Bond (Eds.), *Aging in society: Selected reviews of recent research* (pp. 115–138). Hillsdale, NJ: Lawrence Erlbaum Associates, Inc.

Markides, K. S., Martin, H. W., with Gomez, E. (1983). *Older Mexican Americans: A study in an urban barrio*. Monograph of the Center for Mexican American Studies. Austin, TX: University of Texas Press.

Menck, H. R., et al. (1975). Cancer incidence in the Mexican-American. *Journal of the National Cancer Institute, 55*, 531–536.

Morris, D. L., Buechley, R. W., Key, C. R., & Morgan, M. V. (1978). Gallbladder disease and gallbladder cancer among American Indians in tricultural New Mexico. *Cancer, 42*, 2472–2477.

Moy, C. S., & Wilder, C. S. (1978). Health characteristics of minority groups, United States, 1976. Advance data from *Vital and Health Statistics*, Public Health Service (No. 27). Washington, DC: U.S. Government Printing Office.

Nall, F. C. & Spielberg, J. (1967). Social and cultural factors in the responses of Mexican Americans to medical treatment. *Journal of Health and Human Behavior, 8*, 299–308.

National Center for Health Statistics. (1974). *Summary report: Final mortality statistics, 1970* (Vol. 22, No. 11). Rockville, MD: Public Health Service.

———. (1977). *Blood Pressure Levels of Persons 6–74 Years: United States 1971–1974* (National Health Survey, Series 11, No. 207). Hyattsville, MD: Author.

———. (1978). Total serum cholesterol levels of adults 18–74 years: United States, 1971–1974 (National Health Survey, Series 11, No. 205). Hyattsville, MD: Author.

———. (1980). *Health practices among adults: United States, 1977* (No. 64, HHS Publication No. 81-1250). Hyattsville, MD: Public Health Service.

———. (1980b). *Health United States—1979*. Public Health Service. Washington, DC: U.S. Government Printing Office.

Newell, G. R., & Boutwell, W. B. (1981). Cancer differences among Texas groups: An hypothesis. *The Cancer Bulletin, 33*(3), 113–114.

Newton, F. (1980). Issues in research and service delivery among Mexican American elderly. *The Gerontologist, 20*, 208–213.

Relethford, J. H., Stern, M. P., Gaskill, S. P., & Hazuda, H. P. (1983). Social class, admixture, and skin color variation in Mexican-Americans and Anglo-Americans living in San Antonio, Texas, with special reference to diabetes prevalence. *American Journal of Physical Anthropology, 61*, 97–102. Unpublished manuscript.

Research Group for Population-Based Cancer Registration. (1976). Cancer registries in

Japan: Activities and incidence data. *Annual report of the Center for Adult Diseases* (Vol. 16, pp. 12–31). Osaka, Japan: Center for Adult Diseases.

Roberts, R. E. (1977). The study of mortality in the Mexican-American population. In C. H. Teller, L. F. Estrada, J. Hernandez & D. Alvirez (Eds.), *Cuantos somos: A demographic study of the Mexican-American population* (pp. 131–155). Austin, TX: Center for Mexican American Studies.

Roberts, R. E., & Askew, C. (1972). A consideration of mortality in three subcultures. *Health Services Reports, 87,* 262–272.

Rotkin, I. D. (1973). A comparison review of key epidemiological studies in cervical cancer related to current searches for transmissible agents. *Cancer Research, 33,* 1353–1367.

Rubel, A. (1966). *Across the tracks: Mexican Americans in a Texas city.* Austin, TX: University of Texas Press.

Samet, J. M., Key, C. R., Kutvirt, D. M., & Wiggins, C. L. (1980). Respiratory disease mortality in New Mexico's American Indians and Hispanics. *American Journal of Public Health, 70,* 492–497.

Samet, J. M., Schrag, S. D., Howard, C. A., Key, C. R., & Pathak, D. R. (1982). Respiratory disease in a New Mexico population sample of Hispanic and non-Hispanic whites. *American Review of Respiratory Diseases, 125,* 152–157.

Saunders, L. (1954). *Cultural differences in medical care: The case of the Spanish-speaking people of the Southwest.* New York: Russell Sage.

Schoen, R., & Nelson, V. F. (1981). Mortality by cause among Spanish-surnamed Californians, 1969–1971. *Social Science Quarterly, 62,* 259–274.

Shanas, E. & Maddox, G. L. (1976). Aging, health and the organization of health resources. In R. H. Binstock & E. Shanas (Eds.), *Handbook of the aging and the social sciences* (pp. 592–618). New York: Van Nostrand Reinhold.

Siegel, J. S., & Passel, J. (1979). Coverage of the Hispanic population of the United States in the 1970 census. *Current Population Reports* (Series P-23, No. 82). Washington, DC: U.S. Bureau of the Census.

Sievers, M., & Fisher, J. R. (1983). Cancer in North American Indians: Environment versus heredity. *American Journal of Public Health, 73,* 485–487.

State of New Mexico. (1980). *Unpublished Raw Data.* Santa Fe, NM: New Mexico State Department of Health.

Stern, M. P., & Gaskill, S. P. (1978). Secular trends in ischemic heart disease mortality from 1970 to 1976 in Spanish-surnamed and other white individuals in Bexar County, Texas. *Circulation, 58,* 537–543.

Stern, M. P., Gaskill, S. P., Allen, C. R., Jr., Garza, V., Gonzales, J. L., & Waldrop, R. H. (1981). Cardiovascular risk factors in Mexican-Americans in Laredo, Texas. I. Prevalence of overweight and diabetes and distributions of serum lipids. *American Journal of Epidemiology, 113,* 546–555.

———. (1981). Cardiovascular risk factors in Mexican-Americans in Laredo, Texas. II. Prevalence and control of hypertension. *American Journal of Epidemiology, 113,* 556–562.

Stern, M. P., Gaskill, S. P., Hazuda, H. P., Gardner, L. I., & Haffner, S. M. (1983). Does obesity explain excess prevalence of diabetes among Mexican-Americans? Results of the San Antonio Heart Study. *Diabetologia, 24,* 272–277.

Stern, M. P., Haskell, W. L., Wood, P. D., Osarin, K. E., King, A. B., & Farquhar, J. W. (1974). Affluence and cardiovascular risk factors in Mexican-Americans and other whites in three northern California communities. *Journal of Chronological Disease, 28,* 623–636.

Terris, M., et al. (1967). Epidemiology of cancer of the cervix. V. The relationship of coitus to carcinoma of the cervix. *American Journal of Public Health, 57,* 840–847.

Thomas, D. B. (1979). Epidemiologic studies of cancer in minority groups in the United States. *National Cancer Institute Monograph, 53,* 103–113.

Trevino, K. M. (1982). Vital and health statistics for the U.S. Hispanic population. *American Journal of Public Health, 70,* 979–982.

Vernon, S. W., Tilley, B. C., Neale, A. V., & Steinfeldt, L. (1985). Ethnicity, survival, and delay in seeking treatment for symptoms of breast cancer. *Cancer, 55,* 1563–1571.

Weaver, J. L. (1973). Mexican-American health care behavior: A critical review of the literature. *Social Science Quarterly, 54,* 86–102.

West, K. M. (1978). *Epidemiology of diabetes and its vascular lesions.* New York: Elsevier.

Young, J. L. (1982). Cancer in minorities. In D. L. Parron, F. Solomon, & C. D. Jenkins (Eds.), *Behavior, health risks, and social disadvantage* (pp. 19–31). Washington, DC: National Academy Press.

Young, J. L., Percy, C. L., & Adire, A. J. (Eds.) (1981). Surveillance, epidemiology, and end results: Incidence and mortality data, 1973–1977. *National Cancer Institute Monograph, 57,* 1087.

A COMPARATIVE ANALYSIS OF NEED, ACCESS, AND UTILIZATION OF HEALTH AND HUMAN SERVICES

Margarita C. Treviño

INTRODUCTION

This chapter describes selected aspects of the nature of the demand for health and human services by the Hispanic elderly within the framework of the aging process as well as the health status of nonwhites in the United States. Barriers to access and utilization are presented as experiential commonalities of the poor and nonwhites, and the chapter concludes with suggestions for bridging the gap between providers of health and human services and the Hispanic elderly.

THE NATURE OF THE DEMAND FOR HEALTH AND HUMAN SERVICES

Personal health constitutes a principal area of concern for the Hispanic elderly in the United States (Cartwright et al., 1969; Newton & Ruiz, 1981; Szapocznik, 1982). They are not alone in this case. Hickey (1980) writes:

However we view good health—as a goal to be attained, a state to be sustained, or even a basic right to be enjoyed, we all, at least eventually, perceive the process of aging as a threat to health. It is not an unreasonable perception, since the accumulated effects of aging result in decreased immunities and resistance to disease and in acute illnesses of longer duration; the multiple effects of chronic problems and declining potencies give the elderly greater reason to be concerned about the state of their health. (p. ix)

COMPARATIVE FRAMEWORKS

As noted in table 4.1, irrespective of the scarcity of ethnic-specific data about the health and human service needs of Hispanic elderly, areas of shared needs can be identified and transferred from the majority of older adults in the general population to the Hispanic aged. One of these transferable indices is the socio-economic profile of the elderly in general. Measurable descriptors define the older adult in American society as having low levels of educational attainment; having low income; being retired from service or farm jobs; and living in sub-standard housing. The majority are also urban dwellers (Kart et al., 1978; Newton & Ruiz, 1981; Smith, 1973). Unique to the Hispanic elderly is the fact that the majority were born in another country and communicate principally in Spanish (Newton & Ruiz, 1981).

Types of illness constitute a second area of commonalities among the elderly. According to Wantz and Gay (1981), of the nearly 30 million people over age 65 in the United States today, 86 percent report having at least one chronic condition (persistent and degenerative diseases). Approximately half of these individuals encounter limitations in their daily activity because of poor health (Wantz & Gay, 1981). Other common health disorders of the elderly are heart disease, hypertension, cancer, arthritis, diabetes, and chronic pulmonary problems (Hickey, 1980; Kart et al., 1978). Comparable illness conditions have been reported in the Hispanic elderly (Torres-Gil, 1983).

In addition, the older population is also at risk for poor nutrition (Smith, 1973). This problem is usually compounded by loneliness, depression, a lack of companionship, poor health, and limited economic resources (Feldman et al., 1982). Inadequate income, reports Abeyta-Behnke (1982), is considered to be the most important cause of malnutrition. For the Hispanic elderly, economic limitations mean inadequate amounts of food consumption and reduced choices of foods. According to Abeyta-Behnke (1982), the groups who are least informed and least concerned about nutrition are the poor, minorities, and the elderly. The area of nutrition for health maintenance and health promotion is an additional area of need that is superimposed upon the Hispanic elderly as a consequence of poverty, ethnic minority status, and the aging process. Lacking hard data, it is safe to describe the Hispanic elderly as an at-risk population for malnutrition.

With regard to mental health, Cuellar (1981) notes:

Older populations are believed to have an increased incidence of numerous events or conditions which correlate highly with mental problems. At present, there is no evidence to believe older age groups have a decreased incidence of mental illness. On the contrary, older populations are believed to have an even greater incidence of mental health problems. (p. 189)

Smith (1973) quotes Grollman: "Year in and year out, the older people rank at the bottom of the list for suicide threats and attempts. Annually, they top the statistics of those whose suicide has been completed" (p. 21).

4.1

Comparative Analysis of Socioeconomic Characteristics and Types of Illnesses among the Elderly

Characteristics/ Illnesses	Majority Older Adults in the General Population	Hispanic Older Adults
Socioeconomic charac- teristics		
Low levels of edu- cation	X	X
Low income	X	X
Retired from ser- vice or farm jobs	X	X
Living in substan- dard housing	X	X
Urban dwellers	X	X
American born	X	
Foreign born		X
English speaking	X	
Spanish speaking		X
Types of illnesses		
Heart disease	X	X
Hypertension	X	X
Cancer	X	X
Arthritis	X	X
Diabetes	X	X
Chronic pulmonary problems	X	X
Mental illness	X	Not known
Poor nutrition	X	Not known

Brandt (1982) refers to the Epidemiologic Catchment Area Program conducted by the National Institute of Mental Health as the first attempt to gather data on the prevalence and incidence rates of mental health disorders as classified in the psychiatric manual and diagnosed and treated in clinical practice. Although this project develops an epidemiological profile of mental health disorders across a broad spectrum of the general population, the survey has been augmented to include a larger number of older adults. Brandt (1982) states: "The aging, of course, are important not only for today's planning for public health policy, but for the decades ahead as well. However, at present, we do not have the kinds of data that are essential for intelligent public health planning for this segment of the population'' (p. 401).

Referring specifically to the Mexican-American elderly, Cuellar (1981) points out that "for older Mexican-American populations there well might be a multiple effect of aging and socioeconomic and cultural factors which produces an especially high risk of developing mental problems. This hypothesis, however, has yet to be tested empirically'' (p. 189). With reference to the Hispanic elderly in general, little information is currently available concerning the nature and distribution of mental health problems, misuse of drugs, and alcoholism.

The nature of the demand for health and human services among the Hispanic elderly is thus characterized by multiple threads of commonality with the life experiences of majority older adults in the general population. As a universal process, aging establishes a common base of human needs among the elderly.

An additional framework against which the health and human service needs of the Hispanic older adult can be assessed is the health status of racial and ethnic minorities in the United States. The characterization of need can be exemplified by the commonality of health conditions shared by minority populations in contrast to nonminorities. Two common indices are low income and low levels of education (U.S. Department of Health, Education, and Welfare, 1980). Other health-specific data include higher death rates; shorter life expectancy; deaths more frequently attributed to heart disease, cancer, stroke, and diabetes; higher prevalence rates of arthritis, asthma, impairments of the spine, tuberculosis, and vision problems; and higher incidence of limitation of activity due to chronic conditions (U.S. Department of Health and Human Services, 1980).

The report *Health Status of Aged Medicare Beneficiaries* (1983) indicates that the lower the levels of education, the higher the reported cases of activity limitation. It was also found that the number of unreported conditions was higher for persons with low income and that perception of health status varied directly with education and family income, with perceptions improving in conjunction with increasing levels of education and income.

Older Mexican-Americans have been reported as rating their physical health as "poor" more often than their counterparts in the majority population (Project MASP, 1978) p. 2. Health is rated more frequently as "poor/very poor" by Mexican–American elderly women (Project MASP, 1978) p. 2. The Mexican–American elderly have also reported poor physical health as the reason for retirement more frequently than have the nonminority elderly in the general population. This is especially true for elderly Mexican–American men (Project MASP, 1978) p. 3.

In the process of describing the nature of the demand for health and human services, it becomes readily apparent that the needs of the Hispanic elderly derive from a base of multiple causation. Their problems do not change from the time when they were younger; their needs only become greater in magnitude and more complicated with age. Three case histories demonstrate this point. The names of the persons have been changed to ensure their anonymity. The setting for all three cases is an urban barrio located in the shadow of the downtown skyline. The dilapidated houses and unkept streets reflect decay, and poverty is prevalent.

Case One

Juanita Garcia is sixty-three years of age. She is a retired farm worker with a third grade education and does not speak English. Juanita lives with her husband in a crowded, worn-out frame house in the outlying fringes of the barrio. Their four children are married and have relocated to more affluent parts of the city. Religious relics adorned with faded plastic flowers and different types of festive Christmas ornaments decorate the front porch. Plants fill the few empty spaces left near the entrance.

Juanita has just been released from the county hospital after undergoing abdominal surgery. She does not know why she had the surgery nor what it consisted of. She is weak and unable to care for herself. The edible food in the house has been brought in by a neighbor. The utilities have been turned off. Juanita's husband does yard work occasionally but has not been employed for several months. The family car is broken, and there are signs of destitution about the house.

The Garcias' children keep themselves occupied with their own families. The one daughter who visits her parents fairly frequently is a single parent. She is struggling to raise her three children while her husband is serving a prison term. Juanita's husband, who is usually shy and withdrawn, has assumed an active role in helping his wife during her convalescence. Juanita herself is certain that things are going to work out.

Case Two

Pedro Lopez is seventy-two years of age and suffers from hypertension. He is a retired unskilled worker with a second grade education and does not speak English. He came to the United States from Mexico as a young man.

The barrio clinic is Pedro's primary source of health care, but he has difficulty keeping appointments. He is the guardian and sole caregiver for his only child, a mentally retarded thirty-six-year-old daughter, since his wife died several years ago. He refuses to institutionalize his daughter, and he does not attend the nutrition clinic in the barrio because he does not want to leave her under anyone else's care.

Case Three

Adolpho Martinez is eighty-three years of age and lives alone. He has no formal education and does not speak English. Adolpho has hypertension, diabetes, and limited mobility. His seventy-six-year-old brother, who checks on him from time to time, took him to the barrio clinic because of a sore on Adolpho's foot. Adolpho had had the sore for several weeks and had been soaking his foot in warm water, but the pain was severe and the home treatment was not working. After an examination at the clinic, Adolpho was diagnosed as exhibiting the onset of advancing gangrene and was referred to the county hospital emergency room for care.

Summary

The nature of the demand for health and human services by the Hispanic elderly can be characterized by a series of predisposing factors. These are needs derived from the general socioeconomic conditions of this population group, the health condition of minorities, and the inherent problems of the aging process. These predisposing factors, in turn, have a direct bearing on the accessibility and utilization of health and human services.

DETERMINANT PARAMETERS OF ACCESS AND UTILIZATION OF HEALTH AND HUMAN SERVICES

Given the nature of the demand for services by the Hispanic elderly and that of the general elderly population and nonwhites, transferable considerations are also apparent in the areas of access and utilization. According to Szapocznik (1982), although the elderly constituted only 11 percent of the total population in 1977, they accounted for 29 percent of the total health dollars spent in the United States. Two-thirds of this money came from the public sector. Persons over 65 years of age accounted for 35 percent of all visits to physicians. Medical care was thus consumed by the elderly at a rate far in excess of their numbers in the total population. The health needs of the elderly population in general, therefore, require increased access to and utilization of health services.

A growing number of studies has identified the problems of access to and utilization of health services by the poor and nonwhites (Riessman, 1981; U.S. Department of Health and Human Services, 1980; U.S. Department of Health, Education, and Welfare, 1979; Weaver, 1976). This is an additional framework against which the problems of access and utilization of the Hispanic elderly may be examined. A national profile of the utilization patterns of low-income and nonwhite persons reveals the following:

—Twelve percent of the U.S. population had no regular source of medical care in 1977

—Minorities experienced the greatest difficulty in acquiring and regularly utilizing medical services

—Low-income families (annual income of less than $7000) were 5 times as likely as families in the $15,000 plus income bracket to have no health insurance coverage

—When health care was required, lower income groups were most likely to utilize hospital outpatient clinics and emergency rooms, public health clinics, and neighborhood health centers

—Whites, in general, had greater access to health care facilities than nonwhites and took advantage of medical services more frequently because of greater access

—Hispanics were less likely than all others to have visited a physician's office

—Persons from poor minority backgrounds were likely not to make dental visits (U.S. Department of Health and Human Services, 1980).

Additional national data show that nonwhites are underrepresented in nursing homes and institutions for the mentally retarded and overrepresented in institutions for the mentally ill (U.S. Department of Health, Education, and Welfare, 1979).

Predictors of utilization have been identified in some studies as race, income, and education (Riessman, 1981). Other studies list the illness behavior of the client and the client's evaluation of the physician as influencing factors (Kane et al., 1976). Others attribute the underutilization or nonutilization of health services by the poor to (1) unequal purchasing power; (2) ignorance of where to go for help; (3) cultural differences in perception of illness and treatment required; and (4) feelings of alienation, self-image, and a lack of confidence in the medical care system (Kane et al., 1976). The list of barriers to service utilization also includes: (1) the professional and organizational "culture" which results in inadequate clinic operations; (2) the long waits, impersonality, and bureaucratic procedures with which the client must deal; and (3) social distance between user and provider, medical jargon, and lack of effective communication (Riessman, 1981).

Many of these structural/organizational and sociocultural factors have implications for access and service utilization among the Hispanic elderly; added to these are their preference for Spanish as the dominant language and their use of folk medicine as an alternative treatment modality. A history of discrimination for Hispanics as a minority of color compounds the complexity of access and utilization of health and human services by the Hispanic elderly (Ruiz & Olmedo, 1977; Szapocznik, 1982; Torres-Gil, 1983).

A common misconception about the Hispanic elderly is that they are taken care of by the extended family. Estrada (1977) writes that "the stereotype which views the Spanish-origin elderly as living with their children and being adequately cared for in their old age is incorrect" (p. 13). He states that the Spanish-origin elderly are "three times as likely to live alone than in someone else's home . . . especially elderly Spanish-origin women" (p. 9). In a survey of older Mexican-Americans, Crouch (1972) reports that the respondents had less expectation of aid from their families than from the church or the government. Maldonado (1977) continues: "Sociologists have theorized that aged Mexican-Americans are adequately cared for through the extended family patterns common to their culture. This popular viewpoint, based on factual data and historical observation, is now being questioned'' (p. 18). He asserts that, conse-quently, ''a serious shortage of services for the Mexican-American elderly has developed'' (p. 18). Suarez (1982) maintains that ''our experience to date in-dicates that there are more Puerto Rican elderly living in an atmosphere of rejection and isolation while surrounded by family than we care to admit. Many are systematically excluded from participation in family activities, discussions, and decisions which affect their lives'' (p. 127). Although these multiple pa-rameters are not exhaustive, they are representative of some of the well-recog-nized factors that function as determinants of health and human service utili-zation patterns of the Hispanic elderly.

BRIDGING THE GAP

One way to bridge the gap between the health and human service needs of the Hispanic elderly and the accessibility and utilization of resources is to de-velop a better understanding of providers' and clients' expectations of each other. The provider can expect that the Hispanic elderly's receptivity to the service and compliance behaviors will depend upon the client's perception of (1) the seriousness of the problem; (2) the severity of the case; (3) the vulner-ability to other problems (social and physical); and (4) the benefits of taking action in light of the barriers to be overcome. The expectations of major ref-erence groups such as family and peers are also important in the decision-making process for the Hispanic elderly. An additional influence will be the nature of previous experiences with service providers. If the Hispanic elder has been treated with indifference, ridiculed, or was unable to communicate with the provider, he or she will likely not return for services (Rosenstock, 1974).

The provider can expect that the emotional/attitudinal tone with which ser-vices are provided will be used as a measure of the acceptability of those ser-vices. The provider can also expect that sameness of language facility or ethnic identity will not be an automatic passport for acceptance by the Hispanic el-derly. An enabling attitude accompanied by supportive action is more effective.

On the other hand, the Hispanic elderly client has certain expectations from providers. Hispanic clients expect freedom from stereotypic characterization. The best way to know or to find out what is culturally relevant or acceptable to the Hispanic elderly is to get to know the individual. The Hispanic elderly also expects compatibility of communication systems. This does not mean com-monality of language usage but, rather, understandability of messages and terms.

Hispanic elderly clients also expect sensitivity on the part of the provider to their religious and cultural beliefs and practices. The provider is expected to be sensitive to the Hispanic elder as a whole person. The Hispanic client wants to be viewed and treated as someone who is subjected to the requirements to adapt to the dynamics of a technical society and an ever-changing and stressful en-vironment.

The promise of provider-client partnerships in joint problem solving has yet to become a reality in the provision of services for the Hispanic elderly. Guidelines for the cultivation of collaborative partnerships include involving the Hispanic elderly in the development of action plans for problem resolution. They must be given choices. Providers can also identify significant others in the life of the Hispanic elder. They may be family members, friends, or neighbors. These persons can serve as a part of the support system which may, in turn, encourage the use of services. The need to facilitate language translation cannot be overemphasized. If necessary, a translator network should be established. This could be done by identifying bilingual employees or volunteers and training them to the specifics of the services provided. It is also important to determine the Hispanic elderly's degree of literacy before handing them forms and questionnaires. Being given forms in another language can be an intimidating experience, particularly in the absence of the ability to read or write.

If a Hispanic elder is to be referred to another community service agency, it is important to make every effort possible to know the service system before making the referral. A contact person should be identified in the second agency, and facilities for language translation in that agency should be explored in order to inform the Hispanic client of whether a translator will need to accompany him or her.

The number of race/ethnic and age-specific community service organizations is growing throughout the country. An additional way to increase the accessibility and utilization of health and human service organizations for the Hispanic elderly is for providers to have a working knowledge of community resources with a specific focus on service provision for the Hispanic elderly. An additional resource that can be helpful in bridging the gap between providers and the Hispanic elderly is the Hispanic leadership in the community. There are growing numbers of Hispanic leaders in media, education, business, politics, and religion who can assist in the articulation of need and can lend sensitivity to the special concerns of the Hispanic elderly.

CONCLUSIONS

The nature of the need and the demand for health and human services by the Hispanic elderly carries an inherent urgency to disassemble the obstacles to service access and utilization. The similarity of the need of the Hispanic elderly transferred from the life experiences of the elderly in the general population, the poor, and minorities of color provides a beginning knowledge base from which to propel planning and provision of services toward higher planes of needs satisfaction. A wealth of technology is available to design effective service delivery systems for any population group in this country. The essential nontechnical component needed is the attitudinal commitment to close the gap between the need and the service—between the Hispanic elder and the provider.

REFERENCES

Abeyta-Behnke, M. A. (1982). A nutrition profile of the Hispanic elderly. In P. Vivo & C. Delgado (Eds.), *The Hispanic elderly: La fuente de nuestra historia, cultura, y carino* (pp. 114–117). Washington, DC: U.S. Department of Health and Human Services.

Brandt, E. N., Jr. (1982). Prevention as policy. *Public Health Reports, 97,* 399–401.

Cartwright, W. J., et al. (1969). Use of community resources among aged Mexican-Americans. In *Proceedings of the Southwestern Sociological Association,* 1969.

Crouch, B. M. (1972). Age and institutional support: Perceptions of older Mexican-Americans. *Journal of Gerontology, 27,* 524–529.

Cuellar, I. (1981). Service delivery and mental health services for Chicano elders. In M. Miranda & R. A. Ruiz (Eds.), *Chicano aging and mental health* (p. 189). Washington, DC: U.S. Department of Health and Human Services.

Estrada, L. (1977). The Spanish-origin elderly: A demographic survey. *Research Utilization Report, 4,* 13–14.

Feldman, E. B., Greene, J. M., & Kirchhofer, A. (1982). "Nutrition." In R. B. Taylor (Ed.), *Health promotion: Principles and clinical applications* (pp. 161–195). Norwalk, CT: Appleton-Century-Crofts.

Hickey, T. (1980). *Health and aging.* Monterey, CA: Brooks/Cole.

Kane, Robert L. et al. (1976). Poverty, illness, and medical utilization: An overview. In R. L. Kane (Ed.) *The Health Gap: Medical services and the poor* (pp. 8–9). New York: Springer Publishing Co.

Kart, C. S., et al. (1978). *Aging and health, biologic and social perspectives.* Menlo Park, CA: Addison-Wesley.

Maldonado, J. D. (1977). La familia Mexico Americana and the elderly. *Research Utilization Report, 4,* 9, 18.

Newton, F., & Ruiz, R. A. (1981). Chicano culture and mental health among the elderly. In M. Miranda & R. A. Ruiz (Eds.), *Chicano aging and mental health* (DHHS Publication No. ADM 81-952, pp. 38–75) Rockville, MD: National Institute of Mental Health.

Project MASP Health Factsheet. (1978, August). Ethel Percy Andrus Gerontology Center, Los Angeles, CA: University of Southern California.

Riessman, C. K. (1981). Improving the use of health services by the poor. In P. Conrad & R. Kern (Eds.), *The sociology of health and illness* (pp. 541–557). New York: St. Martin's Press.

Rosenstock, I. M. (1974). The health belief model and preventive health behavior. In M. H. Becker (Ed.), *The health belief model and personal health behavior* (pp. 27–59). Thorofare, NJ: Charles B. Slack.

Ruiz, R., Ruiz, O. & Esteban, L. (1977, September–December). The identification of mental health research priorities for the hispanic elderly in the United States. *Research Bulletin.* University of California, Los Angeles: Spanish Speaking Mental Health Research Center.

Smith, B. K. (1973). *Aging in America* (p. 21). Boston: Beacon Press.

Suarez, J. (1982). The elderly Puerto Rican in the United States: Some observations. In P. Vivó and C. D. Votaw (Eds.), *The Hispanic elderly la fuente de nuestra historia cultura y cariño* [The fountain of our history, culture, and love] (pp.

127–130). Rockville, MD: U.S. Department of Health and Human Services, Public Health Service.

Szapocznik, J. (1982). A non-physician's view of geriatric medical education and training. In P. Vivó and C. D. Votaw (Eds.), *The Hispanic elderly la fuente de nuestra historia cultura y cariño* [The fountain of our history, culture, and love] (pp. 46–52). Rockville, MD: U.S. Department of Health and Human Services, Public Health Service.

Torres-Gil, F. (1983). Social policy and elder Hispanics: A preliminary analysis of health status, rehabilitation needs, and barriers to service utilization. In R. A. Orgren (Ed.), *An assessment of the rehabilitation, physical, and mental health status of the elderly Hispanic* (pp. 61–72). Downey, CA: Professional Staff Association of Rancho Los Amigos Hospital, Inc.

U.S. Department of Health and Human Services. (1980). *Health of the disadvantaged* (DHHS Publication No. [HRA] 80-633). Washington, DC: Author.

———. (1983, September). *Health status of aged Medicare beneficiaries* (Series B, Descriptive Report No. 2) (pp. 5–6). Washington, DC: Author.

U.S. Department of Health, Education, and Welfare. (1979). *Health status of minorities and low-income groups* (DHEW Publication No. [HRA] 79-627). Washington, DC: Author.

———. (1980). *Health United States, 1979* (DHEW Publication No. [PHS] 80-1232). Washington, DC: Author.

Wantz, M. S., & Gay, J. E. (1981). *The aging process: A health perspective.* Cambridge, MA: Winthrop.

Weaver, J. L. (1976). *National health policy and the underserved, ethnic minorities, women, and the elderly.* St. Louis: C. V. Mosby.

Part III
POLITICS AND PUBLIC POLICY

5

INTEREST GROUP POLITICS: EMPOWERMENT OF THE *ANCIANOS*

Fernando Torres-Gil

INTRODUCTION

Alexis de Tocqueville's observation that "in no other country . . . has the principle of association been more successfully used" than in the United States (de Tocqueville, 1945, p. 198) underlies the contemporary phenomenon of individuals organizing to promote their particular interests. This phenomenon has led to a proliferation of groups organized to promote specific objectives through political lobbying. Older persons have also learned to play the interest group politics game, but to what extent have older Hispanics become a special interest group advocating for the issues that affect them as elders and as members of the Hispanic community?

With the Hispanic population projected to be the largest minority group in America after the year 2000 (McKay, 1981) and with the Hispanic elderly as the fastest-growing age group in the country, it is important to know whether they are following the same pattern as older persons in general. Are they actively involved with organizations that represent older persons? Do they have the same interests and attitudes about politics as the general elderly population? Have they had an influence on public policies for older persons? Or do they have different political behavior patterns? The investigation of these questions is timely, contemporary, and important to our understanding of older Hispanics as a new ethnic aged group. With the empowerment of the Hispanic community—as evidenced by the increase of elected Hispanic officials and growing media attention to the political potential of Hispanics—it becomes essential to know what role older Hispanics are playing in politics and the direction their involvement is taking.

The purpose of this chapter is to analyze the role of older Hispanics as a developing special interest group by describing the potential for age-based politics to occur in the Hispanic community and to explore the effects that the empowerment of *ancianos* will have on the Hispanic family, Hispanic politics, and senior citizen interest groups. The remainder of the chapter will explore the extent to which the literature has addressed this issue, examine the historical transition undergone by older persons in traditional Latino society, and identify the pressures that create the potential for older Hispanics to become an interest group.

POLITICS, POLICY, AND THE HISPANIC ELDERLY

An obstacle in examining the role of Hispanic elders in politics and their status as an interest group lies in the dearth of literature focusing on these issues. In the last fifteen years, there has been a dramatic growth in Hispanic political literature. Much is being written about the political developments in the Mexican-American, Cuban, and Puerto Rican communities, from the civil rights era of the 1960s to the decade of the Hispanics in the 1980s (Acuna, 1981; Garcia, 1974). Investigations have been conducted on political behavior, historical events, political philosophy, attitudes and values, and contemporary events occurring in Hispanic communities.

For example, Garcia and de la Garza (1977) examined Chicano politics and such areas as attitudes, politics, and the Hispanic community but made no mention of elders. The journal *Aztlan,* a major intellectual platform for new ideas, features no articles that focus on the role of older Hispanics (e.g., see Garcia, 1983).

If the general Hispanic political literature has ignored the role of older persons, the literature on the politics of aging has hardly done more. In recent years, several books have been published that deal exclusively with politics, public policy, and the elderly. Lammers (1983) explored public policy issues and the role of older persons. Hudson (1981) presented a series of readings on various aspects of politics and policy. Williamson et al. (1982) articulated a historical and theoretical context for understanding the politics of aging. Other than a brief mention made by Lammers (1983) about the development of interest groups representing minority elderly, however, nothing on the role of Hispanic elders is presented in these major works.

On the other hand, Hudson and Binstock (1976) made direct mention of the development of aged-based organizations representing minority elders in their discussion of the National Caucus on the Black Aged. They asked, "How does the political activities of the Caucus compare with those of other black organizations, and how does its behavior compare with that of other organizations such as the Asociación Nacional pro Personas Mayores?'' (p. 387). This question was posed in the context of the potential for minority aged-based organizations to reflect the interest group nature of politics and as such suggests that attention must be given to the development of aged-based organizations representing minority elders.

More recent literature has begun to explore the role of older Hispanics. Torres-Gil and Becerra (1977) presented the results of a study on political participation of Mexican-American elderly and found that this group had low participation rates but high interest in political issues. Further elaboration on the issues affecting Mexican-American elderly participation in politics was presented by Torres-Gil (1982) in a book describing the theoretical, political, and historical dimensions of Hispanic elderly political behavior.

Recent publications have also addressed various aspects of social and political participation of minority elders (Manuel, 1982; McNeely & Colon, 1983; Torres-Gil, 1986a and 1986b). Several chapters in these books examine social policies affecting the minority aged and the political involvement of older members in minority groups. Their focus, however, is illustrative of a preoccupation with the role of professionals and organizations in advocating for the political interests of older minorities. They describe the growth of national organizations representing the minority elderly, the gains and accomplishments in promoting research and acquiring services, and the development of a cadre of researchers and advocates for the Hispanic elderly.

Yet, these publications do not address to any great extent the actual involvement and, more importantly, the leadership of elders in advocacy activities, nor do they examine the traditional patterns of political behavior among Hispanic elders and the extent to which they are influenced by American interest group politics. In effect, they have not addressed the question of older Hispanics actively and directly involved in representing their own interests and acting as a special interest group, as older persons in general are now doing. Gerontologists have devoted little attention to how older persons have shaped political developments in the Hispanic community and whether they have been active in the empowerment of Hispanics. The focus appears to be the political activity of the elites—professionals, national organizations, researchers—and their quest for influence, status, and benefits. To this extent, much work remains to be done in Hispanic gerontology to address the key issue of this chapter: the potential for the Hispanic elderly to develop as an interest group.

ANCIANOS' ROLES IN TRANSITION

Shifting Gears

It is important to shift our focus from the role of professionals and advocates in representing the needs of older Hispanics and organizational politics to the political involvement of older Hispanics in representing their own interests.

Several factors create pressure for greater assertion by elders in providing leadership. First, the number of elders in the Hispanic population is growing. Hispanics comprise 6.4 percent of the U.S. population; 4.9 percent of them are age 65 and over (U.S. Department of Commerce, 1981a). Although Hispanics are a relatively young group with a median age of 23.2 years, the increase in life expectancy for all Americans presumably has begun to generate a larger cohort of Hispanic elders.

Data show that, in the five-year period from March 1975 to March 1980, the Hispanic population age 60 years and over increased at a rate nearly 2.5 times that of the remaining Hispanic population (25 percent v. 9 percent). The increase in the 65 and over age group (34 percent) was substantially higher than the increase of persons 60 years of age and older. The growth rate of older Hispanics during that period was more than twice the rate for older Hispanics in the same age group (25 percent v. 10 percent) (U.S. Department of Health and Human Services, 1981). In fact, a recent report from the Bureau of the Census projects that the Spanish-origin population age 65 and older may quadruple by 2015 and be 7 times its present size in 2030 (U.S. Department of Commerce, 1986).

Second, the growth of the older population in the United States is reflected by the expansion of public benefits and public programs for older persons, such as Social Security, Medicare, the Older Americans Act, nutrition projects, and transportation services. But these public services have not been equally beneficial for the Hispanic elderly. For a variety of reasons—including inadequate access, discrimination, and lack of bilingual and culturally sensitive staff— older Hispanics have underutilized these programs (Cuellar & Weeks, 1980; Guttman, 1980). Elderly Hispanics face multiple jeopardies, putting them in a precarious position in their old age: they tend to have lower incomes, greater difficulties accessing health care, less education, fewer retirement and pension benefits, and are concentrated in neighborhoods that are more prone to crime and provide inadequate housing (Berger, 1983; Freeman et al., 1987).

These multiple jeopardies place older Hispanics in a vulnerable position as they age. Traditionally, they have relied on the family and their culture to ensure that they receive the emotional, physical, and financial support necessary to maximize independence and dignity. The Hispanic culture has been characterized by the extended family, which provides the older person with meaningful roles within an intergenerational milieu (Sotomayor, 1973). This culture, at least in larger cities, is changing, and it no longer ensures that the older person will find support in the neighborhood or in family or cultural institutions such as the church (Becerra & Shaw, 1984; Korte, 1982). This incongruency of culture has led to conflict, role loss, alienation, and in some cases, depression (Kruszewski et al., 1982). What we are seeing perhaps is a crisis developing in the Hispanic community—a crisis for both older persons and their families. If they are faced with major social, economic, and personal needs; if the traditional institutions can no longer provide for them; and if they are living longer and growing in numbers, what will replace the traditional roles of older Hispanics? Where will they exercise their energies and talents?

The situation facing older persons in general gives important clues to the answer. Many elderly face the same dilemmas. Their response has been to organize as an age-based constituency, using their numbers to become active in politics and policy. Will Hispanic elders respond in the same manner? We cannot be certain that they will use the same strategies. But, in order to better understand the potential for older Hispanics seeking political interest group politics as a new vehicle for asserting their identity and responding to the challenges and crises of aging in a new society, it is useful to examine the historical evolution of older persons in traditional Latin cultures.

Evolutionary Changes

The general literature on ethnic studies, anthropology, sociology, and history demonstrates that older persons have had significant roles to play in traditional Latin American society. These roles were a product of the familial, religious, and political systems of that society, where gerontocracies prevailed. Rural agrarian societies of Latin America were based on the extended family, where age was rewarded with respect, deference, and leadership. The older person served as the patriarch or matriarch (generally the former); dispensed wisdom; was the transmitter of culture, language, and history; and played the role of arbitrator.

In turn, older persons were responsible for providing cohesion, continuity, and social stability. The church and religion played a central role in the lives of older persons, serving as the spiritual, social, and political center of power, leadership, and stability. It was a central, unifying, cohesive force, and its traditions of custom, *compadrazgo*, respect, dominance, submission, and authoritarianism served elders well by reinforcing the dominance of gerontocracy in Latin society. In later years, when the church faced the opposition of progressive Latin governments—particularly in Mexico—because of its hold on social and economic resources, the elders were most vehement in supporting the established power of the church (Hough, 1982).

The dominance of the elderly in Latin society was not altogether one of benevolence or the moral superiority of Latin culture. It was partly based on the scarcity of older persons—life expectancy was low. Their influence was also a reflection of political customs in Latin American society—customs characterized by "caciquism" (Machado, 1982). The political traditions of Mexico, the Caribbean islands, and other Latin countries constituted an important element in the role of those older persons engaging in politics. Local caciques (bosses) were individuals with absolute control over local areas, based on the relative geographic isolation between the villages and the administrative hubs of capitals. The caciques would exercise virtual control over an area, through alliances with other powerful members of a village. Sometimes these unions resulted from familial ties, sometimes *compadrazgo* played a role, and at other times wealth elevated an individual to power within a village.

In the evolution of the cacique system, a transmutation of the concept of nobility has occurred. The *don,* a title of respect generally applied to the Spanish gentry (and to the Indian nobility who became integrated into the Spanish system), was eventually granted to any powerful individual who possessed some political influence in a village. The beneficiaries were the elders of the community, where "old men were venerated with the title Don" (Machado, 1982, p. 57). This *don* concept had its roots in the widely scattered haciendas of Latin countries and was predicated upon an interdependence between the patron (employer) and his workers. The traditional mores of caciquism, *don,* and *patron* lent themselves well to the role of elders in political activities. With elders' engagement in politics, these customs guaranteed that, along with respect for them as older persons, they could expect submissiveness and deference.

Revolution in Latin America, particularly Mexico, the end of the *hacendado* economic order, and immigration to the United States brought an end to the traditional political roles of the elderly. Immigration to the United States and the accompanying social, political, and economic changes created tremendous pressures to redefine the traditional roles of the church, caciques, patrons, and donships—the very customs that guaranteed elders a measure of social and political control. The changes brought about through urbanization, acculturation, and American political customs created cultural conflicts that are still evident today. These changes did not occur overnight but are the product of several decades and are now, with the aging of the immigrants from the turn of the century, finally playing themselves out.

Transitional Period

A transitional period, marked by change from traditional roles to the incongruence of cultural expectations, began around the turn of the century. During the past eight decades we have witnessed the exclusion of elders from traditional leadership roles in the political, social, and family life of Latin cultures. By the 1960s, older Hispanics had lost their traditional roles and moved to the background of political life. During that period, Mexican-American and Puerto Rican militancy reached its height, generally led by the young. Since the 1960s, elders have played a minimal role in the tremendous political advancements in the Mexican, Puerto Rican, and Cuban communities. Why has there been such a dramatic shift from the traditional roles of elders in Latin culture to submissiveness and invisibility? A short history describing the transitional period will help to illuminate the reasons why this shift has occurred and why elders may be ready to reassert their political identity in a different fashion.

The Mexican Revolution of 1910–1920 ended the old economic order and eliminated the system of servitude and peonage characteristic of the *hacendado* system. It also led to the exodus of many poor peasants seeking to escape the civil disorder and looking for jobs and a new life in the United States. Prior to that time, their experience of the United States was tempered by the Treaty of Guadalupe Hidalgo (1848) and the subsequent repression and secondary status experienced by Mexicans and Mexican-Americans along the border areas of the United States.

Immigration to the United States uprooted this cohort of elderly from traditional customs and life-styles, but also led to the economic and social advancement of their children and grandchildren. The Depression tested the fortitude of this cohort and provided its members with independence and strength that exist yet today and which some scholars assert is a strength in a society where they are no longer appreciated. The Depression also instituted fear of authorities because of the numerous deportations that occurred at that time, further dislocating families and extended relationships. The fact that many individuals did not acquire citizenship added to their sense of insecurity in this country.

Subsequent events counterbalanced the negative experiences of revolution, migration, and deportation (McLemore, 1980). The sons of these elders joined the armed services in great numbers to fight for the United States during World War II, and their daughters were able to work in the war industries and acquire a measure of independence. It was this generation that returned from the war and began the great political organizations that are still with us today. The GI Forum, begun by veterans, is perhaps the best known civil rights group of the World War II generation. The 1950s and 1960s saw the evolution of a more assertive, militant, and nationalistic group of Hispanics: the grandchildren of today's elders. Their political strategies and causes brought gains to the Hispanic community but served to further distance them from political traditions.

Puerto Ricans experienced a different set of events, but with similar consequences for their elders. The surplus labor existing in Puerto Rico after World War II, the inclusion of Puerto Ricans in the armed services during the war, and the great migration to the mainland encouraged today's elderly Puerto Ricans to move to New York and other mainland cities to find work and enjoy a better life-style. The urbanization of the Puerto Rican population in the United States changed the political traditions enjoyed by elders on the island, just as in the Mexicans' situation. In the Puerto Ricans' case, however, many elders have attempted to return to the mainland, after working for twenty or thirty years, only to find that the traditional life-styles have been greatly altered by American influences.

Today's Cuban elderly are recent immigrants to the United States, having arrived as political refugees from Castro's revolution of 1958. The Cuban population is characterized by a high median age, reflecting the middle-income middle-aged group that comprised the first wave of refugees. They were better prepared than Mexicans and Puerto Ricans to cope with American society and to prosper as older persons. Having learned the language of their host society, they quickly used their education and skills to develop the economic base of south Florida and become the middle class of the Cuban-American community.

The conclusion of this historical overview is that today's cohorts of Mexican-American, Puerto Rican, and Cuban elders have witnessed tremendous changes during their lifes. They reflect the dramatic transition from the elderly Latin immigration to the United States to an acculturated, growing, and influential segment of society in this country. But they also reflect the burden they have had to carry, which is now affecting their abilities to live out their lives: the effects of immigration, economic and social dislocation, assimilation of children and grandchildren, and loss of traditional social and political norms have led to a political behavior termed the *politics of deference* (Torres-Gil, 1982).

The politics of deference is characterized by several features: (1) elders' acquiescence to the young to provide political leadership; (2) a more cautious approach to political involvement; (3) alienation from contemporary political gains in the Hispanic community; and (4) a vulnerability reflected in the fears and insecurities that they are not yet fully accepted as American citizens. Many Mexican-American elderly are not yet citizens and assume that they are ineligible for Social Security, despite the fact that they have worked for many years in the United States, raising their families and paying into the system. Puerto Rican and Cuban elderly are more likely to speak Spanish than English and to hold to traditional customs. In many respects, they are not as well educated or economically secure as their children and grandchildren.

This is not to say that today's cohort of elderly have not played political roles. In many cases they have. The Mexican-American elderly created the League of United Latin American Citizens (LULAC) and fought the first battles against discrimination and repression. They provided support to Cesar Chavez in his early days. The Cuban-American elderly took the initiative of leaving Cuba and opened the doors of advancement for the the current economic and political gains of the Cuban-American community. The Puerto Rican elderly were the first to travel to the mainland to seek jobs and raise their families.

However, this political participation was not based on cultural or traditional norms that emphasized leadership by elders (the gerontocracy of Latin society) but, rather, on individualism—individual efforts by energetic and committed persons. Today we find a situation where the effects of this transitional period have crystallized and where "political ageism," the alienation of elders from political leadership, has been institutionalized in the Hispanic community. No longer are elders expected to be given deference simply because of age; now they must prove themselves as individuals. No longer are they automatically approached for advice by political leaders; they are more likely to be ridiculed for maintaining old political styles associated with the cacique and patron systems.

At one time elders took consolation in their continued importance in maintaining the family and participating in church activities. The respect they received and the roles they played throughout this transitional period, particularly in rural and urban enclaves, gave them an important and significant position in their communities. This, too, however, is eroding. It took longer than the political erosion, but the change is unmistakable. What has resulted is a set of political and cultural conflicts occurring among today's cohorts of Hispanic elders—conflicts that have placed elders in a precarious situation and created political, emotional, and social distress. Their leadership in the Hispanic community is all but ignored by younger political leaders. The assimilation and upward mobility of their children and grandchildren have left them behind. Their historical experiences have made them cautious and fearful of expressing their opinions. In short, they are facing a crossroad in determining whether they will live out their lives in this fashion or redefine their relationship to their families, their communities, and society at large.

EMPOWERMENT OF THE *ANCIANOS*

This fundamental alteration of traditional roles is being supplanted by a modern set of norms and values that are only now being detected in the Hispanic community, marking an end to the transitional period. This change and modernization will directly affect relationships of elders with their families, their communities, and the political empowerment occurring in the Hispanic community. The thesis of this chapter is that Hispanic elders will face increasing pressures to become an interest group model (albeit in a limited fashion) to address the dislocation of traditional roles and once again to assert their influence.

Jackson (1980) foretold these occurrences among minority elderly, particularly black, Asian, and Native American groups—groups that have faced similar transitional events. In her pioneering book on minorities and aging, Jackson examines the social and political participation of minority elders. She notes that "voting behavior of different age cohorts . . . seems to be affected by period effects" (p. 150), and that the political powerlessness of the oldest age cohorts does not include lower voting records. Jackson defines this as reflective of a more traditional and less militant political behavior. She concludes that currently "minority aged have not formed a prime organizing factor for their political activity . . . but in the future age interests will probably assume greater priority, given the proliferation of age-specific organizations and increasing age-segregated housing" (p. 150).

New Roles in Politics: Influence for Change

Minority elders may, in the future, acquire age as a primary interest for political behavior, particularly if they have also undergone a transition from traditional cultural norms to a modern set of norms and values. To what extent does this forecast apply to the Hispanic elderly? A number of factors will compel Hispanic elders to consider and develop new roles that will move them from the politics of deference characteristic of the transitional period to a new period characterized by interest group politics.

Politics of Aging

The politics of aging has set an example for all older persons. The elderly in general have undergone similar transitional periods, albeit in different ways. Previous historical periods reflect a traditional pattern—with extended families, significant community roles, and a political gerontocracy, where age was an important factor in defining leadership. The difference, perhaps, is that the elderly in general lost those roles at an earlier period and gained the added advantages of assimilation to American culture: they have been in this country for several generations, are able to speak English, are socialized to the American political culture, and know how to use the American political system.

Overcoming the effects of ageism has lent itself well to elders organizing as an interest group, with age as the specific criterion. Many organizations exist at all levels of government and represent many issues of concern for the elderly. Some have been active since the 1950s, particularly the American Association of Retired Persons (AARP); others have resulted from specific struggles, such as the National Council of Senior Citizens formed to support the passage of Medicare. With few exceptions, however, these organizations have not included large numbers of Hispanics and other minorities. The minority elderly play no leadership position in these mainstream age-based groups, and no active efforts have been undertaken to include them in significant numbers.

The reason for this is unclear, but the effect has been to encourage the separation of several independent groups representing each of the specific elderly ethnic groups. These groups include the National Hispanic Council on Aging, the National Caucus on Black Aging, the Asociación Nacional pro Personas Mayores, the National Indian Council on Aging, and the Pacific/Asian Resource Center on Aging. The political evolution of older persons in this country has set a model that other age groups can emulate.

The Social and Economic Conditions of the
Hispanic Community

The Hispanic community, with its economic and social problems and with the changes occurring in family life-styles and expectations, can no longer guarantee its elders a measure of economic and social protection. Despite its poverty and isolation, the Hispanic community served as a haven for the older person throughout the transitional period from a societal gerontocracy. In the barrio, the elder could speak Spanish, interact with friends and acquaintances, be secure from crime, and have the family near for support. In this haven, the elder retained a measure of status that minimized the effects of the transitional period. And, when the time came that the elder was too frail or poor to remain independent, family, friends, and the church would be available to assist.

As mentioned earlier, the family is now less capable of providing traditional supports for elders. Those who are upwardly mobile and educated leave the barrio and move to the suburbs and other cities for opportunities and are thus no longer readily accessible. For those who have been unable to take advantage of what society has to offer and remain poor, the ability to provide assistance is more limited. The higher costs of housing, the need for both husband and wife to work, smaller families, and the effects of inflation have made it more difficult for families to assist elders and has imposed strains on these limited resources. There are also the effects of assimilation, which lessen the obligations of the second and third generations, and families are unable or unwilling to assist. In the barrio, crime, housing, and transportation have become serious problems, making elders vulnerable to the forces of the outside environment—forces that were held at bay in a time when traditions, isolation, and customs allowed neighborhoods to prosper, despite their poverty. In short, elders are no longer secure in their own communities and increasingly have had to fend for themselves.

Visibility of Public Policy Issues

The politics of aging and the visibility of organized efforts are directly linked with media and public attention to policy issues affecting the elderly. In recent years, major social policy concerns and political controversies have centered around the fiscal viability of Social Security, the budget crisis facing Medicare and Medicaid, the elimination of mandatory retirement, the raising of eligibility ages for public benefits, the provision of catastrophic health care coverage, and the increasing costs associated with public benefits and programs for older persons. The growing interest of the media, opinion-makers, and the public at large has served to focus attention on the effect and implications of policy issues affecting older persons from the entire society.

This interest has not escaped the Hispanic community. It is difficult for even the most isolated ethnic communities to be ignorant of the public debates swirling around Social Security and Medicare, particularly since they are the major programs benefiting the poor and physically disabled—a large proportion of the minority elderly population. Added to this consciousness is the public interest in major political events such as the 1991 White House Conference on Aging and efforts to promote long-term care and quality nursing homes at the state and local levels. The Hispanic elderly are increasingly concerned with the outcomes of such debates. This concern is serving to convince many elders in general that they have a stake in the debates and outcomes, and it serves to influence many Hispanic elders in particular to recognize that perhaps they, too, must be influential as older persons and not simply as Hispanics in an intergenerational milieu.

Lack of Advocacy by Hispanic Political Leaders

The Hispanic community has made great political strides in the last twenty years. From initial grassroots organizing and farm worker-related advocacy in the late 1960s to the election of congressmen, mayors, and state officials throughout the country, the Hispanic community is now recognized as an important political force in American society. Their activities have generated the development of new political leadership—bright and educated young men and women who are providing sophisticated, dynamic representation for the Hispanic population.

Yet, a conspicuous element of these successes and developments is the abrogation of interest in senior citizen concerns and the abolishment of age as a variable in defining political leadership; no longer are elders in their communities automatically sought for advice, leadership, or participation by Hispanic political figures. When political leaders do seek them out, it generally borders on patronization at best (e.g., including senior concerns in political platforms, visiting senior centers during election campaigns) and derision at worst (e.g., criticizing the caciquism and political traditions of the elderly). A vacuum is thus created whereby elders are not expected, and perhaps no longer expect, to play a role other than through individual efforts. When elders are concerned with the outcomes of public policy debates, they must depend on the generosity and sensitivity of Hispanic political leaders not to ignore their interests. This dependence may increasingly be violated. In recent debates over Medicare, Medicaid, and Social Security, Hispanic political leaders have not taken a leadership role in defining, influencing, and determining the outcome of these debates other than pronouncements that they support the preservation of these programs.

Ageism

The promotion of aging services has had an unintended effect of making the Hispanic elderly more comfortable with ageist strategies—with elders moving from intergenerational activities to ones where they develop primary allegiance to other older persons. For example, the creation of multipurpose senior centers under the auspices of the Older Americans Act and the integration of nutrition and social services have made them highly popular in the Hispanic community. Most housing projects for the elderly have a senior citizen center and generally a senior citizen club where elders seek recreational and social activities.

Cuellar (1978) was one of the first to investigate the role of senior citizen clubs as voluntary associations in the Mexican-American community. He suggests that there is an emergent senior citizen subculture in the Hispanic community, unlike anything the traditional culture has envisioned, and that Mexican-American elderly, like other Americans, have adopted the cultural ideology of the dominant society. Although their numbers are small, the rapid proliferation of senior citizen centers suggests that the elderly are seeking their own culturally satisfying solution to offset loss of status.

AGGREGATE EFFECTS

Hispanic elders can no longer depend on traditional social support to protect them and to give them stability and security. They are becoming aware that they, like older persons in general, must protect their interests. More than ever, older Hispanics and their families depend on Social Security, Medicare, and other social services for independence and security, and, if political leaders are not representing their interests in the political sphere, they may conclude that they will have to become more involved.

Some people still feel that elders are essentially conservative and passive and prefer to give their time and energy to the church. Although elders are certainly more religious than younger cohorts, the role of the church in their lives has been exaggerated (Hough, 1982). The church has failed to reach large segments of the Hispanic population as they strive for greater influence in American society. As the Hispanic community has become more active—politically and socially—the church has been left behind. Only in the last ten years has the church become socially active. To the extent that it has been involved in social issues, the church has taken an increasingly greater leadership role in social concerns. The creation of the United Neighborhood Organizations (UNO) in Los Angeles and Communities Organized for Public Service (COPS) in San Antonio was intended to galvanize the barrios to directly confront issues of discrimination, jobs, housing, and crime. These programs have drawn out many elders who can remain active with the church as well as become politically organized. Therefore, the church cannot be blamed as a disincentive for older persons to become more assertive; if the church becomes uninvolved, elders will move without it.

Neither can the family be expected to draw the attention and energies of older persons. As Hispanics assimilate and become affluent, the cohesive elements of the family will decline. As younger generations move out and up and lose interest in culture, language, and intergenerational relationships, elders will become increasingly isolated. The more socially ambitious attempted to break away from old patterns that offered parents and grandparents security in an alien land, and as Machado (1982) aptly states, "older family members . . . saw desertion as a serious threat" to their status in the family and the community (p. 50).

The potential for elders to exercise political influence is revealed by data from the 1980 general election. It demonstrates that, even though the Hispanic community had lower registration and voting rates than the general population, among those who were registered and did vote the young-old and the old-old in the Hispanic population had the highest rates. For example, 44.9 percent and 40.2 percent of Spanish-origin elderly age 55 to 64 years and 65 to 74 years, respectively, voted, compared to only 27.5 percent for persons age 25 to 34 years (U.S. Department of Commerce, 1981b). Jackson (1980) has also found this to be the case among other older minority persons; older members consistently had the highest voting rates, although males were more likely to vote than females. It can be expected that, as politicians discover the voting power of elders, they may begin to take their political leadership more seriously.

ANCIANOS AS A SPECIAL INTEREST GROUP

The potential empowerment of elder Hispanics as an interest group was evident in the 1970s. The first National Conference on Hispanic Aging in 1973 brought together Cuban, Puerto Rican, and Mexican-American elders to discuss common issues and concerns and to formulate a national organizing strategy for influencing public policy (Hernandez & Mendoza, 1975). The outgrowth of the conference was the creation of the Asociación Nacional pro Personas Mayores, a national advocacy group engaged in technical assistance and political lobbying. The 1981 White House Conference on Aging amply demonstrated the development of a cadre of older Hispanics providing leadership on political issues, serving as delegates to their areas, and representing local organizations.

The advancements in this ten-year period provided important evidence that Hispanic elders were adopting new roles to supplant the loss of traditional ones. In several important respects, however, the rise of Hispanic professionals during this period deterred the development of elder leadership, at least on a national level. Elders were represented on state boards and commissions and on boards of directors of Hispanic aging groups, and they participated at conferences, workshops, and gatherings. However, professionals—generally younger—were in control and dominant in articulating the concerns of the elderly and in determining the agendas for organizing. Their need to lead was understandable, given the complexities of public policy, and during this period they provided effective leadership.

Additional resources were provided by the federal government, programs were expanded, legislation and regulations were revised to benefit minority elderly, and research was conducted to better understand the issues affecting minority elders. The election and subsequent events of 1980 have proven that professionals may not be up to the task of protecting the interests of elders in the turbulent decade of the 1980s. Programs have been significantly cut back; control has passed to the states, making it difficult to rely on federal support and protection; research dollars are limited; and national organizations are struggling for survival.

In short, during a climate of retrenchment and federal insensitivity to the needs of this group, professionals have not had the political leverage or influence to prevent the loss of services and programs. The elder Hispanic, who was previously willing to rely on professional leadership, is more vulnerable than ever under the policies of a conservative administration, and professionals do not have the political clout to effect those changes. Therefore, the conditions and necessity exist for Hispanic elders to become an interest group, providing their own leadership in an organized fashion and determining which issues will have priority. Their empowerment will become a necessity. Public policy is influenced only by groups with the financial, political, and constituent support to make their needs known and with the ability to respond when they are not met. Hispanic elders possess the numbers and the issues around which to coalesce. Increasingly, they will face a need to develop a sense of community, given the loss of traditional roles and practices. An interest group composed of elderly Hispanics may serve to provide the forum for meeting their needs.

IMPLICATIONS

If the above scenario occurs, what will it mean for the Hispanic community, the family, and the elderly? The answer to this question is important and raises a host of issues. If the older Hispanic increasingly participates in organized activities that have political interests as priorities, there will be important benefits. Hispanic elders will be able to voice their concerns, to participate with like-minded individuals, and to derive a sense of emotional and social satisfaction. This will increase their importance in the Hispanic community and make them a political force to be reckoned with, much like the elderly in general, who are now catered to by the political establishment. They will be able to bargain, negotiate, and make compromises with Hispanic elected officials and aged-based organizations. In short, they may reassert the political gerontocracy they enjoyed in traditional Latin culture, only now it will be a variation of the American model of politics, where they will act as political equals to other interest groups.

Not all of the implications will be positive. First, the family will no longer have precedence in the elder's time. As older persons spend more time attending meetings, organizing registration drives, and engaging in political dialogue and debates over the issues affecting them, they will be less likely or able to assume whatever traditional roles are expected of them, generally related to the care of grandchildren. They will be less likely to pass on language, history, and culture. In short, the family may find the older person unavailable.

Second, the church will no longer have a monopoly on elders' time or allegiance. The church will find older persons a force pressuring it to become more socially responsive and to develop an agenda for promoting senior citizen concerns.

Third, politicians—particularly Hispanic elected officials—will be made more accountable. No longer will it be enough to visit a senior citizen center to win votes. Now politicians will have to demonstrate that they are keeping their promises and that they are effective advocates of senior concerns. Politicians will need to court the elder vote, particularly with their greater propensity to be registered and to exercise voting rights.

Fourth, Hispanic elders as interest groups will inject a new element into the politics of aging. Established aged-based organizations will be forced to confront the growing cultural diversity of the aging population. Not only will Hispanics organize, but blacks and Asians may become interest groups as well. Aged-based organizations will need to decide whether they want to involve and co-opt these groups or treat them as potential competitors or allies. If they choose to integrate them, the elders may become an important force in these organizations. If they choose to ignore them, then Hispanic elderly groups will relate to them as interest groups.

The reality of Hispanic elders organizing in significant numbers is still in the future. But signs that older Hispanics are developing priorities as older persons who happen to be Hispanic are unmistakable. As Hispanic senior citizen organizations develop, there are several possible directions they can take. These include greater involvement in Hispanic political activities with age-related politics or development as separate groups. The integration of Hispanic aging interest groups with general Hispanic political activities is possible because the participants need each other. The elder needs the political support of Hispanic elected officials, especially to influence public policy, while political officials need the numbers and votes of older adults. On the other hand, established age organizations need Hispanics as allies and as constituents with a common purpose—promoting the concerns of the elderly. The Hispanic elderly need these groups for the same reasons. It is also possible that Hispanic elderly may seek to form their own clubs, organizations, and institutions that cater solely to Hispanic elderly and to exercise their political involvement with the groups with which they can make the best deal.

The extent to which any of these directions unfolds will depend on how quickly Hispanic political leaders, non-Hispanic aging organizations, and the Hispanic elderly themselves understand the potential for empowerment of older Hispanics as an interest group. In addition, it will depend on the cohort changes occurring in the Hispanic community. Today's cohort of elder Hispanics is still a part of their historical and traditional experiences. The cultural conflicts they face and the incongruencies these conflicts generate mask the very real need many elders have to continue participating with the family, the church, and their communities as respected *dons* and *doñas*. If the Hispanic community fosters an intergenerational environment, this cohort may not fully exercise its role as a senior interest group. Subsequent cohorts will not be as tied to these traditional expectations.

The young-old—the Hispanics of the World War II era—are less tied to the political socialization of Latin cultures and more ingrained with American political behaviors. They may be the first cohort to fully exercise their potential as active senior citizens, proud of their Hispanic heritage, yet determined to influence aging policy and politics. Following them will be the generation from the 1950s and 1960s, the Hispanic baby boomers, who will someday be the Hispanic seniors. Perhaps then we will see the full flowering of organized Hispanic elders influencing public policy to benefit them as older persons, as Hispanics, and as United States citizens.

REFERENCES

Note: Appreciation is extended to my students in GERO 433; Ethnicity and Aging, for their inspiration and assistance, in particular, Hank Chapjian and Bettina Erives.

Acuna, R. (1981). *Occupied America: A history of Chicanos* (2nd ed.). New York: Harper & Row.

Archdeacon, T. (1983). *Becoming American: An ethnic history.* New York: Free Press.

Becerra, R., & Shaw, D. (1984). *The Hispanic elderly: A research reference guide.* Lanham, MD: University Press of America.

Berger, P. (1983). The economic well-being of elderly Hispanics. *Journal of Minority Aging, 8,* 36–46.

Binstock, R. (1972). Interest group liberalism and the politics of aging. *The Gerontologist, 12,* 265–280.

———. (1979). A policy agenda on aging for the 1980s. *National Journal, 41,* 1711–1717.

Campbell, J., & Strate, J. (1981). Are old people conservative? *The Gerontologist, 21,* 580–591.

Cueller, J. (1978). El senior citizens club: The older Mexican-American in the voluntary association. In B. Myerhoff & A. Simic (Eds.), *Life's career—aging: Cultural variations on growing old* (pp. 207–230). Beverly Hills: Sage.

Cellular, J., & Weeks, J. (1980). *Minority elderly Americans: The assessment of needs and equitable receipt of public benefits as a prototype for area agencies on aging* (Final Report). San Diego: Allied Home Health Association.

Cutler, N. (1977). Demographic, socio-psychological, and political factors in the politics of aging: A foundation for research in political gerontology. *American Political Science Review, 71,* 1011–1025.

Dahlie, J., & Fernando, T. (Eds.). (1981). *Ethnicity, power, and politics in Canada.* Toronto: Methuen.

de Tocqueville, A. (1945). In P. Bradley (Ed.) *Democracy in America.* New York: Vintage Books. (Original work published, 1835).

Estes, C. (1979). *The aging enterprise.* San Francisco: Jossey-Bass.

Freeman, H., Biendon, R., Aiken, L., Sudman, S., Mullinix, C., & Corey, C. (1987, Spring). Americans report on their access to care. *Health Affairs, 6,* No. 1, 6–18.

Garcia, C. (1974). *La causa politica: A Chicano politics reader.* Notre Dame, IN: University of Notre Dame Press.

Garcia, C., & de la Garza, V. (1977). *The Chicano political experience.* North Scituate, MA: Duxbury Press.

Garcia, J. (1983). Chicano political development: Examining participation in the "Decade of Hispanics." *La Red/The Net, 72,* 8–18.

Gordon, M. (1981). Models of pluralism: The new American dilemma. *America as a Multicultural Society: The Annals, 454,* 178–188.

Guttman, D. (1980). *Perspective on equitable share in public benefits by minority elderly* (Executive Summary. Administration on Aging Grant No. 90-A-1671). Washington, DC: Catholic University of America.

Hernandez, A., & Mendoza, J. (Eds.). (1975). *National conference on the Spanish-speaking elderly.* Kansas City, MO: National Chicano Social Planning Council.

Holzberg, C. (1982). Ethnicity and aging: Anthropological perspectives on more than just the minority elderly. *The Gerontologist, 22,* 249–257.

Hough, R. (1982). Religion and pluralism among the Spanish-speaking groups of the

Southwest. In A. Kruszewski, R. Hough, & J. Ornstein-Galicia (Eds.), *Politics and society in the Southwest* (pp. 169–195). Boulder, CO: Westview Press.

Hudson, R. (1981). *The aging in politics: Process and policy*. Springfield, IL: Charles C. Thomas.

Hudson, R., & Binstock, R. (1976). Political systems and aging. In R. Binstock & E. Shanas (Eds.), *Handbook of aging and the social sciences* (pp. 369–400). New York: Van Nostrand Reinhold.

Jackson, J. (1980). *Minorities and aging*. Belmont, CA: Wadsworth.

Korte, A. (1982). Social interaction and morale of Spanish-speaking rural and urban elderly. *Journal of Gerontological Social Work, 4,* 57–66.

Kruszewski, A., Hough, R., & Ornstein-Galicia, J. (Eds.). (1982). *Politics and society in the Southwest*. Boulder, CO: Westview Press.

Lammers, W. (1983). *Public policy and the aging*. Washington, DC: Congressional Quarterly Press.

Lowi, T. (1967). The public philosophy: Interest group liberalism. *The American Political Science Review, 61,* 5–24.

Machado, M. (1982). The Mexican-American: A problem in cross-cultural identity. In A. Kruszewski, R. Hough, & J. Ornstein-Galicia (Eds.), *Politics and society in the Southwest.* (pp. 47–66). Boulder, CO: Westview Press.

Manson, S., Murray, C., & Cain, L. (1981). Ethnicity, aging, and support networks: An evolving methodological strategy. *Journal of Minority Aging, 6,* No. 1, 2.

Manuel, R. (1981). Leadership factors in service delivery and minority elderly utilization. *Journal of Minority Aging, 5,* 218–232.

———. (Ed.). (1982). *Minority aging: Sociological and social psychological issues*. Westport, CT: Greenwood Press.

McKay, E. (1981). *Hispanic statistics summary: A compendium of data on Hispanic Americans*. Washington, DC: National Council of La Raza.

McLemore, D. (1980). *Racial and ethnic relations in America*. Boston: Allyn & Bacon.

McNeeley, R., & Colon, J. (Eds.). (1983). *Aging in minority groups*. Beverly Hills: Sage.

Morrison, B. J. (1983). Sociocultural dimensions: Nursing homes and the minority aged. *Journal of Gerontological Social Work, 5,* 127.

Pratt, H. (1976). *The gray lobby*. Chicago: University of Chicago Press.

Ralson, P., & Griggs, M. (1981). Factors affecting participation in senior centers: Race, sex, and socioeconomic differences. *Journal of Minority Aging, 5,* 209–217.

Sotomayor, M. (1973). A study of Chicano grandparents in an urban barrio. Unpublished doctoral dissertation, University of Denver, Denver.

———. (1986a). An examination of factors affecting future cohorts of elderly Hispanics. *The Gerontologist, 26,* 140–146.

———. (Ed.). (1986b). *Hispanics in an aging society*. New York: Carnegie Corporation.

Torres-Gil, F., & Becerra, R. (1977). The political behavior of the Mexican-American elderly. *The Gerontologist, 17,* 392–399.

Torres-Gil, F. (1982). *The politics of aging among elder Hispanics*. Washington, DC: University Press of America.

U.S. Department of Commerce, Bureau of the Census. (1981a). Age, sex, race, and Spanish origin of the population by regions, divisions, and states: 1980. *1980*

Census of the Population: Supplementary Reports. Washington, DC: U.S. Government Printing Office.

———. (1981b). Voting and registration in the election of November 1980. *Current Population Reports* (Series P-20, No. 359). Washington, DC: U.S. Government Printing Office.

———. (1986). Projections of the Hispanic population: 1983–2080. *Current Population Reports* (Series P-25, No. 995). Washington, DC: U.S. Government Printing Office.

U.S. Department of Health and Human Services, Human Development Services, Administration on Aging. (1981). Characteristics of the Hispanic elderly. *Statistical Reports on Older Americans.* Washington, DC: U.S. Government Printing Office.

Williamson, J. B., Evans, L., & Powell, L. A. (1982). *Politics of aging.* Springfield, IL: Charles C. Thomas.

6

SOCIAL POLICY AND ELDERLY HISPANICS

Alejandro Garcia

INTRODUCTION

The literature addressing the degree of availability, accessibility, and utilization of social services by elderly Hispanics is fairly extensive.[1] It is generally perceived that, even when services are available, questionable accessibility and concomitant underutilization are prevalent. Reasons given for this low utilization rate include factors such as language, geography, lack of information, discrimination, and others (e.g., see Bell, et al., 1976; Crouch, 1972; Gilfix, 1977; Torres-Gil, 1976; U.S. Commission on Civil Rights, 1982; U.S. Senate, 1968–1969). However, the literature has not readily addressed the impact of social legislation upon traditional intervention modalities. What has been the impact of social policy on the traditional support networks of the Hispanic elderly?

A policy is generally a vehicle used to address the resolution of a certain social problem. In evaluating the impact of that policy, we tend to focus only on the degree to which the problem is addressed, resolved, or modified. Glazer (1981) suggests that "it is illusory to see social policy only as making an *inroad* on a problem; there are dynamic aspects to any policy, such that it also *expands* the problem, *generates* further problems. And, for a number of reasons, social policy finds it impossible to deal adequately with these new demands that follow the implementation of the original measures" (p. 157).

It appears that the literature has addressed the insensitivity of social policy to the needs of elderly Hispanics, but has not considered the impact of that policy on the traditional mechanisms used to resolve such issues or to address other needs. Glazer (1981) notes:

Every piece of social policy substitutes for some traditional arrangement, whether good or bad, a new arrangement in which public authorities take over, at least in part, the role of the family, or the ethnic and neighborhood group, or of the voluntary associa- tion. In doing so, social policy weakens the position of these traditional agents and further encourages needy people to depend on the government, rather than on the tra- ditional structures, for help. Perhaps this is the basic force behind the ever-growing demand for social policy and its frequent failure to satisfy the demand. (p. 197)

This chapter will examine a number of major programs for the elderly to determine the extent to which they have been insensitive to traditional coping mechanisms of Hispanic families, with particular emphasis on elderly Hispan- ics. From a Glazerian perspective, the intent of this chapter is to determine whether the government has overextended the limits of social policy in attempt- ing to address certain social problems of elderly Hispanics and, in so doing, has created additional difficulties for them. The chapter will then propose ways of ensuring that social policy is sensitive and responsible to Hispanic elderly while minimizing any iatrogenic effects that it may carry with it.

There are numerous social programs for the elderly. This discussion will be limited to the Social Security Old Age Insurance program, the Old Age Assis- tance program under the Supplemental Security Income program, housing pro- grams, Title III of the Older Americans Act, and Medicare and Medicaid.

SOCIAL SECURITY OLD AGE INSURANCE PROGRAM

The Social Security Old Age Insurance program is the major income-provid- ing program for elderly persons in the United States. It provides full benefits to retired persons age sixty-five and over who have worked a total of forty quarters in covered employment. The benefit level is based on the level of contributions that have been indexed over a number of years, with specified minimum and maximum benefit amounts. A person may choose to retire as early as age sixty-two and draw actuarilly reduced benefits.

As Garcia (1980) has noted, the present cohort of elderly Mexican-American men does poorly when compared to its white counterparts. The reasons for this phenomenon are numerous. There are problems in eligibility; Garcia found that only 82 percent of Mexican-Americans were Social Security insured at age 65, compared to 92 percent of non-Hispanic whites in the same age group. An additional 6 percent of Mexican-Americans and 2 percent of whites had re- ceived insured status on a special age 72 provision (Garcia, 1980, p. 184). Factors contributing to this low level of benefit eligibility included extensive work in noncovered employment (such as agriculture prior to its incorporation into covered employment in the 1950s), intermittent work patterns, the holding of multiple Social Security numbers, and the nonreporting of contributions by employers.

Mexican-Americans were also found to have lower benefit levels than their white counterparts. Garcia found that 43 percent of white recipients were receiving benefits in the upper one-third bracket while only 8 percent of Mexican-Americans were in the same category. In addition, 28 percent of elderly Mexican-Americans were not receiving Social Security Old Age Social Insurance (OASI) benefits at all, compared with only 7 percent of white elderly males. A majority of this percentage were simply not eligible for benefits, but a smaller percentage appears to have been eligible yet was not receiving benefits (Garcia, 1980, p. 172). A number of causes may have accounted for this phenomenon, including lack of knowledge of how to apply, no knowledge of eligibility criteria, fear of authorities, and language problems.

For those Mexican-Americans receiving OASI benefits, the level of benefits was considerably lower than that received by their white counterparts. Only 11 percent of elderly Mexican-American men receiving benefits were in the upper one-third in terms of monthly benefits, compared with 44 percent of white elderly males (Garcia, 1980, p. 176). The fact that employment for elderly Mexican-Americans has been concentrated in the unskilled levels in agriculture and industry contributes to this discrepancy. Intermittent work patterns are another factor. Although most Hispanics are now in covered Social Security employment, it is anticipated that they will continue to be eligible for low levels of benefits due to persistent problems in the areas of education and employment.

In testing Glazer's hypothesis in evaluating the Old Age Insurance program, one would find that the introduction of this problem had an impact on familial responsibility in care for elderly relatives as well as on the formalization of retirement age. In addition, it had a positive impact on traditional voluntary social service agencies in that it changed their clientele.

For Hispanics, a delay ensued before Social Security legislation affected the family, due primarily to the fact that Hispanics were extensively involved in the agricultural sector when the Social Security Act was passed in 1935, and agricultural workers and farmers were not covered by the initial legislation. The introduction of this legislation may have been responsible to some degree for elderly Hispanics remaining in their own homes rather than living with and being dependent upon adult children or other relatives. It is difficult to separate the influence of economics from that of culture in making this determination.

There is concern that the impact of familial assistance, coupled with benefits from the OASI program, was still so low for some elderly Hispanics that, in Garcia's (1980) study, disproportionate numbers of them were still in the work force compared to their white counterparts. Nevertheless, questions arise about the nature of the familial and neighborhood support system prior to the advent of this program and the changes that may be directly attributable to OASI. In addition, questions must be raised about the roles and responsibilities of elderly Hispanics in an extended family (Sotomayor, 1973) and to what extent they may have changed if the elderly Hispanic was no longer living in the home.

SUPPLEMENTAL SECURITY INCOME PROGRAM

For those elderly Hispanics whose income from Social Security and/or other sources is extremely low, the Social Security Supplemental Security Income Old Age Assistance program is available. The Old Age Assistance program is a means-tested program for persons age 65 and over. Benefit levels from this program vary, with states having the option of supplementing the amount provided by the Social Security Administration.

It should be noted that the 1980 census reported that nearly 22 percent of elderly Hispanics who headed families were poor, as were 44 percent of elderly Hispanics who were unrelated individuals (table 6.1). On the basis of this finding, one might say that persons who live with relatives tend to be less poor, but there is a disincentive to living with relatives.

Eligibility for the Old Age Assistance program is based on need. To the extent that this is the case, benefit levels are reduced if the elderly person is living with others, regardless of their income level. For the Hispanic elderly and their families, this may be a disincentive to living together, and, if this is the case, families would lose the benefit of the presence of elderly relatives in their traditional roles. Sotomayor (1973) points out that

Aged parents always have had a place of considerable significance within the Mexican traditional family. The grandmother was delegated a good share of the nurturing tasks toward the young grandchildren; it was she who provided the continuation of religious education and ritual within the home as well as encouragement of general education achievement. The grandfather assumed the function of transmitter of history, perpetuator of values and heritage. If, for example, the married sons or sons-in-law did not fulfill the expectations of support of their wives and children, it was the primary responsibility of the grandfather to confront them and to ensure that they met their obligations. In times of crisis, including economic need, the grandparents stood willing to share and lend every support. In turn, a mutual, helping, reciprocal relationship was expected of the grown sons and daughters, not only for economic support of the elderly but for emotional needs as well. (p. 9)

It can be argued that the above situation is one with little relation to reality. One can also question the degree to which economic considerations account for an extended family living together and to what extent this is a matter of culture. The reality of the situation is that only about one of every six elderly Hispanics lives with relatives. Although this is a larger percentage than is found among whites, it is still a minority. Torres-Gil (1976) has broadened the conceptualization of the extended family to include those families which live in close proximity and have frequent contacts.

6.1
Summary of Characteristics of Spanish- and Mexican-Origin Families by Poverty Status, March 1979 (in Thousands)

Population Group	Spanish Origin			Mexican Origin			Non-Spanish		
	Total	Poor		Total	Poor		Total	Poor	
		N	%		N	%		N	%
Families	2,741	559	20.4	1,620	301	18.6	55,063	4,721	8.6
Persons 65 and over maintaining a family	214	47	22.0	115	30	26.3	8,296	665	8.0
Unrelated individuals[a] 65 and over	119	52	43.6	61	25	41.0	------	-----	---

Source: Population Characteristics, Persons of Spanish Origin in the United States: March 1979, CPS Reports, Series P - 20, No. 354 (issued October 1980), Tables 31 and Q.

[a]Persons not living with any relatives may (1) constitute a one-person household, (2) be part of a household including one or more families or unrelated individuals, or (3) reside in group quarters such as a rooming house.

The question of whether a reduction of benefits is a disincentive for elderly Hispanics to live with their relatives, then, is a complex one. If Hispanic elderly live with their adult children and grandchildren, they could engage in the variety of activities that Sotomayor (1973) enumerates. However, there are also drawbacks in this situation in that elderly persons may wish to live by themselves in their own homes. If this is the case, Supplemental Security Income (SSI) benefits may provide them with some degree of assistance in doing so. Ideally, SSI benefits should not be reduced if elderly Hispanics are living with relatives so that they can decide where to live on the basis of other factors.

HOUSING PROGRAMS

Congregate living facilities that are government subsidized or sponsored are usually insensitive to the needs and cultural priorities of elderly Hispanics. A number of concerns arise in this regard, many of which were elucidated by Carp (1966) in her study of Victoria Plaza in San Antonio, Texas. The reasons for elderly Hispanics' refusal to move into these facilities may include their location outside of the Hispanic barrio or neighborhood, which meets a number of needs for this group, including church, neighbors, ethnic stores, language, and a sense of belonging. An additional concern is that some of these facilities may be high-rise buildings, whereas elderly Hispanics may prefer apartments that allow them to do some leisure gardening. Furthermore, a majority of these facilities are age-segregated and do not allow extended visits by children. To the extent that elderly Hispanics are still committed to an extended family, regulations promoting age segregation would dissuade Hispanic elderly from seeking to be housed in these facilities. The negative impact of such policies includes the loss of sense of community, loss of extended family, and inability to continue leisure activities such as gardening, visits with friends and relatives, ethnic shopping, and other important activities.

THE OLDER AMERICANS ACT

The Older Americans Act (OAA) was first passed in 1965 "as one of the first major attempts by the federal government to address the social needs of all older persons on a national level" (U.S. Commission on Civil Rights, 1982, vol. 1, p. 5). Since that time, it has been amended on a number of occasions. It presently has two major titles that provide services to elderly persons and are relevant to the focus of this paper. Title III-B includes the provision of information and referral, transportation, outreach, housing, legal, and health services. Title III-C includes nutrition services that may be delivered to individual homes or provided in congregate meal facilities (U.S. Commission on Civil Rights, 1982, vol. 1, p. 11).

In providing this breadth of services, the Older Americans Act attempted to fill perceived major service voids for the elderly. In so doing, it is questionable whether lawmakers considered the resources that already existed in the Hispanic community; and additional questions are raised about whether they endeavored to use these resources, to support their continued use, or to build upon them. It appears that the response to these questions has to be negative. Although there may have been an intention to be sensitive to the Hispanic elderly's needs in the initial legislation, this commitment appears to have later been modified in the 1978 amendments and apparently operationalized only to a limited extent while it existed.

First of all, the U.S. Commission on Civil Rights found that little was done to reach monolingual elderly. In a study conducted by the commission it was found that "Older Americans Act programs generally did not have bilingual employees, although a need for them was often evident. Despite the need, nowhere was there a requirement for any bilingualism among program staff" (U.S. Commission on Civil Rights, 1982, vol. 2, p. 47). The commission also found that Hispanics were "rarely" involved in key decision-making positions.

The Commission found that, despite the fact that minority organizations were often in a position to render unique services (e.g., information and referral and ethnic meals), minority firms received few Title III and Title IV awards under the Older Americans Act. Even though minority organizations had low representation among Title III and Title IV funded groups, few formal mechanisms existed to increase their participation. (U.S. Commission on Civil Rights, 1982, vol. 2, p. 48)

Based on the above information and other evidence, it is not surprising that the commission found that, in almost every city visited, older minorities generally were not participating fully in the available programs. In addition, although few minorities participated in Older Americans Act programs, "little outreach to minority elderly existed" (U.S. Commission on Civil Rights, 1982, vol. 2, p. 48). The commission did raise concern about

the removal in 1978 of several statutory provisions and sections of the act that referred explicitly to the inclusion of minorities in Older Americans Act programs. (For example, the 1975 amendments to the model project provisions of the Older Americans Act provided that the Commissioner on Aging must give special consideration to projects that provided needed services to minorities, American Indians, and limited-English-speaking elderly. The 1978 amendments removed these provisions. The Administration on Aging, following Congress's lead, revised the Older Americans Act regulations to eliminate requirements for establishing preferences or priorities for minorities. For instance, the regulations issued under the 1978 amendments had no explicit requirements for minority participation in grants and contracts.) Since the Commission found a seeming disregard for responsibilities by program administrators to enforce compliance with Title VI of the Civil Rights Act of 1964, the Commission also questions the commitment of program administrators to minority participation in Older Americans Act programs without such legislation. (U.S. Commission on Civil Rights, 1982, vol. 2, p. 48)

Even when existing legislation mandated a variety of activities designed to improve the participation of older Hispanics in OAA programs, it was not fully operationalized. When the 1978 amendments removed any requirements for establishing references or provisions for minorities, services to Hispanics were substantially reduced.

To the extent that it appears that Hispanic elderly have been served minimally by Older Americans Act programs, there is little or no evidence that this legislation has had a negative impact upon the ongoing formal and informal support systems of this group. However, to the extent that Hispanic elderly tend to be poor and in need of a variety of ethnic-sensitive social services, there is grave concern that these needs are still unmet.

MEDICARE AND MEDICAID

Medicare is the major health service provider in the United States. Part A, the hospitalization component of this program, requires that a person be age 65 or over *and* be eligible for Social Security Old Age Insurance benefits. As noted previously, a relatively high percentage of elderly Mexican-Americans are not eligible for OASI, and thus they are ineligible for Part A of Medicare.

It should be noted that, for those elderly Hispanics eligible for the hospitalization component of Medicare, a deductible must be paid which amounts to the first day of hospitalization. This amount was $540 in 1988. It is possible that this amount may represent a major roadblock to elderly Hispanics seeking inpatient treatment and may result in acute conditions becoming chronic. It should be noted that Part A is available for persons not eligible for OASI benefits, but the premium may be prohibitive ($234 per month in 1988).

Most persons age 65 and over are eligible and may participate on a voluntary basis in Part B of Medicare, the outpatient component. Participation requires a monthly premium of $24.80 per month (as of January 1988) plus a $75 deductible and 20 percent co-insurance.

Persons ineligible for OASI may qualify for the means-tested SSI. If they are eligible for SSI, they would also be eligible for Medicaid, in which case the state would have the option of enrolling the individual in the Medicare program and paying the premium, deductible, and co-insurance.

A major concern is medical coverage for persons who do not fit in the categories of eligibility for Medicare and Medicaid. For Hispanics, one such group is the near elderly, persons age 50 to 64 who may have deteriorating health but may not be eligible for these programs. Although some states may extend Medicaid eligibility to persons who fall into the category of "medically needy," this practice is not compulsory.

The limits of social policy can be assessed with regard to this particular issue in terms of who is authorized to receive reimbursement for services. Clearly, licensed medical doctors and related licensed professionals are eligible to receive reimbursement. However, *espiritistas* and *curanderos,* Puerto Rican and Mexican folk healers, are not. For those elderly Hispanics who use these service providers, the failure of Medicare and Medicaid to reimburse for them will result in a disincentive to use them and an incentive to use more traditional medical services, which some elderly Hispanics find cold and distant. It should be noted that not all elderly Hispanics use *espiritistas* and *curanderos*. In addition, although some Hispanics may see folk healers as valuable providers of services (e.g., see Bell et al., 1976, p. 31), others regard them as charlatans who exploit poor, unsophisticated people and who may cause delays for some individuals seeking timely and appropriate medical attention.

RECOMMENDATIONS

From the above analysis, it appears that policies have had a negative impact on the systems of traditional support that exist for elderly Hispanics. Obviously, the response is not to eradicate programs that may be helpful to this group, but to change them in ways that will maximize their effectiveness while preserving traditional support systems.

A solution is a high degree of individualization according to ethnic/racial group. The immediate response from bureaucrats typically focuses on the administrative difficulty that such proposals would create. Too often a major concern of policy administrators is administrative ease rather than the ability of a program to respond to an identified problem area.

If individualization is implemented, additional caveats should be noted. One is the close examination of Hispanics according to their national origin, socioeconomic status, degree of English fluency, and level of adherence to their respective group's cultural tradition. With regard to national origin, program developers should be aware of the substantial differences among national origin groups; lumping them together as "Hispanics" obfuscates their cultural uniqueness. Mexicans, Puerto Ricans, and Cubans carry their respective cultural identifications with them into old age.

Other characteristics that should be taken into consideration in creating programs for Hispanic elderly are their urban or rural orientation, and their degree of fluency in English and Spanish (it is possible that, if a Hispanic person is functually illiterate in English, he or she may be functionally illiterate in Spanish as well). Over and above these concerns, questions must be posed as to the status of the Hispanic elderly along a cultural continuum. As noted in the scale below, their degree of acculturation may range from being totally unacculturated to being totally acculturated, and service design must be responsible for making this determination.

Hispanic Cultural Continuum

←――――――――――――――――――――――――――――――――――→

| Maintenance of traditional Hispanic culture; predominantly Spanish-speaking | Bilingual and bicultural | Totally acculturated; may not speak Spanish; little or no identification with Hispanic culture |

CONCLUSION

The intent of this chapter has not been to dismiss all social policy that has been insensitive to elderly Hispanics, but to ensure that policy-makers are aware of the heterogeneity of elderly Hispanics, their traditions and needs, and the impact that social policies have on the support networks of this group.

NOTE

1. The term "Hispanic" is used to represent persons of Spanish heritage such as Mexican-Americans, Puerto Ricans, Cubans, etc.

REFERENCES

Bell, D., Kasschau, P., & Zellman, G. (1976, April). *Delivering services to elderly members of minority groups: A critical review of the literature.* Santa Monica, CA: Rand Corporation.

Carp, F. M. (1966). *A future for the aged: Victoria Plaza and its residents.* Austin: University of Texas Press.

Crouch, B. M. (1972). Age and institutional supports: Perceptions of older Mexican Americans. *Journal of Gerontology, 27,* 524–529.

Garcia, A. (1980). The contribution of Social Security to the adequacy of income of elderly Chicanos. Unpublished doctoral dissertation, Brandeis University, Waltham, MA.

Gilfix, M. (1977 Summer). A case of unequal suffering. *Generations, 2,* No. 2.

Glazer, N. (1981). The limits of social policy. In N. Gilbert and H. Specht (Eds.) *The emergence of social welfare and social work* (2nd ed.), (pp. 190–204). Itasca, IL: F. E. Peacock Publisher.

Sotomayor, M. (1973). A study of Chicano grandparents in an urban barrio. Unpublished doctoral dissertation, University of Denver, Denver, CO.

Torres-Gil, F. (1976). The politics of los ancianos. Unpublished doctoral dissertation, Brandeis University, Waltham, WA.

U.S. Bureau of the Census. (1980, October). *Population characteristics—persons of Spanish origin in the United States: March 1979* (Current Population Reports, Series P-2Q, No. 354). Washington, DC: U.S. Government Printing Office.

U.S. Commission on Civil Rights. (1982). *Minority elderly services: New programs, old promises* (Parts I and II). Washington, DC: U.S. Government Printing Office.

U.S. Senate Special Committee on Aging. (1968–1969). *Availability and usefulness of federal programs and services to elderly Mexican-Americans.* Washington, DC: U.S. Government Printing Office.

7

INCOME MAINTENANCE AND THE HISPANIC ELDERLY

Daniel T. Gallego

INTRODUCTION

If we were to single out an indicator that would best predict the general welfare of the Hispanic elderly of America, that indicator would be income adequacy. Adequacy of income and the assurance that income will remain constant are definite preconditions of an individual's general welfare. Degree of income is inseparable from three other variables: social class, power, and prestige.

Social class basically determines one's life-style and opportunities. Social class is measured by using more than income as an indicator. Education, occupation, religion, and material possessions contribute to the development of an individual's value system and determine the manner in which he or she chooses to live.

Adequacy and/or availability of income is also directly related to the power or lack of power that an individual will have in competing in the marketplace for goods such as food and services. Adequacy of income can be correlated to other variables such as degree of education and occupational status. Once again, a value system is determined—one which curtails poorer individuals from rising above their low economic status.

Although income is not directly used in determining the prestige one receives, indirectly it is an important indicator. Prestige can be defined as "society's principal symbol of an individual's or group's standing" (Eisenstadt, 1971, p. 26). The basis for prestige apparently centers around three conditions:

(1) belonging to a group; (2) occupying an important position in that group; and (3) being a symbol of the main goals of the group. The group may well be a social class grouping in a community.

Money, oftentimes referred to as "income," is not the only means of purchasing goods and services. Other variables within the community or family system—such as prestige, social class, and power—can acquire those commodities as well. It should also be understood that what is defined as an "adequate income level" for one segment of society may not be so for another segment. Income needs are relative, not absolute. We may even argue about "essential" or "basic" needs of an individual. Is it possible to set an absolute figure that distinguishes between those who are in need and those who are not? Yet, a figure has been established, and we measure all individuals using that gauge.

PERSPECTIVES ON THE AMERICAN STRATIFICATION SYSTEM AND THE MINORITY ELDERLY

Recent immigrants and minority groups, presently and in the past, have had disproportionate percentages of their members exhibiting the following characteristics: (1) a high majority below the poverty level; (2) unemployment rates frequently two or three times higher than that of the general population; (3) educational attainments considerably lower than those of the general population; (4) participation in federal programs far below the rates of participation of the general population; and (5) high proportions clustered in low occupational positions of nontransport, operative, and nonfarm labor.

It is easy to blame the victims and say that the same opportunities have been available to them as to the general population. This creates the impression that equal opportunities in the areas of education, occupation, and the economic market exist in all segments of society, an assumption that, in light of what historians and social scientists have written, is both unrealistic and unfounded.

Another explanation of why new immigrants and minorities occupy an unfavorable socioeconomic position in society is that "keeping minorities down" may be serving a positive function for society. Society is, in fact, benefiting by keeping minorities in lower socioeconomic brackets, thus reducing tension between the majority and minority groups in a competitive system. Other benefits might include ensuring that undesirable jobs get done, giving privileged positions to members of the majority group, displacing aggression, maintaining power, and protecting the self-esteem of majority group members.

In reality, the explanation of why minority groups in the United States often have low socioeconomic status cannot be clarified by an either/or answer.

SOURCES OF INCOME FOR THE HISPANIC ELDERLY

In 1978, over 90 percent of the Hispanic elderly's income came from Social Security. In the general population, 15 percent of the individuals who were categorized as being unrelated and about 6 percent of the families who were headed by an individual age 65 or over claimed that Social Security was their sole source of income. Twenty-five percent of persons who were unrelated and about 40 percent of families headed by a person age 65 or over reported that they had received income from private and federal pensions; 12 percent of the elderly who were unrelated and 8 percent of families with an elderly head of household received Supplemental Security Income (SSI). Sixty-two percent of the elderly who were unrelated and 70 percent of the families with an elderly head of household reported that they had received some income from annuities, dividends, and rental properties; the average amount of money received from such sources was $1013 per year (U.S. Senate, 1980b).

In a national study conducted by the Asociación Nacional pro Personas Mayores (1980), it was reported that the main sources of income varied greatly for Hispanics, with Cubans having the highest monthly incomes from all sources. This is understandable since Cubans also have the highest educational levels of all Hispanic groups (see table 7.1).

When we compare the Hispanic elderly with those of the general population, the data suggest the following:

1. There is a higher percentage of Hispanic elderly who claim Social Security as their main source of income.

2. Hispanic elderly have a higher percentage of individuals (20.0 percent) who supplemented their income with SSI than did the general population (12 percent for unrelated persons and 6 percent for families).

3. The percentage of Hispanic elderly who received money from retirement was considerably lower than that in the general population (8.1 percent, compared to 25 percent for unrelated persons, and 40 percent for families with heads of households over 65 years of age).

4. Whereas 70 percent of the individuals from the general population reported receiving income from annuities, dividends, and rental properties, none of the Hispanic categories included annuities or dividends as a source of income and only 4.4 percent claimed rental properties as a main source of income.

5. Eleven percent of the general population claimed welfare as their main source of income, compared to 8.5 percent of the Hispanic elderly.

Differences between the general population and the Hispanic elderly seem to be greatest in the areas of dependence on Social Security and SSI as main sources of income. The differences seem to be exacerbated when we take into consideration the fact that there are fewer individuals drawing Social Security among Hispanics than in the general population (approximately 50 percent compared to almost 90 percent). The area that distinguishes the Hispanic elderly from the general population with regard to sources of income is annuities and dividends. Hispanic elderly do not have these sources as supplemental income in the retirement years. This is understandable when we consider the

7.1
Sources of Income of Cuban Elderly

Type of Income	Percentage
Social Security retirement	34.4
Employment (full- or part-time)	19.5
Supplementary Security Income	20.0
Retirement pensions (job)	8.1
Social Security widow's benefits	6.9
Social Security disability	8.5
Welfare	8.5
Rental	4.4
Family member assistance	2.8

Note. Sources are not mutually exclusive.

mean educational attainment, the traditional occupations of the Hispanic elderly, and the number of young Hispanics who have poverty level incomes.

EMPLOYMENT AND THE HISPANIC ELDERLY

When the overall employment picture is considered, Hispanics fare relatively well. One out of 19 persons who were employed in 1981 was of Spanish origin, compared to one out of 25 in 1973. The total Hispanic population participates in the labor market at a rate similar to that of all workers in the United States, as indicated by comparative statistics for 64 percent of the total population and 63.8 percent of the Hispanic population. Although the rate of participation was similar to that for the general population, there were differences within age categories. Other than those Hispanics age 20 to 24 years and 55 years and over, adult Hispanic men were slightly less likely to participate in the labor force (Roth, 1981).

When we look specifically at the labor force of those individuals 65 and older, Hispanic men fare relatively well. This is indicated by participation rates of 19.1 percent for all men 65 and over as compared to 19.4 percent for Hispanic men 65 and over. Hispanic women 65 and older have considerably lower labor market participation than women overall in the United States, as indicated by proportions of 4.9 percent and 8.1 percent, respectively.

As a population category Hispanics account for a disproportionate share of unemployed individuals. The total Hispanic population accounts for approxi-

7.2

Percentage Distribution in Civilian Labor Forces and Percentage of Unemployment for Persons Aged 65 and Over

Group	Labor Force Distribution	Unemployment
All workers	2.8	3.2
Mexican-Americans	0.9	7.3
Puerto Ricans	0.3	0.0
Cubans	2.9	5.4

Source: Roth, 1981.

mately 5.5 percent of the civilian labor force and at the same time makes up 6 to 7.5 percent of the nation's unemployed. This percentage is anywhere from 40 to 50 percent greater than the overall rate of all anglo workers but lower than the unemployment rate of blacks in the nation. When specific ethnic categories were analyzed, it was noted Puerto Ricans had the highest unemployment rate and Cubans had the lowest.

Observing the unemployment rate for individuals 65 and older, it was noted that Hispanic men did not fare as well as all workers in the labor market. Table 7.2 illustrates the disproportionate unemployment among the elderly, compared to the percentage distribution of the civilian labor force.

Even though 57 percent of the working age Hispanic population was employed, compared to 59 percent of the total overall population, this does not explain why a disproportionate number of Hispanics are considered to be at the "below poverty" level. The answer, then, must be found in the types of occupations in which they are employed.

If the assumption is made that older individuals maintain occupations held in earlier years, it follows that the majority of the Hispanic elderly are employed in nontransport, operatives, nonfarm labor, and service occupations. These occupations are overrepresented among the Hispanic population. It can also be concluded that women who are still working (4.9 percent) are in clerical, nontransport operatives, or service occupations.

In addition to being underrepresented in the labor market and having a high percentage of unemployment, the Hispanic elderly also retire at a younger age than does the general population. The average age of retirement for Hispanics is 61.5 years, with the Puerto Rican adult retiring at least three years earlier. The main reason given for early retirement was poor health. Other reasons were age (52.5 percent), and "no work" (4.4 percent) (Asociación Nacional pro Personas Mayores, 1980).

7.3
Actual Earnings Replacement Rates Provided by Social Security for Couples Retiring in 1968–1974

Pre-Retirement Earnings	Actual Replacement Rates
$1,000-$3,999	63%
$4,000-$5,999	52%
$6,000-$7,999	48%
$8,000-$9,999	45%
$10,000-$12,499	37%
$12,500-$14,999	32%
$15,000 and over	25%

Source: U.S. Senate Special Committee on Aging, Part 1, 1980a.

THE HISPANIC ELDERLY AND SOCIAL SECURITY

Statistical data concerning Hispanic elderly and Social Security are sparse and inconclusive. The author has perused census material, but because of small samples the Census Bureau has reached no conclusions. Data on the Hispanic elderly and Social Security will be taken from regional studies that have not focused specifically on Social Security.

Overview

Social Security, as originally established, was intended to provide workers and their families with a floor of income protection, providing that circumstances merited assistance. Eligibility was established by premature death, disability, or retirement. Social Security was not intended to be the sole base but, rather, to provide one-third of income. The other two-thirds were to come from supplementary insurance, savings, investments, and individual retirement programs.

The founders of the Social Security program recognized that individuals with low earning power would have difficulty providing protection for the income. As a result, the benefits were weighted to give a higher replacement of earnings to low wage earners. As shown in table 7.3, individuals who are in the lowest economic category will receive 63 percent of their income in Social Security benefits, whereas those in the highest economic category will receive only 25 percent. The higher replacement of earnings has been nullified as inflation has eroded the fixed income of the elderly. In recent years, the "escalator" provision has been added to the Social Security program, giving recipients automatic cost of living adjustments (COLAs) based on the consumer price index (CPI). These adjustments have averaged a 3 percent increase from the first quarter of the previous year to the first quarter of the current year.

Hispanic elderly suffer greatly from inadequate incomes even with increases and adjustments made by the Social Security Administration. In a study by the Allied Home Health Association of San Diego (Cuellar, 1980), it was found that 85 percent of the Hispanic elderly recorded their income to be under $5000 a year (p. 29). More specifically, an Asociación Nacional pro Personas Mayores study (1980) reported that the average Social Security payment for Hispanics nationally was $249; 3 percent of $250 is $7.50 a month, hardly enough to keep up with inflation.

Enrollment in the Social Security program for the Hispanic elderly has always been problematic. As indicated above, 90 percent of the general population used Social Security as an important source of income. In contrast, only 56 percent of the Hispanic elderly were drawing Social Security benefits (White House Conference Report, 1981).

Looking at the lower participation rates of the Hispanic elderly in the Social Security program, one might ask what the participation rate is in survivor's benefits and disability benefits. The Hispanic population may be reaping benefits from Social Security long before they reach age 65. Of the approximately 1.9 million individuals who received retirement (worker's and disability) work benefits in 1978, approximately 88,000 were born outside the United States. This figure is only 5 percent of all retired workers and 4 percent of all disabled workers. The European-born, however, had the largest percentage of individuals in the categories of foreign-born and language-identified persons. Only 7000 disabled workers were born in Spanish-language countries. Nine percent of Hispanics who were awarded benefits under liability were between 62 and 64 years of age. This was a much smaller percentage than those who were foreign-born. The average PIA (Primary Insurance Amount) was $284 a month. This was less than the average for all foreign-born persons ($312 per month) and all disabled persons ($324 per month). These findings were substantiated by the Asociación Nacional pro Personas Mayores study.

The lower percentage of Hispanic elderly participating in the Social Security program has at least three explanations: (1) misconceptions of citizenship requirements; (2) language difficulties; and (3) eligibility for Social Security benefits.

Misconceptions of Citizenship Requirements

One of the major misconceptions of elderly Hispanics is the requirement of U.S. citizenship for Social Security eligibility. Traditionally, Hispanic elderly have resisted U.S. citizenship. In the past, they have enjoyed the privileges of living in America without pressure to change their citizenship. They moved to parts of the country where barrios existed, and their lives were not drastically altered. The process of accommodation and cultural pride have been major factors causing low citizenship rates among Hispanic elderly. Cases have been documented in which Hispanic elderly desiring Social Security have given up citizenship in their native country; later they learned that U.S. citizenship was not required in order to benefit from Social Security—payment into the Social Security program was the only criterion.

Language Difficulties

The degree of Hispanic elderly participation in the Social Security program is related to the amount of information printed in the Spanish language. Also important is the number of individuals in local agencies who speak Spanish. Agencies located in predominantly Spanish-speaking areas with Spanish-speaking personnel have a higher rate of enrollment in the program than those lacking native language assistance. Studies on enrollment in Social Security suggest that friendship is a primary factor. Agency facilities and relatives are also factors. In the case of the Hispanic elderly, two of the three sources were Spanish-speaking.

Eligibility for Social Security Benefits

The final problematic area seems to be eligibility for Social Security benefits. The Hispanic elderly are clustered predominantly in occupations that are transitory: nontransport, operatives, and nonfarm labor. Hispanic women are employed as operatives and in service areas. Employers in these fields often cut corners by not withholding Social Security taxes, thus reducing the individual's eligibility in later life. This practice is further complicated by the citizenship status of persons applying for these occupational positions.

SUPPLEMENTAL SECURITY INCOME (SSI)

The Supplemental Security Income (SSI) program was enacted in 1972 as Title XVI of the Social Security Act. It provided income for the blind, aged, disabled, and individuals with little or no income or resources. The SSI program is funded by general tax revenues and is administered by the Social Security Administration. Prior to 1972, SSI was state operated, often by welfare departments using federal financial assistance.

Eligibility requirements for individuals applying for SSI benefits include: (1) age 65 or older, but not exclusively; (2) blind or disabled; (3) meet income limitations; and (4) assets not exceeding $1500 for an individual or $2250 for a couple. Not included in the assets test is the value of the applicant's home.

The applicant, however, may not own a car valued at more than $4500 or have more than $2000 equity in household goods and personal effects. The excess value of an automobile and personal effects is applied to the asset limitation for eligibility. These requirements also include certain miscellaneous assets such as insurance policies (to be figured into the assets requirements).

Although the SSI program previously dealt predominantly with the elderly and, to a lesser degree, with the blind and disabled, that trend seems to be changing to benefit blind and disabled individuals. In 1981, 66 percent of those receiving SSI payments were awarded benefits for disability or blindness; the remainder were awarded for age. The explanation for the reduction of elderly in the program is that SSI may still be stereotyped as being "welfare" assistance rather than tied into the Social Security program. In a study entitled "SSI Aged: Pilot Study of Eligibility and Participation in SSI," a number of variables were found to affect participation in the program regardless of ethnic background, as shown in table 7.4.

FUTURE TRENDS AND PROSPECTS

Looking at the future trends and income prospects of the Hispanic elderly, the following facts must be considered, for the young people of today are the elderly of tomorrow.

1. The Hispanic population is the nation's fastest-growing minority; it constituted 6.4 percent of the population in 1980; this will increase to a projected 10.8 percent in the year 2000 and 14.7 percent in the year 2020.

2. By the year 2025, the Hispanic population will see a large segment of its population turn 65 years of age. The projected percentage of elderly in the population will be 10 percent.

3. Eighty-eight percent of the Hispanic population live in metropolitan areas, compared to 75 percent of the general population and 81 percent of the black population.

4. The crude birth rate for all Hispanics is 25.5 births per 1000 population. For every 1000 women between the ages of 15 and 44 there are 100.5 births. This is compared to 14.7 births for 1000 of the Anglo population and 63.2 births for women between the ages of 15 and 44 in the Anglo population.

5. Hispanic life expectancy may now be slightly higher than that of Anglos in the United States. Among males, life expectancy is 71.4 years, compared to 70.2 years for the Anglo population.

6. Hispanics are less likely than the general population to be living in married couple families and much more likely to be in families headed by a single parent, almost always the mother. Seventy-three percent of Hispanics live in married couple households, compared to 82 percent of the Anglo population who live in married couple households.

7. Even though the younger Hispanic child spends more time in school than his or her parent, Hispanics lag behind blacks and far behind Anglos in educational attainment.

Summary of Differences between SSI Participants and Eligible Non-Participants

Variable	Findings
Sociodemographic	
Age	Non-participants are younger.
Sex	Non-participants are more likely to be female.
Race	No difference.
Language	No difference.
Marital status	Non-participants are more likely to be married.
Living arrangements	Non-participants are more likely to be living with someone.
Education	Non-participants are more educated.
Income	
Amount of income	Non-participants have higher income; the difference is greater for couples than for individuals.
Type of income	Non-participants are more likely to receive Social Security benefits.
Assets	
Home ownership	Non-participants are more likely to be home owners.
Liquid assets	Non-participants are more likely to have liquid assets.
Amount of liquid assets	Non-participants have greater liquid assets
Type of liquid assets	No difference.
Experience with and Attitudes toward Other Government Programs[a]	
Extent of contact with other government programs[a]	Non-participants are less likely to have applied to other government programs for benefits.
Receipt of benefits from other government programs[a]	Non-participants are less likely to have received benefits from other government programs.

Variable	Findings
Satisfaction with other government programs[a]	No difference.
Attitudes toward welfare	Non-participants are less positive than participants about welfare assistance, although over half would apply for benefits if they thought they could get them.
Attitudes toward Social Security	No difference.
Experience with and Attitudes toward SSI	
Knowledge of SSI	Almost one-half of non-participants have never heard of SSI; for non-participants who are aware of the SSI program, they understand it about as well as participants do.
Experience with SSI	About one-quarter of non-participants have tried to find out whether they are eligible for SSI; about 9% have received SSI in the past; non-participants are less likely than participants to have had someone help them complete an application for SSI benefits.
Attitudes toward SSI	Non-participants who have applied for SSI in the past are more likely than participants to be negative about the experience; most non-participants would apply for SSI benefits if they knew they were eligible.
Other	
Social contact	Non-participants are more likely to read a newspaper and listen to a radio daily.
Mobility	No difference.
Size of potential SSI benefit	Non-participants are eligible for smaller benefits.

[a]Includes welfare, food stamps, and Medicaid.

8. Because of poor educational attainment, Hispanics remain clustered in low-paying blue-collar and semiskilled jobs in fields like construction and manufacturing. These jobs are highly seasonal and subject to high layoffs.

9. For the Hispanic women who have a high probability of being single because of divorce or separation, 75 percent who are working will be clustered in the clerical, machine operator or "nontransport operative," or service worker fields.

10. Although the income of Hispanics is higher than that of blacks, it is still only 70 percent of Anglo income.

11. The percentage of Hispanics in poverty will remain 2.5 to 3 times higher than that in the Anglo population.

When we project these trends into the future and look at the effects which they have on generations to come, we can make the following predictions, assuming no major changes.

1. The number of Hispanic elderly will grow dramatically by the year 2020.

2. Most of the elderly will be urban dwellers.

3. The elders will come from large families. The families or orientation and procreation will provide a strong natural support system for the Hispanic elderly.

4. The Hispanic elderly will be poorly educated and thus will have held low-paying jobs throughout their lives.

5. The Hispanic elderly will be likely not to be covered by a company or personal pension program.

6. A higher percentage of women will be in the poverty category because of single-parent marital status, as well as working in the categories of clerical, operative, and service workers. As such, older women will have a higher probability of being totally dependent on Social Security than will Anglo women.

7. Coming from large families, having large families, and working at low-paying jobs, the Hispanic elderly will have poor health, which will lead to earlier retirement.

Prospects of economic conditions being better for the Hispanic elderly in the future seem rather remote. Economic improvement is unlikely unless the economic cycle is broken for the younger Hispanic population today. There must be a concerted effort on the part of the Hispanics themselves, politicians, and educators to break the economic cycle to guarantee economic opportunities for this growing untapped resource. Hispanics themselves must become involved in the political arena, where they can influence decisions that will provide opportunities for other Hispanics. Political role models must convince their constituents to embrace the best of the two cultures. The Cubans have succeeded in improving their socioeconomic status because of their education and orientation toward professional success. Politicians must recognize that, when a group of people is economically repressed, the whole nation suffers higher taxes to pay for social programs. Although education cannot be used as a panacea for all the ills of a culture, it must be recognized that it is one of the main indicators for obtaining a high-paying job, which, in turn, allows the individual to save and to invest in the future. It must be observed that, in other segments of the population, as incomes increase, fertility rates decrease, a variable that must be addressed if the Hispanic population is to make economic improvement.

REFERENCES

Asociación Nacional pro Personas Mayores (1980, December). *A national study to assess the service needs of the Hispanic elderly.* Los Angeles: Author.

Cuellar, J. B. (1980). *Minority elderly Americans: A prototype for area agencies on aging.* San Diego: Allied Home Health Association.

Kennedy, L. (1982). *Disability insurance program participation: Financing and disability determination and review process, with some SSI comparisons.* Washington, DC: U.S. Government Printing Office.

Roth, D. M. (1981). *Hispanics in the U.S. labor force: A brief examination.* Washington, DC: Congressional Research Service.

U.S. Senate, Special Committee on Aging. (1980a). *Developments in aging* (Part 1). Washington, DC: U.S. Government Printing Office.

———. (1980b). *Developments in aging* (Vol. 1). Washington, DC: U.S. Government Printing Office.

White House Conference on Aging. (1981). *Executive Summary of Technical Committee on Retirement Income.* Washington, DC: U.S. Government Printing Office.

Part IV

FAMILY, COMMUNITY, AND NATURAL SUPPORT SYSTEMS

8

THE HISPANIC ELDERLY AND THE EXTENDED MULTIGENERATIONAL FAMILY

Marta Sotomayor and Steven R. Applewhite

INTRODUCTION

An effort to identify and examine the various institutions, cultural modes, life-styles, and values of the various Hispanic populations in this country was initiated only recently, more specifically since the 1960s and 1970s. This endeavor has been primarily an in-group search and/or self-discovery process, guided mostly by Hispanic academics. It was prompted by a need to assess the internal cultural norms and values and the socioeconomic and political effects of the ascribed low status given to most Hispanics by the dominant group in the United States. The goal is to develop interventions to ameliorate existing conditions.

Numerous examples have been cited to support the theory that the extended family has been and continues to be the most important institution for Hispanics regardless of their country of origin, length of residence in the United States, racial and/or ethnic ancestry, social class, and even religious preference. A central theme in the ongoing dialogue has been the recognition of the roles and the functions that the elderly assume and their importance to the well-being of the family. The attention now being given by gerontologists to the multigenerational family and its similarities to the Hispanic extended family, which by its nature is multigenerational, will no doubt encourage further dialogue on this topic.

The recent attention given to the multigenerational family has been prompted by certain demographic trends. For example, the proportion of older persons with children has remained largely unchanged in the past twenty years. Many individuals are now both adult children and grandparents. Approximately 40 percent of all older persons who have children are heads of four-generation families. Forty percent of the individuals in their late 50s have surviving parents, and 20 percent of persons in their early 60s have a surviving parent (Brody, 1981).

There is no question that for Hispanics the family has provided a significant amount of support during times of social and economic stress as well as emotional nurturing and protection from discrimination and racism suffered by most Hispanics in this country (Sotomayor and Curiel, 1988). For example, it is clear that the racism encountered by Hispanic children early in their educational experience, focusing on the transmission of the dominant culture from generation to generation at the expense of other cultures, results in a negative self-concept and low self-esteem that have devastating effects on their learning process, sense of autonomy, and mastery. Under these conditions, it is assumed, the family has had to play an even more important and meaningful role due to the absence of other reinforcements and supports available and accessible to the children of the dominant culture.

The lack of access for adult members of minority groups to the various avenues of opportunity has played a significant role in the perpetuation of a negative self-perception and low sense of worth experienced by Hispanics, a condition that has had to be mitigated and balanced by other positive influences and institutions within the Hispanic culture itself. Who else could have provided the support, the nurturing, the sense of protection, and the comfort but the members of the one "friendly" system, the family?

It is believed that the elderly in particular provide most of the support since they have survived—whether well or not too well—despite the deleterious psychological, economic, and political effects of discrimination. Support has consisted of physical care, financial help, assistance in household tasks, provision of discipline and *consejos* (advice) across generations, and intervention in crisis situations, particularly during times of illness and economic need. Certainly the elderly have been mediators between the two cultures and the various generations within their own families. They have bridged the emotional gaps between the various generations as well as between the dominant culture's institutions and those of the Hispanic culture. Undoubtedly, the skills required to survive and to cope have been transmitted by the elderly to the younger generations. The respect required by the traditional Hispanic culture for the elderly has helped to legitimize and to give a good portion of the responsibility for carrying out certain key functions to them.

ROLES OF THE ELDERLY IN HISPANIC
EXTENDED FAMILIES

It has been hypothesized that the elderly, more than any other age group in the Hispanic extended family system, assume an important role in at least three key areas: (1) the socialization of the younger generations; (2) the provision of emotional support, particularly in times of need and crisis; and (3) the transmission across the generations of a point of cultural and linguistic reference that gives meaning and direction in a hostile environment to individual family members.

The functions ascribed by the Hispanic family are not necessarily different than those that most family theoreticians ascribe to the families in the general population. The main difference is that in the dominant groups of society, the role of the elderly in carrying out the above-mentioned functions has not been specifically ascribed, nor shared to a significant degree with the elderly as it has in the Hispanic culture. The reasons for this have been attributed to a variety of factors, among which are the following:

1. Demographic level studies of the general population have tended to be based on individuals rather than on family events and/or units.
2. The needs of the elderly have been regarded separately from those of the younger generations.
3. Identification and assessment have been lacking regarding specific family members' circumstances and abilities to provide certain types of care and to perform certain functions at different stages of the family's life cycle (Lateva & Heuman, 1982).
4. Family theoreticians have overlooked the fact that a considerable number of families go through different phases and stages characteristic of nuclear families and of the extended family at other times.
5. Certain youth-oriented values are supported and reinforced by policy positions and practice considerations that lead to serious gaps in the understanding of the roles and the functions of the elderly within the family unit.

In effect, some social welfare policies can be antifamily. For example, SSI regulations can penalize parents whose children assist them by reducing benefits and/or by declaring the elderly ineligible for health benefits provided through Medicaid community-based long-term care, a service that is crucial to families who care for their relatives (Brody, 1981).

Family life developmental stage theories have tended to ignore developments within three- or four-generation families, and family development schemas have minimized factors related to the aging family; further, family life cycle states have usually been associated with child development (Steinglass, 1978). There has been a tendency to ignore the fact that there are certain life cycle events that are predominant at an older age than a younger one but that have specific antecedents in earlier years.

Bearing and rearing of children, marriage of children, later years without children, illness, and death are events which by their very nature encourage or discourage emotional interaction, involvement, and reaction at certain points in the life cycle of families (Glick, 1957). Although some of these events have transitional effects, they can provide indications of the many different ways in which a family as a system handles conflict and stress, its resilience, and its adaptability. Similarly, family influence at a given time and age might be stronger and more important than in others; further, we have tended to ignore this influence on contemporary events. There is little in the gerontology literature that provides an understanding of the stress signals that are evident in earlier years but that can have serious repercussions as one reaches the age of 65 years or over.

MULTIGENERATIONAL FAMILY RELATIONSHIPS

Although there are differences of opinion among Hispanic academics—as there are within any other group—as to whether the Hispanic extended family is a myth or in the process of transformation and/or extinction, the available evidence shows that at this point in time the nature, the extent, and the quality of familial relationships among most Hispanics are more characteristic of the extended multigenerational family pattern, at least to a greater degree than that found among dominant population groups (Cantor, 1975; Velez, 1983). Differences of opinion regarding the status or prevalence of the extended family found among the various Hispanic groups are certainly related to issues of definition and a dearth of systematic research that can allow generalizations.

Traditionally, the extended family has been defined as an interdependent and interactive kin network that allows for mutual and reciprocal help among its various members and generations within the family system. The concept of the Hispanic extended family has always considered the inter- and multigenerational interactions and relationships that are inherent in it, but it has differed from that of the dominant groups in this country in at least two main aspects: (1) for the dominant society, the extended family is seen as a kin system organized along consanguinal rather than conjugal lines; and (2) it is composed of a network of subfamilies often residing in the same household (Laslett, 1965).

For Hispanics, on the other hand, the extended family often includes relationships other than those defined by consanguinal and/or conjugal lines. For the Mexican-American family, for example, the traditional extended family includes additional kinship layers formed by networks of *compadres,* which can include blood kin but also nonblood-related members. It can include members related by marriage or not so related. These networks can increase with a series of events such as baptism, marriage, or the coming of age ceremony for fifteen-year-old girls *(fiesta de quince años).* At least three pairs of *padrinos* (god-fathers and godmothers) could be acquired at a marriage ceremony, and this network could be even further extended by intra- and interrelationships of *compadres, padrinos,* and *ahijados* and *compadres* of *compadres*.

The literature reports that Puerto Rican families can be similar to Mexican-American families in this regard:

Frequently it encompasses more than the nuclear unit and includes grandparents, uncles, and cousins and also goes beyond what is usually called the extended family to take in persons who are not blood relatives. . . . The institution of *compadrazgo,* a coparenthood, often plays a significant role. (Glijansky & Staples, 1978, p. 77)

Thus, arguments such as the one presented by Coale (1955) to the effect that high mortality and short life expectancy limited the extension of the family either vertically or horizontally in groups of lower economic means and limited access to resources do not apply to the above-cited examples simply because these types of families do not depend solely on blood related and/or conjugal relationships for their existence.

The most significant characteristic of the *compadrazgo* relationship is the reciprocal responsibilities which can last a lifetime, often into old age and then be passed on to one's kin after death. The existence of a large household to accommodate the extended family based on the *compadre* system is not necessary as the different layers of this network do not have to reside in the same household—or the same neighborhood, for that matter—to exercise the functions that characterize it. Thus, the expected reciprocal and mutual help responsibilities are not dependent on the place of abode or geographical proximity. They can be carried out by the different members of the *compadre* network at different times and places in the life course of the family.

In addition to providing economic assistance when needed, this type of network provides a sense of belonging, loyalty, and responsibility for its members. In this type of family, transactions and interactions take place as individuals and family units move through a variety of network layers, and are often determined by events intrinsic to the family cycle over time. Change or the ability to adapt to change has to be a main characteristic of the network's members. For those families that suffer discrimination and often economic need, maximizing whatever resources are available has to be a requirement to respond to stress. This point of view maintains that Hispanics not only prefer but should support and encourage the extended family rather than the nuclear family that is organized along consanguinal and conjugal lines.

It is now supported by new empirical evidence that, by and large, the nuclear family has been a fiction of the imagination of sociologists. Until recently, we were told that the nuclear family was the inevitable outcome of modernization (Kerckhoff, 1972; Murdock, 1949; Nimkoff & Middleton, 1960; Osmond, 1969) and that, because of its smaller size, it was more capable of adapting and changing and of being simultaneously stable and mobile, thus being able to provide more emotional support to individual family members during times of change brought about by industrialization (Vincent, 1967). We were actually led to believe that the nuclear family was the preferred mode of economically developed and affluent nations (Linton, 1936; Parsons, 1943). The extended family was seen as being more suited to the ''less privileged'' classes as it was more conducive to economic survival. However, it retarded in many ways the process of industrialization by discouraging individual initiative (Segre, 1975), and, since industrialization was seen as a priority goal, the implication has been that the extended family is a deterrent to its achievement.

RESEARCH FINDINGS

Current evidence shows that most individuals today, regardless of social class and despite some fundamental changes such as smaller households, access to Social Security benefits, and public housing for the elderly, live and interact with families whose characteristic features include extensive kinship relationships (Litwak, 1965), even though they may be housed in nuclear units. Approximately 80 percent of people over 65 years of age with children live less than an hour away from at least one of their children (Shanas, 1979). Only 3 percent of the noninstitutionalized older population is homeless (Troll, 1971). It is estimated that 7 to 17 percent of the impaired elderly who are able to remain in the community can do so largely due to the efforts of family members (Brody, 1981; Shanas, 1979b).

Contrary to the myth that families abandon their elderly relatives, families do provide the majority of in-home care and are in frequent contact with their aged kin. One-half of all elderly women and one-third of all elderly men who are widowed, separated, or divorced share a home with their children, and many other elderly are semi-independent due to the help they receive from their families (Brody et al., 1978).

Research findings show that most elderly are part of their own family networks, see their adult children and other close kin at least several times per week, and interact regularly by telephone or letter with relatives who live at a distance from them (Bild & Havighurst, 1976; Cantor, 1975; Rathbone-McCuan & Hashimi, 1982; Troll, 1971). Most elderly seem to prefer to turn to their families and friends rather than to formal service delivery systems, at least when they need social support, household management, and home care (Shanas, 1979). Thus, there is enough evidence to challenge the belief that the nuclear family is isolated from the larger kin network and that its members are more receptive of and/or slower to change or to adapt to change than the nuclear family (Rao, 1973).

Seventy-eight percent of elderly caregivers are women relatives (Steinitz, 1981). As women who have surviving parents or parents-in-law advance to their early 60s, they will be more likely to have their parents dependent upon them or to spend more time caring for their parents, to do more difficult care-giving tasks, and to have the parents in their own household (Lang & Brody, 1983, p. 193–202).

Given this situation, the responsibilities of middle-aged women peak at a time when they are experiencing their own age-related transitions, thus increasing their vulnerability (Ward, 1978). As women continue to enter the work force, their responsibilities as wives, homemakers, parents, and grandparents will also increase. More responsibilities will be placed upon grandparents to carry out a variety of tasks in maintaining the household and caring for young children.

INTERVENTION CONSIDERATIONS

Practice expertise and interventions on behalf of the Hispanic elderly and their families have been seriously and negatively influenced by a number of factors:

1. Lack of access to the service delivery systems where Hispanic elders could receive assistance with their problems
2. Limited knowledge about the type of cultural/linguistic differences in problems and needs and those related to the economic and social discrimination that places this group of elderly at a greater risk than other poor elderly
3. Lack of foresight on the part of program planners and administrators to look ahead and prepare for the growing number of Hispanic elders in the coming decades
4. The absence of adequate theory building about the process of aging in the Hispanic extended multigenerational family
5. The low priority given by policy-makers and by private and public funding sources to study the age-/family-related issues that could provide insight and direction to program planners and practitioners

Rising costs of housing, energy, food, transportation, and health care added to the chronic poor economic conditions faced by the Hispanic elderly will no doubt continue to reinforce intergenerational and multigenerational relationships. Understanding certain maintenance functions and the lead roles taken by certain family members at different points in the life cycle of the Hispanic extended multigenerational family could provide direction regarding various types of interventions that may be undertaken on behalf of the elderly.

Although psychotherapists working with families have addressed primarily mental and emotional problems of children and their parents and have relied upon assessments of individuals and family functions based on clinical acumen and judgment (Forman & Hagan, 1983), their conceptual frameworks can be used to increase the understanding of the Hispanic multigenerational family.

Family therapy has been influenced by two broad and interrelated theoretical developments, learning theory and systems theory (Ackerman, 1958; Haley, 1971; Stanton, 1979). Learning theory emphasizes changing behavior and how change affects the behavior of another family member (Patterson, 1971; Patterson et al., 1968; Stuart, 1969). Systems theory emphasizes that no member of a system acts in isolation and that the actions of each member affect the actions of another member. The general systems paradigm is also appropriate to an understanding of the relationship between the Hispanic family and society's interactions.

An important element in these two conceptual frameworks is the interdependence of family members when the family is viewed as a system. Most family therapists agree that the whole family has to be involved in solving the individual's problems and/or meeting his or her needs; each family member is equally considered in the therapeutic process. The family structure, the problem/need at hand, the resources available to the family, and the particular skill of the therapist determine the outcome of the intervention.

A FAMILY MODEL

An important point to be kept in mind in developing a family model to work with the Hispanic elderly is that the "family" is common to all individuals and that it is a conceptual unifier. As such, it can lead to the discovery of common antecedents and provide an interpersonal and transactional context in which different types of behavior originate, continue, or are discontinued. The behavior of an individual family member cannot be interpreted in isolation from the rest of the family's behavior, and, although some types of behavior can be assessed as detrimental and/or dysfunctional to the family, some can be seen as potentially beneficial. In summary, the family must be seen as the crucial intervening variable for a significant number of individual outcomes and behaviors.

The strengths, needs, and problems of the Hispanic elderly need to be assessed within the context of an array of issues, such as proximity to the extended multigenerational family, long-term family relationships, styles, and patterns of communication, the degree and rate of acculturation of younger generations, historical events precipitating migration to the United States, current individual needs as the result of the aging process of certain developmental stages, family management styles, approaches, and available resources, real or perceived loss of power and self-esteem of the elderly, variations in reciprocity, dependence/independence issues in more than three-generation families, and others.

Other elements also need to be considered. For example, Quinn and Keller (1983) identify a number of dimensions associated with the quality of intergenerational relationships between the older parent and adult children, of which the expression of affection and effective communication are most important. Affection, or the expression of sentiment and values, is seen as essential in meaningful relationships. Close ties are based upon mutual affection, interdependence, and reciprocal giving. Affective bonds with children are formed because parents and children have similar interests and values and thus are able to arrive at consensus and seek each other for closeness. Jacobsen et al. (1975) claim the existence of a "test of values" in which family members gather and communicate, through which their liking for each other is increased. Effectiveness in communication is based on meeting role expectations and consists primarily of transmitting what is expected by the other. This includes an ability to negotiate those expectations that are possible to fulfill.

CASE STUDY

The following excerpts from a case situation illustrate a number of the above-mentioned factors and their interplay in family situations that allow the strengths of an elderly woman to be expressed but also demonstrate how the family can intervene during vulnerable and stressful situations on her behalf.

Mrs. C is a Mexican-American widow in her mid-80s who migrated to this country in the early 1920s; she has resided in a southwestern state since that time. She has four living daughters, twelve grandchildren, six great-grandchildren, one stepson, and one stepdaughter from whom she has four additional grandchildren and five great-grandchildren. There are a number of significant persons in her life, among whom is the daughter of a *compadre* who is now deceased. For all purposes this woman is treated as a family member to the extent of experiencing sibling rivalry with the other daughters. Mrs. C raised four of her grandchildren and assumed major responsibility for the full-time care of two of them; the other two usually returned to their parents' home at the end of the work day.

Despite her advanced age, Mrs. C is in relatively good health after a bout with breast cancer, removal of her gallbladder at the age of seventy-nine, and eye surgery for the removal of a cataract. She receives Social Security benefits, SSI, and Medicaid. She does not move as fast as she once did, and her daughters and granchildren worry that she might fall, which she often does, or burn herself at the cooking range. She has consistently refused to give up her independent living arrangements, yet most of her recent difficulties have been related to her place of residence, and consequently she has moved several times in the last five years. She now rents an apartment owned by her oldest daughter, A, for which she pays one-third of the actual amount of the rent. Some of her daughters are now putting pressure on her to consider other living arrangements, and she has recently begun to talk about moving to another state where her "favorite" daughter resides or to another city where most of her daughters were born.

Mrs. C seems to have considerable influence in the lives of her daughters, grandchildren, great-grandchildren, stepchildren, sons, and daughters-in-law, and others in the extended family, and has a particularly close bond with three of the grandchildren whom she raised even though these grandchildren are themselves adults and one has two small children of her own.

This family is characterized by a great deal of interaction among the various generations: small groupings form to cope or deal with different situations and/ or events, consisting of cousins, daughters and children, or daughters and nephews/nieces, and so on. At times groups of "allies" form to solve a particular crisis or to "rescue" a particular family member from a particular situation. Information about the family is related and transmitted regularly among all of its members via the telephone or by visiting one another's homes; crises are usually communicated to Mrs. C, who in turn relays them to the rest of the family.

At this time individual family members are persuaded and/or influenced by Mrs. C. as to the type of action that is necessary at a given time, place, and on behalf of someone. For example, one of her granddaughters, B, a young woman of about twenty-three years of age, was recently found unconscious in front of her apartment by the landlord. Mrs. C was called by the landlord, at which time she mobilized a number of family members, including the granddaughter's divorced father (Mrs. C's ex-son-in-law), who had been kept informed of his daughter's problems by Mrs. C. Through her persuasion, it was agreed that each immediate family member of B would contribute a monthly amount of money to pay for her support and counseling sessions to deal with her apparent alcoholism. Further, Mrs. C arranged with her older daughter to promise an apartment close to her as soon as one became vacant. This took place within one month of the above incident. No one seemed to question the process followed or the decisions made and the actions taken; rather, Mrs. C's daughter, D, the mother of B, seemed relieved to see the results of Mrs. C's efforts on behalf of B, particularly in getting the cooperation of the ex-husband and B's siblings in contrast to her own inability to do so in the past. The strong, resourceful, thoughtful, "therapy"-oriented eighty-five-year-old grandmother played a key role in this situation.

A different event, taking place during the same time, illustrates the vulnerability of this same woman and her inability to handle a crisis directly by herself. At the time of this event, Mrs. C had another daughter residing with her, who had recently obtained a divorce after twenty years of marriage. This daughter had recently experienced the marriage of her one daughter, who had moved out of town and given birth to her first child, and her son was having a number of difficulties adjusting to his parents' divorce and becoming independent. Thus, this daughter seemed to be experiencing a number of stresses associated with a particular phase in her own life, but aggravated by an unexpected divorce and the realization of the need to start her own independent life. This daughter, who in the past had been thoughtful, respectful, and considerate of her mother, had recently become harsh, inconsiderate of the limited financial resources of her mother, controlling, impatient, and in many ways abusive. She accused her mother of "gossiping" about her and telling her affairs to the rest of the family, thus violating the trust placed in her; of not providing enough support to her; and at the same time of interfering with her freedom.

The situation at Mrs. C's small apartment had become intolerable for the two women, but particularly for Mrs. C, who was beginning to feel the pinch of the added financial burden, the lack of privacy, and the humiliation experienced due to the "disrespect" shown to her by her daughter. Mrs. C felt trapped in a painful situation, angry at herself for not taking stronger action and encouraging the daughter to become self-sufficient a year after her divorce, and angry at the daughter for the pain she was inflicting; at the same time, however, she felt guilty for wanting her daughter out of her home. Mrs. C complained of feeling ill; she could not eat or sleep and was afraid that she might suffer a stroke. Finally, Mrs. C communicated with her "favorite" daughter, who flew into town, and, after discussion with the other three sisters, it was decided that she must ask her sister E to move out of their mother's apartment. Obviously, this was a painful experience for all those involved, yet it was this crisis that prompted Mrs. C to get help from another daughter and forced E to resume her own independent life and initiate a process of self-help and reconstruction.

CONCLUDING REMARKS

In their interventions practitioners must understand and utilize the family's composition, the role that each family member plays and/or has the potential for assuming, and the underlying family structure, including hierarchical factors as well as the many resources that can be mobilized within the family. It is only within this context that practitioners from the service delivery system can identify their own role(s) and intervene appropriately on behalf of the family and its individual members.

REFERENCES

Ackerman, N. (1958). *Psychodynamics of family life*. New York: Basic Books.

Bild, B. R., & Havighurst, P. J. (1976). Senior citizens in great cities: The case of Chicago. *The Gerontologist, 16,* 63–69.

Brody, E. M. (1981). Women in the middle and family help to older people. *The Gerontologist, 21,* 471–480.

Brody, S., Poulshock, W. W., & Masiocchi, D. (1978). The family caring unit: A major consideration in the long-term support system. *The Gerontologist, 18,* 556–561.

Cantor, M. (1975). Life space and the social support system of the inner city elderly of New York. *The Gerontologist, 15,* 23–24.

Coale, A. (1965). *Aspects of the analysis of family structure*. Princeton, NJ: Princeton University Press.

Fennell, V. I. (1977). Age relation and rapid change in a small town. *The Gerontologist, 17,* (5) 405–411.

Forman, D. B., & Hagan, J. B. (1983). A comparative review of total family functioning measures. *The American Journal of Family Therapy, 11*(4), 25–38.

Glick, P. (1957). *American families*. New York: Wiley.

Glijansky, A., & Staples, R. B. (1978). Utilizing family therapy with Puerto Rican families in community settings: Special considerations. In *Hispanic report on families and youth*. Washington, DC: National Coalition of Hispanic Mental Health and Human Services Organization.

Jacobsen, R. R., Berry, K. J., & Olson, K. F. (1975). An empirical test of the generational gap: A comparative intrafamilial study. *Journal of Marriage and the Family, 37,* 840–852.

Kerckhoff, A. G. (1972). Conjugal relationships in industrial societies. In M. Sussman & B. Cogswell (Eds.), *Cross-national family research* (pp. 54–65). London: E. J. Brill.

Lang, A., & Brody, E. M. (1983). Characteristics of middle-aged daughters and help to their elderly mothers. *Journal of Marriage and the Family, 45,* 193–202.

Laslett, T. R. (1965). *The world we have lost*. London: Methuen.

Lateva, L. S., & Heuman, L. F. (1982). The inadequacy of needs assessment of the elderly. *The Gerontologist, 22,* 324–330.

Linton, R. (1936). *The study of man*. New York: Appleton-Century-Crofts.

Litwak, E. (1965). Extended kin relations in an industrial democratic society. In E. Shanas & G. F. Streib (Eds.), *Social structure and the family*. Englewood Cliffs, NJ: Prentice-Hall.

Murdock, G. P. (1949). *Social structure*. New York: Macmillan.

Nimkoff, M. R., & Middleton R. (1960). Types of family and types of economy. *American Journal of Sociology, 66,* 215–217.

Osmond, M. W. (1969). A cross-cultural analysis of family organization. *Journal of Marriage and the Family, 31,* 302–310.

Parsons, T. (1943). The kinship system of the contemporary United States. *American Anthropologist, 45,* 22–38.

Patterson, G. (1971). *Families*. Champaign, IL: Research Press.

Patterson, G., Ray, R., & Shaw, D. (1968). Direct intervention in families of deviant children. *Oregon Research Institute Research Bulletin, 8*(9), 1–62.

Quinn, W. H., & Keller, J. (1983). Older generations of the family: Relational dimensions and quality. *The American Journal of Family Therapy, 11*(3), 23–24.

Rao, L. (1973). Industrialization and the family: A world view. *International Journal of Sociology and the Family, 3,* 179–189.

Rathbone-McCuan, E., & Hashimi, J. (1982). *Isolated elders: Health and social interventions*. Rockville, MD: Aspen Systems.

Segre, S. (1975). Family stability, social classes, and values in traditional and industrial societies. *Journal of Marriage and the Family, 37,* 431–436.

Shanas, E. (1979). Social myth as hypothesis: The case of the family relations of old people. *Gerontologist, 19,* (1) 3–9.

Shanas, E. (1979b). The family as a social support system in old age. *Gerontologist, 19,* (2) 169–174.

Sotomayor, M., & Curiel, H. (1988). *The Hispanic elderly: A cultural signature*. Edinburg, Texas: Pan American University Press.

Sowder, B., Dickey, S., & Glynn, T. J. (1981). Family therapy: A summary of selected literature. Rockville, MD: U.S. Department of Health and Human Services, National Institute on Drug Abuse.

Stanton, M. D. (1979). Family treatment of drug problems: A review. In R. L. DuPont,

A. Goldsten, & J. O'Donnell (Eds.), *Handbook on drug abuse*. Rockville, MD: National Institute on Drug Abuse.

Steinglass, M. (1978). The conceptualization of marriage from a systems theory perspective. In T. J. Paolino & S. McCrady (Eds.), *Marriage and marital therapies*. New York: Brunner/Mazel.

Steinitz, L. (1981). Informal supports in long-term care: Implications and policy options. Paper presented to the National Conference on Social Welfare.

Stuart, R. (1969). Operant interpersonal treatment for marital discord. *Journal of Consulting and Clinical Psychology, 33*, 675–682.

Troll, L. E. (1971). The family of later life: A decade of review. *Journal of Marriage and the Family, 33*, 263–290.

Velez, M. T. (1983). The social context of mothering: A comparison of Mexican-American and Anglo mother-infant interaction patterns. Unpublished doctoral dissertation, Wright Institute, Los Angeles Graduate School, Los Angeles.

Vincent, C. (1967). Mental health and the family. *Journal of Marriage and the Family, 29*, 18–39.

Ward, R. A. (1978). Limitations of the family as a supportive institution in the lives of the aged. *Family Coordinator, 27*, 365–373.

9

EL BARRIO: PERCEPTIONS AND UTILIZATION OF THE HISPANIC NEIGHBORHOOD

David Maldonado

INTRODUCTION

It is almost impossible to discuss any aspect of the Hispanic population and experience without reference to the barrio. In fact, many studies and observations simply assume the significance of the barrio in explaining and understanding Hispanics. The barrio has been incorporated into numerous studies and/or used in research interpretations, yet few have made it central to their focus of analysis. The purpose of this chapter is to explore the significance of the barrio in the Hispanic experience by presenting a preliminary study designed to explore the perception and utilization of a Texas urban barrio by older Hispanics.

THE BARRIO: DIVERSITY OF UNDERSTANDING

The Barrio

That the barrio has been widely accepted as a key element in the Hispanic literature does not mean that there is universal agreement about the meaning or usage of the term. On the contrary, it means many things, at times even being undefined as if there is a universal understanding of what a barrio is. In reality, conflicting opinions exist in the literature regarding the significance, value, and function of the barrio. What is clear, is that the term *barrio* is heavily laden with value, bias, emotion, and romanticism.

The barrio is always more than a simple neighborhood. It is also more than a locality where most of the residents are Hispanic. For many, the barrio is either a crime-ridden concentration of poverty from whence Hispanics seek to escape, or it is the cultural sanctuary where Hispanics find caring neighbors and supportive social networks. For others, the barrio is a political colony externally controlled, while for many, it is a phenomenon that exists only because of historical segregation and thus, something that never should have existed in the first place. For some, it is the lost paradise that unfortunately is disappearing.

A common practice is to equate the term *barrio* with that of ghetto and to describe it in terms of the traditional inner-city setting. Even scholars who have broader views of the barrio cannot avoid making comparisons between the barrio and the ghetto (Cuellar 1978; Sotomayor 1971). The barrio as ghetto and the elderly as older slum dwellers imply that negative residential environments hold consequences detrimental to older persons. This view presents the barrio as a pathological setting with extremely limited resources and threatening elements.

At the other end of the continuum is a more romanticized view of the barrio. This view tends to present the barrio as an idyllic community environment in which Hispanics find sociocultural harmony, mutual caring and support, and a broad sense of belonging and acceptance. Becerra (1983) suggests that barrio friendships and mutual help from barrio residents may even take the place of family interaction for older Hispanics. Valle and Mendoza (1978) also tend to present an almost exclusively ideal interpretation of barrio life. Although they do not use the term *barrio,* preferring *vecindad* instead, their view of the barrio is that of a network of supportive relationships in regards to the Hispanic elderly. Again, these views tend to overemphasize the positive aspects of the barrio to the extent that the limitations and constraints of the barrio are overlooked and a romanticized image is created. This is not to deny the positive observations that these scholars have made, but only to note that their overemphasis on the positive can create an idyllic image.

A third view of the barrio is the political perspective. This approach builds more upon historical and economic analyses, and emphasizes the power relationship between the barrio and the social structure beyond its boundaries. Two excellent representatives of this perspective are of Sotomayor (1971) and Acuna (1977). Using the neocolonial model, they suggest that the Hispanic population is a colonized people, making the barrio an internal colony. As such, the barrio is externally controlled by the dominant colonizer through basic political and economic institutions. Such external control results in the draining of resources from the barrio out to the external structures for the benefit of the colonizer. Thus, the barrio is left with extremely limited resources, inferior status, and no self-determination. The colonial model of the barrio tends to place the weight of blame upon political and economic dynamics, especially the action of the colonizers. In fact, the barrio and its residents are seen as the victims of externally initiated colonizing processes.

The barrio has also been presented as the product of historical segregation. For example Grebler et. al. (1970) explain the barrio as the product of historical residential segregation. Moreover, the patterns vary according to specific histories; for example, some barrios emerged from Spanish settlements (plazas), while others were originally labor camps. However, the thrust of this perspective is that barrios emerged in response to a clear pattern of discrimination and segregation. This perspective incorporates economics not in a political sense, but in a sociological approach to explain the emergence and maintenance of barrios. Explicit in this perspective is the notion of separation and isolation.

Still others present the barrio as a haven from the past that is unfortunately disappearing. For example, Galarza (1980) presents the barrio as a passing form of community life that has evolved over a century and a half as a transplant from an earlier form of social life in Mexico. As such, the barrio has been effective in assisting immigrants adjust to the new world by providing a network of human relations developed to meet the needs of its residents. However, the barrio has been dissolving. It has been eroded by migration, urbanization, and social opportunities. Its ethnic and social importance has been diminished. In short, the barrio is a fading phenomenon that has lost its sociocultural functions.

The four views presented above are not meant to be exhaustive, but rather to illustrate the variety of perspectives that have been developed in addressing the barrio. All of these views offer some insight and make valuable contributions to a broader understanding of the barrio. Yet it is probably a combination of all of these in addition to others, that best reflects a realistic understanding of the barrio.

Certainly the barrio is a neighborhood of Hispanic residents. It is the product of historical, racial, and economic dynamics that segregated Hispanics into isolated communities. Such isolation facilitated the development of dynamics and structures within the barrio that reflected the natural and special needs of an ostracized ethnic community. Thus, the barrio reflects the negative consequences of segregation and denial, as well as the positive aspects of social structures emerging to meet the needs of its members. It is also important to note that the barrio is changing, as it must, if it is to meet the current needs of its residents.

A second conclusion of this brief summary is that the barrio is a much more complex phenomenon than might be first expected. A major contribution of the literature is the important observation that there is diversity among barrios. To put it simply: not all barrios are the same. They differ in their historical development, regional characteristics, urban-rural contexts, Hispanic composition, economic resources, and so on. Likewise, it would be ill advised to assume that all residents of the same barrio are homogeneous; not all share community identity, perceptions, and resources. Indeed, barrios and their residents are complex social entities which require from the observer an openness of mind and a diversity of approach.

THE HISPANIC ELDERLY AND THE BARRIO: A HISTORICAL OVERVIEW

The current generation of older Hispanics has emerged from a historical era and set of experiences that binds it to the barrio in ways that are only recently being appreciated. The historical era was the pre-civil rights era and the experiences were essentially discrimination and segregation. These, along with the dynamics of immigration, produced the barrios and the generation of older Hispanics as they are known today.

With almost half (48 percent) of the older Hispanics born outside of the continental United States, immigration emerges as a significant influence in the lives of the elderly. Among Mexican-Americans, 58.7 percent are foreign, while 90.7 percent of the Puerto Rican and 93.1 percent of the Cuban elderly were born on the islands. Foreign birth implies immigration. It is well known that the immigrant tends to follow the path of his/her predecessor through the utilization of informal networks resulting in concentrations of immigrants in particular areas. For the Mexican-American, immigration led to concentrations in southwestern towns and cities, while the Puerto Rican followed paths to northwestern and the Cuban, to southern Florida.

Barrios emerged as ports of entry, as well as hospitable and culturally congruent settings. The immigrant could function in the barrio without fear or trauma. The barrio is where the immigrant arrived; it provided cultural continuity and a network of friends, information, and resources. The barrio made it possible for the immigrant to survive the transition to the new country, establish new roots, and begin a new life. That immigrant is today's older Hispanic. That barrio played an important role in the life of this older generation.

As a port of entry for immigrants and a distinctly Hispanic setting, the barrio might be viewed as an intentional creation by Hispanics. This would suggest that barrios exist because Hispanics value such settings and purposely maintain such neighborhoods. However, such may not always be the case. The other side of the coin is the historical experience of segregation. The separation of ethnic and racial groups into distinct geographic areas is also a function of racist and discriminatory practices. The pre-civil rights generation of Hispanics actually did not have a choice of where to buy into the housing market and where to live. Rather, segregationist policies and practices restricted the Hispanic to the barrio. Thus, the Hispanic elderly of today, whether immigrant or native born, have been historically tied to the barrio—the immigrant because of need, the native because of restriction.

Regardless of whether it was a matter of need or restriction, the barrio was the Hispanic neighborhood. It was the Hispanic turf. Its sounds, aromas, and sights were Hispanic. The people and their culture permeated the totality of its life. For those who were born in the barrio, it was the extension of family and home. For those who arrived there, it was the closest thing to home that they could find. In a true sense, the barrio was the broader context of family life. It was in the barrio that Hispanics found a sense of membership and belonging. In fact, identification with particular barrios contributed to Hispanics' self-identities. The barrio was the context for lifelong friendships and the creation of familial networks through marriage and *compadrazcos*. It was in the barrio that the current generation of elders developed, made friends, married, and raised their families. Indeed, the barrio has been a significant context for critical life experiences of older Hispanics.

Cota-Robles (1980) observes that the barrio also served as a "cultural coping mechanism for the Chicano elderly." Immigrants suffered from discrimination due to language, racial, and cultural differences. The barrio provided a setting where these characteristics were not considered negative or reasons for differential treatment. On the contrary, it reflected their language, culture, and preferences. This included the choice of not interacting with Anglos, in order to live in one's natural cultural environment.

A significant element in the history of the Hispanic population has been the role of land and home ownership. The relationship between the people and the land has always been a very special one. Pre-Columbian heritage has contributed to Hispanic respect for and intimate identification with the land. To own a piece of land became even more important to the generation that passed through rural and agricultural experiences. These dynamics were carried into urban barrios through the values of home ownership. Home ownership is surprisingly high among the Hispanic elderly; surprising, only because of their meager financial resources.

To own *nuestra casa* [own house] is very important. It reflects a sense of belonging and identification. It means that the owner has established roots. They were here to stay. The current elderly generation did not purchase their property for investment purposes or as a temporary step upward, but rather for life-long intentions. This was going to be their home. They identified with it. It was their piece of the barrio. They belonged there and nobody was going to move them. Many intended to die there.

La casa is also *el hogar* (home). It is not merely a house to provide physical shelter; it is *home*, a special place for the family. Here children are born and reared. It's a sanctuary for its members, where comfort and rest are found. *El hogar* is the place where values are taught and meaningful aspects of life are experienced. Probably the most tender life experiences are associated with *el hogar*. Thus, for an older person who has lived most of his/her life in a particular house, that place is most special and holds memories that sustain and continue to give meaning to life. *De aqui solo muerto me sacan.* ("From here, only dead will I leave"). Such common statements by the elderly reflect the value and attachment associated with their homes to the point that only death will pull them away.

It is not surprising that Carp (1969) found that no Mexican-American elderly had made application for public housing in her San Antonio study. Instead, she discovered that the Hispanic elderly judged their present housing favorably, were happy there, and saw no reason to move. In a later study in San Antonio, Markides and Martin (1983) found that 72.9 percent of the older Chicanos owned their homes. An overwhelming 78.7 percent reported that they were very satisfied, and an additional 17.2 percent indicated that they were somewhat satisfied. Lacayo (1980) discovered that 67 percent of Mexican-Americans are homeowners; she also found that only 6.4% of the Mexican Americans planned to move in the near future. In fact, over 50 percent had lived in their present home for twenty years or longer. This information confirms the observation that older Hispanics are long-time residents of barrios, where they tend to be satisfied with their housing situation and have no plans of moving. They are deeply rooted.

Given the diversity of observations regarding the historical significance of the barrio for Hispanics, and especially for the current older generation, it is important to stay close to the thinking and behavior of barrio residents so as not to perpetuate political and cultural myths. With this in mind, an exploratory study was conducted in a large urban setting in Texas to document the perceptions and utilizations of the barrio by older Hispanics. Fifty-five older Hispanics from a large barrio were interviewed (Java, 1983).

It is important to note that the majority of older Hispanics lived alone or with their spouses. This random sample reflected 35.2 percent living alone and 33.3 percent living with their spouses; a total of 61 percent live in one-generation households. It is also of interest to observe that 69.9 percent believed that older persons should reside with persons of their own age. Seventy-four percent of the older Hispanics also disagreed that older persons should live with their children. One hundred percent agreed that older persons should live in their own home as long as possible. These observations indicate that older Hispanics prefer to live on their own. They are rugged survivors, who learned to be self-sufficient. Yet, older Hispanics do not want to be isolated. Ninety-one percent preferred to live near their relatives.

Home ownership is most important for older Hispanics. Ninety-seven percent agreed that home ownership was important and of these, surveyed, 69.1 percent owned their own home while only 5.5 percent rented their homes; the rest of the sample had other living arrangements. They had been long-term residents with 29 percent residing between 20–29 years, 47.3 percent between 30–39 years, and 14.5 percent over 40 years in their current homes. Yet, they were not totally satisfied with the quality of their homes. Only 30 percent rated their homes as good or excellent; 24 percent felt their homes were poor. However, the older Hispanics were not ready to move out. Ninety-two point six percent indicated that they would not move out of the neighborhood. These observations indicate that their homes and barrios are important for older Hispanics. They recognize the limitations yet do not intend to leave. It is their home, no matter how humble and poor; it will always be their home.

Older Hispanics tend to possess a positive attitude toward their neighborhoods. For example, 213 in the Texas study rated their barrio as good or excellent, while only 1.9 percent rated it as poor. In addition, over 20 percent saw their neighborhoods as improving. Ninety-eight percent of the Hispanic elderly also rated their neighbors as good or excellent. The overall conclusion is that older Hispanics are indeed satisfied with their homes, their neighbors, and neighborhoods. They have no plans of leaving, but intend to stay in their barrio. In fact, their travel outside the neighborhood is minimal. They are barrio citizens.

However, in spite of their high regard for their neighborhoods and neighbors, the Hispanic elders tend to have fairly few contacts with their neighborhoods and to be quite dissatisfied with the community services provided in the neighborhood. Over 60 percent rate police protection as poor, and 83 percent rate the bus service and fire protection as fair to poor. Also, over 80 percent rate social services as fair to poor; 48 percent rate public services also as fair to poor. In summary, while they like their barrios, they are not at all satisfied with the public and social services available there.

CONCLUSIONS

The above literature critique and brief report on a study conducted in Texas indicate that the barrio is indeed important to the Hispanic elderly. The barrio reflects their history of immigration, segregation, cultural continuity, and current predicament. Older Hispanics are in the barrio where they own their home. They are happiest there. They like their ambiance but are realistic enough to recognize the problems of life in the barrio—poor public services. It is a predicament that divides their loyalties between their love for and investment in their homes and the harsh realities of the barrio. It is a life of love, conflict, and contradiction.

REFERENCES

Acuna, R. (1972). *Occupied America*. San Francisco: Canfield Press.

Becerra, R. (1983). The Mexican American: Aging in a changing society. In R. L. McNeely & J. L. Colen (Eds.), *Aging in minority groups* (pp. 108–118). Beverly Hills: Sage.

Carp, F. (1969). Housing and minority-group elderly. *The Gerontologist, 9* (1), 20–24.

Cota-Robles, F. (1980). Chicano culture and mental health among the elderly. In M. Miranda & R. Ruiz (Eds.), *Chicano aging and mental health* (pp. 38–75). Rockville, MD: National Institute of Mental Health.

Cuellar, J. (1978). El senior citizen club. In B. G. Myerhoff & A. Simic (Eds.), *Life's career* (pp. 207–230). Beverly Hills: Sage.

Galarza, E. (1980). Forecasting future cohorts of Mexican elders. In M. Miranda & R. Ruiz (Eds.), *Chicano aging and mental health* (pp. 238–240). Rockville, MD: National Institute of Mental Health.

Grebler, L., Moore, J., & Guzman, R. (1970). *The Mexican American people*. New York: Free Press.

Jara, R. (1983). *The significance of the barrio in housing the Chicano elderly*. Unpublished master's thesis, University of Texas at Arlington, Arlington, TX.

Lacayo, C. (1980). *A national study to assess the service needs of the Hispanic elderly*. Los Angeles: Associación Nacional pro Personas Mayores.

Markides, K. & Martin, H. (1983). *Older Mexican Americans*. Austin, TX: University of Texas Press.

Sotomayor, M. (1971). Mexican-American interaction with social systems. *Social Casework*, 316–322.

Valle, R., & Mendoza, L. (1978). *The elder latino*. San Diego, CA: Campanile Press.

10

EMPOWERMENT: STRENGTHENING THE NATURAL SUPPORT NETWORK OF THE HISPANIC RURAL ELDERLY

Juan Paz and Steven R. Applewhite

INTRODUCTION

Empowerment is a key social and psychological construct directly linked to a person's ability to function effectively within his or her immediate nurturing system and the larger society. An ecological approach to the analysis of the socioeconomic problems of the Hispanic rural elderly includes an examination of their strengths as well as their vulnerability. For this purpose, social systems theory is used to study influential force fields in their environment. Within the context of this conceptual model, the Hispanic rural elder is seen as being at the center of his or her social milieu.

EMPOWERMENT

To empower means "to enable"; the root word *power* is derived from the Latin *posse,* meaning "to be able" (May, 1972). Friedrich Nietzsche in *Also Sprach Zarathustra* speaks of the "will to power" as it applies to self-realization and self-actualization. This is comparable to the Hispanic belief *querer es poder* ("to will it so is to make it so"). Power within this conceptual framework is used as it applies to interpersonal relations and other humanistic endeavors. May (1972) defines power as "the ability to cause or prevent change".

In psychology, power is the ability to affect, to influence, and to change other persons. Power is an ego-syntonic concept that builds a person's self-esteem and self-worth: *Creo que puedo* (I think I'm able). In achieving a sense of their own significance, individuals attain self-affirmation, the process of positively validating their existence and life experiences. In aging, empowerment is a process that enhances an individual's values and attitudes; it enhances one's role within the context of society and is fundamental to the effective exercise of interpersonal skills with significant others as well as the broader society.

Powerlessness can manifest itself at two levels, the individual and the societal. Individuals are powerless when their self-perception is negative; these persons will possess low self-esteem and self-worth. When individuals have allocated or abdicated the decision-making process over their lives in interpersonal relations, they are said to be powerless. At the societal level, persons or groups of persons are rendered powerless when they belong to a social group that is not positively valued by the mainstream culture. Persons who belong to racial, age, physical, and geographical groups that are outside the mainstream culture of society are often stigmatized. These persons are subjected to negative valuations by the mainstream culture and are often prevented from fully participating in the total social system.

THE HISPANIC RURAL ELDERLY

Recent changes in the geographic distribution of Hispanics have created a new focus on Hispanic populations removed from traditional Hispanic population centers. Hispanics in the state of Washington are a case in point. In the 1980 census, there were 7584 Hispanics 55 years of age or older in the state, approximately half living in urban areas and half in rural areas (U.S. Bureau of the Census, 1980). Of this number, 4811 were age 60 or over, including 618 persons over 75 years of age. These numbers represent a growth of 380 percent from the 1970 census estimates for this population group. Hispanic elderly use state social services at the lowest rate of any minority. Data from the Washington State Bureau of Aging and Adult Services indicate that only 411 persons of the total Hispanic elderly population participated in state and federal nutrition programs in 1982 (Dept. of Social & Health Services, 1983). Why are Hispanics not participating in these programs?

THE LIFE EXPERIENCE

In order to fully appreciate the elderly's social environment, it is necessary to study their experiences and history. Gamboa has documented evidence that Hispanics arrived in the northwest territory as early as 1774, although significant growth actually began in the early 1900s (Gamboa, 1981). Significant migration patterns developed when Mexican labor was needed by large farm owners in central Washington. Interviews with elderly persons reveal a migration pattern starting in Texas and going to Wyoming, Montana, and Colorado before ending in Washington.

During the early twentieth century, farm growers went to Texas and Mexico to recruit Mexican farm laborers. Many Hispanic families and single individuals went to central Washington to work. Workers and their families often lived in farm labor camps that were provided by growers, often at exorbitant costs. The migrant labor camp left much to be desired. Often as many as three hundred persons lived in the Yakima Chief Ranch in Mabton. Some families traveled in the migrant stream; others decided to settle down in Washington. Work was plentiful, and persons who remained frequently wrote and encouraged their families and friends to move to Washington with the promise of employment.

When families left the labor camp, most did not move far from their employers' farms. Therefore, Hispanics tended to live in rural areas with family and friends in close proximity. Family, friends, and neighbors often helped each other build their homes, a practice that still exists today. This settling out of the migrant stream was responsible for the formation of small rural Spanish-speaking communities. These early settlers are stable persons; a recent study of elderly Hispanics in rural Washington found that most have lived in their communities for 30 years or more, and that 80 percent of these individuals own their homes.

The quality of life for the early settlers was poor. Most persons dedicated their lives to farm labor, which was physically strenuous. Interviews of elderly persons reveal that medical services were nonexistent and social programs were only for whites. Most elders do not speak English because they had few opportunities to learn to do so. Many persons had to hold two or more jobs to make ends meet. The farm owner often controlled the lives of his workers, threatening to take away their jobs or home if he was not satisfied with their work or any other aspect of their lives. The children of farm workers in many instances did not attend school; they, too, had to work and contribute to the family's earnings. Pay for work was low, and often laborers would be left with almost nothing after paying their bill at the camp store. Most leisure time was spent at home or in Hispanic community activities because the majority of the centers of social activity frequented by whites had signs posted saying "No Mexicans Allowed."

The previously cited study of 110 Hispanic elders revealed that their median education level was 2.8 years, and that approximately 25 percent had no formal education at all. The majority are monolingual Spanish-speaking persons; 40 percent were educated in Mexico (Paz, 1982). An analysis of their living arrangements showed that, of the 110 elders, 17 lived alone, 78 lived with their spouses, 5 lived with a spouse and children, 4 lived with a son or daughter, 4 lived with a relative, and 1 lived with a friend. Ninety percent of the respondents had family members living in the same town or county.

Two-thirds of the persons studied had annual incomes of less than $5500, well below poverty level. Major sources of income were Social Security old age pensions and retirement pensions related to their work. Several individuals still worked and supplemented their income by performing agriculture-related jobs. From the total group, 17 percent received no pension, 24.5 percent received a pension of less than $200 a month, and 25.5 percent received a pension of less than $300 a month. It is clear that the life experience of the Hispanic elders is reflected by their current socioeconomic situation and their status within the context of the larger society.

THE DOMINANT CULTURE

The social systems of the dominant culture carry with them cultural norms and values that result in a negative valuation for Hispanic elders and prevent them from fully participating in the larger society. These negative valuations comprise a force field that conflicts with the force field of the Hispanic culture. It is necessary to understand that norms, values, and behavior are the driving forces that establish the social structure that determines status, rewards, and punishments in society. The negative valuations that the larger society holds for the elderly often conflict with the force field of Hispanic elders, which accords them higher status and respect within the context of their communities and social networks. Some of these negative valuations include—but are not limited to—ageism, racism, individualism, language, and a rapidly changing value base. Behavior that is founded on such values and attitudes subjects Hispanic elders to triple or multiple jeopardy.

Ageism is an attitude that views the elderly as undesirable. It views older persons as being unable to continue contributing to society and thus assigns them low status in the social hierarchy of the dominant culture. Preference in modern society is given to youth and places the elderly in a position of powerlessness due to their loss of status and function in society (Bengston et al., 1975).

Racism on the part of the larger society and social service delivery systems is responsible for the nonparticipation of Hispanic elders in aging programs. Today's elderly are the children who lived during the Hoover administration, which took jobs away from "Mexicans" to give to "Americans." They remember being denied welfare, as well as the categorical deportation of "Mexicanos" to Mexico during the Depression because social workers did not want to increase the welfare rolls with Mexicans (Morales, 1976).

The needs of the larger society are often the overriding determinant for designing social service delivery systems. As a result, the needs of ethnic minority collectives such as the Hispanic rural elderly are frequently overlooked in the planning of service delivery systems. Such an approach to the design of service delivery systems planning makes the systems inaccessible to minorities and denies them services to which they are entitled. The Washington State Mental Health and Aging Systems Force in its 1983 report concluded:

Ethnic minority elderly suffer needlessly from both cultural insensitivity and ageism in the mental health and aging service delivery system. Due to such attitudes, as well as language and cultural differences, the unique characteristics and needs of the ethnic minority elderly are not respected in the planning and delivery of mental health and aging services. (Dept. of Social and Health Services, 1983)

The social services delivery system and the aging network are subsystems of the larger society. These subsystems reflect the norms and values of the larger society and function in a manner that leaves Hispanic elders outside or at the periphery of accessibility. For example, some policies create age segregation; others ignore the language needs of the elderly; still others deepen their financial problems. These policies are in conflict with the social systems of the Hispanic culture, which functions with distinct norms and values.

THE HISPANIC CULTURE

The social system of the Hispanic culture carries with it cultural norms and values that reflect a high level of positive valuation for the elderly. Positive valuations such as respect and acceptance give them high status and authority within the hierarchy of the Hispanic social system. In the case of the rural Hispanics in Washington, for example, the elderly perform predetermined roles and functions. The traditional value base of the Chicano culture incorporates values from the larger Mexican culture. In a study of young adolescents in Mexico, Diaz-Guerrero (1967) found that the elderly occupy one of the highest positions of respect in Mexican society.

Anthropological studies of the various indigenous cultures of Mexico have revealed that the elderly occupied a central place in their communities. Among the Aztecs, the elderly performed the vital function of transmitting their culture to subsequent generations. A description of the teachings of the Huebuetlatolli states: "These are several learned treatise and expositions of the elder sages. They contain lessons and instructions directed to inspire children, youth, and those entering marriage with their basic principles, morals, beliefs, and traditions" (Leon-Portilla, 1961, [author's translation]).

Clearly, the elderly were and continue to be highly valued for their role and function as well as their ability to contribute their knowledge and experience to their society. In the contemporary Hispanic culture it is still common practice to seek out the elderly for advice (known as *platicas* [talks] or *pedir consejo* [advice-seeking]). Numerous older Hispanics in central Washington stated that they continue to perform these roles and functions. Their advice is often sought in child-rearing and family relations.

Using the definition of empowerment given at the beginning of this chapter, Hispanic elders are empowered within the context of their own culture. These persons are highly valued; they continue to perform vital roles and functions, and they exercise considerable influence within their families and communities. Hispanic elders occupy a central place within their social system and are seen as an important element in their culture. Persons who are empowered within their own culture may choose to dissociate themselves from the dominant culture, which would subject them to its negative valuations of older persons.

A COMPARISON OF SOCIAL SYSTEMS

To study the relationship that exists between the elderly and their two social systems, it is necessary to compare these systems. The nurturing system is the Hispanic culture, and the sustaining system is the dominant culture. The nurturing system provides a sense of belonging, identity, and validation. The sustaining system is composed of those elements of the larger society with which elders must interact in order to function, such as banks, post offices, the police, and the like. The nature of the relationship between the elderly and their social systems is dynamic. At times a person may be interacting with elements of both systems, which creates conflict situations. For example, a monolingual Spanish speaker may have to visit a physician and not possess thorough information regarding his or her health care. In other cases, it is not uncommon for Spanish elders to be residing in nursing homes where none of the staff providing care speak Spanish. These are situations in which the older person is rendered powerless.

"A great deal of human life can be seen as the conflict between power on the one side and powerlessness on the other" (May, 1972). In the case of the Hispanic elderly, powerlessness can be seen as a result of their conflicting sociocultural systems. Figure 10.1 illustrates the cultural norms and values of the dominant culture that render the Hispanic elderly powerless, and the norms and values of the Hispanic culture that empower them.

This comparison of the social systems of the Hispanic elderly is simplified for the purpose of viewing opposing and conflicting values, norms, and behavior. In the dominant culture, ageism subjects older persons to the stigmas of age; racism is directed to racial and ethnic minority persons; older persons often lose their status in society; and English is the preferred language in the social system. The cumulative effect of these four variables alone is sufficient to render a Hispanic elder powerless from inherent negative valuations. The Hispanic culture, with its positive valuations, is characterized as having respect for the aged, demonstrating acceptance of social differences, enabling older persons to enjoy a higher social status, and employing Spanish as the preferred language of the social system.

Values in both social systems are derived from the culture. The value base of the dominant culture is one that is individualistic, going back perhaps to Darwin's theory of the survival of the fittest. In addition, the pressures of urbanization, modernization, and upward mobility are rapidly changing the value base. The value base of the Hispanic culture is more appropriately seen as that of a gemeinschaft community. In the formation of their small rural communities, today's Hispanic elderly sought to establish their roots. They reinforced their identity by speaking Spanish and formalizing personal and kinship ties

Figure 10.1
Comparison of the Social Systems of Chicano Elders

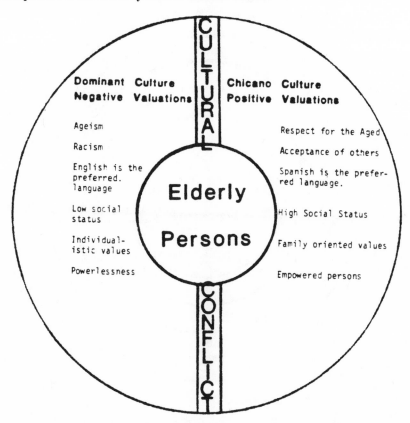

with the persons who could share their experience as well as serve as sources of emotional support. The rapidly changing value base of the dominant culture conflicts with the humanistic value base of the Hispanic culture.

NATURAL HELPING SYSTEMS

A natural helping system is defined as a network of individuals that exists within a Hispanic community. Natural helping systems have a social structure with a hierarchy that places the elderly at the center of the network. Figure 10.2 illustrates a natural helping system; it is conceptualized as the elderly's nurturing system, with the larger society—the sustaining system—at the periphery. The system includes (A) members of the immediate family (husband, wife, children); (B) the extended family (aunts, uncles, cousins); (C) the *compadrazgo* system (godparents, godchildren, church sponsors); (D) the barrio, also known as the *colonia* (the immediate neighborhood environment) and; (E) the

Figure 10.2
Natural Helping System

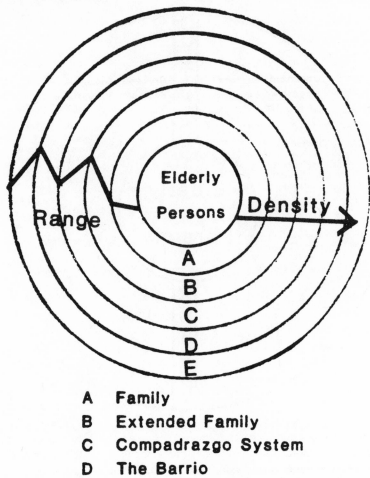

A   **Family**
B   **Extended Family**
C   **Compadrazgo System**
D   **The Barrio**
E   **Larger Society**

larger society, distant from the elderly but with potential to be a support system.

Natural helping systems function as self-help networks; they emerge in response to needs unmet by social institutions. An analysis of the structure of the natural helping system establishes the set of relations that exists between it and an elder. Such systems function on the basis of social exchange of goods and services, and their members help each other with the understanding that they will also receive help when they need it. This practice is known as social reciprocity, and it allows for the redistribution of resources. Natural helping systems vary in type, size, and purpose. They may be small groups or large aggregate networks; they may be formal or informal; they may function actively or on a reactivation basis (Paz, 1982).

CHARACTERISTICS OF A NATURAL HELPING SYSTEM

An examination of the structure and function of natural helping systems leads to the identification of the characteristics of such a system. It is a source of support, stability, expertise, authority, and knowledge. Support is vital for group survival and growth. Support in a natural helping system can take the form of emotional support or the support of ideas, values, beliefs, and practices. Expertise is provided in such systems by persons who are role models or have had varied experiences performing a service, such as *curandera* [natural healer]. Authority is exercised by members who have been accorded respect and the ability to lead or influence other members, such as a *madrina* (godmother), *tia* (aunt), or *abuelitos* (grandparents). Knowledge within the context of this discussion is known as *conocimiento,* the wisdom of life and experience. Within a Hispanic rural community the elderly still occupy the role of transmitters of knowledge and culture; the Sociedad Mutalista is a case in point.

La Sociedad Mutalista de Grander (the Mutual Aid Society) is a mutual self-help society started in the early 1960s in Mabton, a small rural community in central Washington. It originated in response to the needs of Mexican-Americans, who were often denied social services from hostile state and local agencies (Cantu, 1982). For example, when an individual was ill or died, a small group of persons would pool their resources to assist that individual or his or her family and meet their needs collectively. The response of the group consisted not only of tangible goods and services, but also mental and emotional support.

Mutual self-help societies such as these are an organized response to meet the human needs of persons that are left unmet by the various networks of social services. Historically, mutual aid societies have been involved in alternative education and in the collection, distribution, and allocation of goods and services—ranging from food and clothing to banking associations. Some societies are linked to religious institutions that encouraged their activities (Velez-Ibanez, 1983).

The orientation toward personal helping is carried out by attending to a person's needs through being present, listening, and giving advice. When a person has problems that hinder the tasks of everyday living, someone in the natural support network may assume the role of performing functions such as cooking, cleaning, driving, and caring for children. These jobs are done with the understanding that no compensation for the help is expected. Instead, the person assisted may be called upon at a later date to help others.

The Sociedad Mutalista de Granger is illustrative of the central role that elders play within the Hispanic social network. Since its beginnings, older persons were sought for advice because of their perceived high status and experi-

10.1
Frequency of Social Visits: Percentages (N = 110)

Frequency	Visits from Family	Visits to Family	Visits from Friends	Visits to Friends
Never	3.7	7.3	6.4	17.3
At least once a week	80.7	74.5	58.2	44.5
About once a month	11.0	13.6	30.0	36.4
About once every six months	4.6	4.5	4.5	0.9

ence. Presently, the Sociedad Mutalista has grown from an informal collective to a sophisticated formal body with articles of incorporation and by-laws. It also owns a meeting and dance hall where its members sponsor fund raisers as well as numerous cultural events. The leadership is composed largely of elders, drawing from the organizational experience of those members who saw the Sociedad grow. Clearly, the practice of seeking out elders because of their knowledge and authority places them at the center of their social networks.

At this point it is necessary to caution individuals hoping to establish natural support systems for their constituencies. Such systems are developed over long periods of time, typically years. They are time-tested. They afford their members a sense of stability. In this day of programs that last one or two years, it is difficult to develop reliable, time-tested systems. One suggested approach is to analyze a Hispanic elder's existing set of social relations, identify the persons who have a relationship with the elder, and build and strengthen that relationship by empowering them.

THE CASE OF THE CHICANO RURAL ELDER

A study entitled "The Chicano Rural Elderly: A Study of Their Natural Helping Networks and Help-Seeking Behavior" (Paz 1982) conducted in rural central Washington documents the importance of social relationships. The study focused on social reciprocity by analyzing the frequency of social visits with both family and friends. The findings reveal a high level of social contact between elders and their families and friends. Table 10.1 indicates that 80.7 percent of the participants were visited by their families at least once a week, and 74.5 percent visited their family members at least once a week.

Clearly, the family is seen as a primary source of social contact. The Hispanic elderly are at the center of their social support networks, contrary to the elderly of the dominant culture, who are at the periphery. Friends in the community play a secondary role in helping older persons. Fifty-eight percent of

10.2
Levels of Social Reciprocity: Percentages (N = 110)

Frequency of Help Given	To Family	To Friends
Never	10.0	28.2
Once a week	42.7	61.8
Several times a week	29.1	4.5
Daily	15.5	2.7

the participants were visited by their friends at least once a week, and 44.5 percent visited their friends at least once a week.

These findings regarding social visits with family and friends indicate the importance of social relationships. In such visits, the elderly are recipients as well as initiators. Clearly, the Hispanic rural elderly do not experience the social isolation of other groups.

Natural helping systems function on the basis of social reciprocity in which there is mutual understanding and exchange of goods and/or services. All too often the elderly are seen only as recipients of help. The interviews in this study revealed the participants to be active persons with a distinct identity and keen sense of group survival. Table 10.2 indicates the frequency with which they helped members of their family and their friends.

THE EMPOWERMENT PROCESS

The strategies for the empowerment process include dealing directly with power blocks, influencing or changing the nature of the relationship between persons who have power and those who are powerless, and building and strengthening resources to effectively carry out the empowerment process (Solomon, 1976). Empowerment needs to be planned by identifying the driving and restraining forces that prevent older Hispanics from participating in their total environment. Participation refers to the ability to function effectively both within the Hispanic culture and within the dominant culture and its subsystems of social institutions, such as social service agencies (figure 10.3).

Power blocks can be dealt with directly by helping individuals deal effectively with the forces that would render them powerless—individuals, groups, institutions, or society as a whole. It is necessary for powerless persons to attain a sense *(sentimento)* of being, to develop positive self-esteem, self-worth, and self-affirmation. Hispanic elders are empowered by their culture. Their cultural strengths and resources such as their natural helping systems can be used to deal effectively with the negative valuations of the dominant culture.

Figure 10.3
Empowerment Process

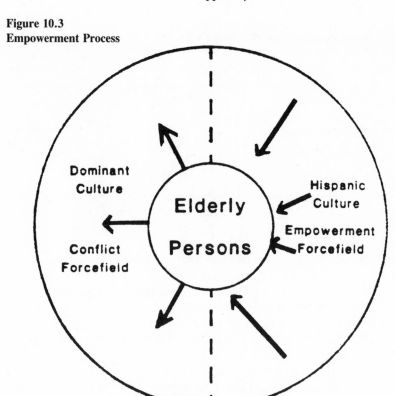

The nature of the relationship between being an empowered elder within the Hispanic culture or powerless within the dominant culture must be further explored. However, social service systems that are reflective of the dominant culture must accept and integrate the norms and values of the Hispanic culture. By incorporating these norms and values the social service systems would empower both Hispanic and non-Hispanic elders.

Figure 10.3 illustrates the empowerment process. It focuses on the strengths of the Hispanic culture with its empowerment force field. The main task is to utilize this force field to strengthen an elder's ability to function effectively within the dominant culture and its conflict force field. The force field can serve to buttress the negative influences of the dominant culture as well as to provide strength.

The quality of life of elderly persons can be enhanced by using natural helping networks as alternative models of service delivery. This is not to advocate using natural helping networks in lieu of current structural models; rather, they are meant to be used in conjunction with existing models and in developing new approaches to service delivery (Sotomayor, 1980). This chapter demonstrates the integral, active role that the Hispanic elderly play in the lives of their families and communities, highlighting the need to involve the families of older Hispanics in the service delivery process. Programs that provide services to elderly persons should be intergenerational and offer services within the context of the elderly's families and communities.

REFERENCES

Bengston, U. L., Dowd, J. J., Smith, S. H., & Inkeles, A. (1975). Modernization, modernity, and perceptions of aging: A cross cultural study. *Journal of Gerontology, 30* (6), 685–695.

Cantu, L. (1982). *La Sociedad Mutalista de Granger: Reflexion* (Interview). Yakima, WA: Hispanic Media Association.

Caso, A. (1945). *La religion de los Aztecas*. Mexico: Secretaria de Education Publica.

Department of Health and Social Services. (1983). *Mental health and aging systems coordination project task force report*. Olympia, WA: Washington State Department of Social and Health Services.

Diaz-Guerrero, R. (1967). *Psychology of the Mexican*. Austin: University of Texas Press.

Gamboa, E. (1971). *Chicanos in the Pacific northwest*. Seattle: National Endowment for the Humanities Grant, University of Washington.

———. (1981). Mexican migration into Washington state: A history, 1940–1950. *Pacific Northwest Quarterly, 72*.

Leon-Portilla, M. (1961). *Los antiguos Mexicanos*. Mexico: Fondo de Cultura Economica.

May, R. (1972). *Power and innocence*. New York: W. W. Norton.

Mental Health and Aging Systems Task Force. (1983). *Ethnic minority elderly*. Olympia: Mental Health Division, Washington State Department of Social and Health Services.

Morales, A. (1976). The Mexican American and mental health issues. In M. Sotomayor (Ed.), *Cross cultural perspectives in social work practice and education* (pp. 2–20). Houston, TX: University of Houston.

Pancoast, D., & Collins, A. (1976). *Natural support networks: A strategy for prevention*. Washington, DC: National Association of Social Workers.

Paz, J. (1982). The Chicano elderly: A study of their natural helping networks and help-seeking behavior. *Proceedings of a symposium on the delivery of health services to the underserved*. Cheney: Eastern Washington University.

Solomon, B. (1976). *Black empowerment: Social work in oppressed communities*. New York: Columbia University Press.

Sotomayor, M. (1980). Alternative models of service delivery for the Hispanic elderly. *Research Bulletin*. New York: Hispanic Research Center, Fordham University.

U.S. Bureau of the Census. (1980). *Census of population and housing: State of Washington county, Olympia, Washington*. Washington, DC: U.S. Government Printing Office.

———. (1983). *Conditions of Hispanics in America today*. Washington, DC.: U.S. Government Printing Office.

Velez-Ibanez, C. G. (1983). *Bonds of mutual trust*. New Brunswick, NJ: Rutgers University Press.

Part V
RESEARCH

AGE- AND GENDER-LINKED NORMS AMONG OLDER HISPANIC WOMEN

Elena Bastida

INTRODUCTION

Until this decade, research on older Hispanics has been limited, but, as Newton Cota-Robles (1980) notes, this is no longer exactly the case. The number of articles and studies on this population has increased appreciably in this decade, with nearly one hundred publications constituting the main body of information. On the negative side, however, Newton Cota-Robles (1980) further notes that critical problems remain with the available data in that they are basically descriptive and often too general to provide more than a superficial understanding of the Hispanic elderly. This results in frequent speculations about the meaning of aging, usually based on assumptions about the traditional modernity continuum as applied to the older Hispanic population.

This study seeks to contribute to the existing body of knowledge on Hispanic Americans by (1) incorporating into the research design subsamples consisting of participants from the largest groups of Hispanic Americans, (namely, Mexican, Puerto Ricans, and Cubans), and (2) exploring age- and gender-linked norms among these subpopulations so that a better understanding of the normative and evaluative components of this group's aging experience may be obtained.

Neugarten et al. (1965) observe that "in all societies age is one of the bases for the ascription of status and one of the underlying dimensions by which social interaction is regulated" (p. 710). In this chapter concern over age-appropriate behavior is examined as illustrated by age norms that implicitly or explicitly are supported by a wide variety of sanctions, ranging from those that relate directly to the transgressor in terms of individual behavior to those that stress the deleterious effects of the transgressions upon the group.

Spicer (1971) describes critical elements of long duration as the "persistent identity system" (p. 795). Collective identity systems are learned like other cultural elements. Such systems allow individuals to maintain continuity in a wide variety of sociocultural environments. Following Spicer, it is proposed that core elements of the collective identity system may be found to exist for the three subpopulations of Hispanic Americans studied here. It is acknowledged that important variations exist among these groups as indicated by differences in national origin, factors leading to emigration, language colloquialisms, geographical residence in the United States, and other less significant characteristics (e.g., food preparation).

However, the author's extensive background experience and field work with all three subpopulations during a six-year period provide ample evidence that cultural similarities far outweigh differences. Even language colloquialisms, which have been suggested to further contribute to research difficulties experienced in the creation of structured instruments and their administration, were not problematic in this study. The same research schedule was administered to all participants regardless of their national origin and/or geographical location. It is expected that much stands to be gained from a comparative study that seeks to integrate the body of knowledge on Hispanic Americans by examining differences and/or similarities in age- and gender-linked norms for the three subpopulations.

RESEARCH DESIGN AND METHODS

A triangulation of methods was incorporated into the research design by conducting extensive field work among all three groups and administering a structured interview schedule containing open and closed questions. Through the application of content analysis, quantifiable measures were obtained for all open-ended questions. A three-member panel representing each of the subgroups under study read all open-ended answers, helped develop the criteria employed in the content analysis to quantify responses, and evaluated one another's coding and interpretations.

One hundred and one respondents were recruited from senior citizen groups and through informal networks. A purposive sample was drawn, and a list was compiled of eligible participants. Respondents were selected at random from this list. Eligibility was determined on the basis of the research design, which called for the participant to possess certain desired characteristics: female; 55 years of age or older; of Mexican, Puerto Rican, or Cuban origin; and noninstitutionalized.

Participants lived in predominantly Hispanic communities, or barrios, and

Spanish was their dominant language. The Puerto Rican and Cuban subsamples were drawn from the Miami metropolitan area, and the Mexican-American sub-sample was drawn from the Kansas City metropolitan area (to include Kansas and Missouri) and smaller towns in Kansas. Structured interviews were approx-imately two hours in duration. Each participant was questioned about age iden-tification, aging, and age- and gender-linked norms. In addition, basic demo-graphic characteristics were elicited from all respondents.

Extensive field work was conducted between 1975 and 1981. Observations obtained during this period led to the elaboration of the research instrument administered to the study population. All interviews were conducted in Span-ish. Whenever applicable, observations based on field work experiences are included in support of the findings presented here.

THE STUDY POPULATION

Data were derived from a population of 101 women over 55 years of age of Mexican (N = 41), Puerto Rican (N = 27), and Cuban (N = 33) origin. The age range was 55 to 84; the median age was 68. Over 2/3 of the respondents (N = 68) were not high school graduates, and only a few (N = 9) had com-pleted 16 or more years of school. Sixty were married, 34 were widowed, and 7 were divorced or never married. Family income ranged from $234 to $1180 per month for 1979. Married women, as might be expected, had the highest incomes; no widowed or single respondents reported family incomes of over $480 a month. The median family income was $415 per month. Each partici-pant was in relatively good health at the time of the study, physically mobile, and functionally capable of taking care of herself. Demographic information about the respondents is presented in table 11.1.

FINDINGS

Pursuit of Realism

Data obtained from the three subpopulations of older women revealed a much greater consensus on age and gender norms among these groups than expected. This consensus appears to be based on a significant and prevalent orientation: "the pursuit of a realistic attitude." This orientation was found to underlie normative expectations on age identification, age- and gender-appropriate be-havior, and aging.

Sanctions that extol the desirability of applying the pursuit of realism to everyday behavior gain in strength as one approaches the fifth and sixth de-cades of life. The desirability of pursuing realism in everyday attitudes and behaviors was found consistently to underlie older women's responses to items on age identification, aging, and age- and gender-appropriate behavior.

Extensive content analysis of all open-ended responses indicated that 83.2

11.1

Socio-Demographic Variables (N = 101)

Variable	N	%
Ethnic origin		
Mexican	41	40.6
Puerto Rican	27	26.7
Cuban	33	32.7
Age		
55-60 years	18	17.8
61-65 years	17	16.8
66-70 years	30	29.7
71-75 years	23	22.8
Over 75 years	12	11.9
Monthly income		
$399 or less	27	26.7
$400-$599	35	34.7
$600-$799	21	20.8
$800-$999	11	10.9
$1,000 and over	6	5.9
Marital status		
Married	60	59.4
Divorced/never married	7	6.9
Widowed	34	33.7
Years of school completed		
0-6	32	31.7
7-9	30	29.7
10-12	22	21.8
13-16	7	6.9
Over 16	9	8.9
Self-reported health status		
Excellent	0	0.0
Good	12	11.9
Fair	40	39.6
Poor	33	32.7
Very poor	16	15.8

percent of the women studied alluded to this value when responding to open-ended questions. Furthermore, even when responding to structured questions, 83 percent of the women relied on the use of a realistic qualifier when elaborating the reasons for their choices. These comments were carefully annotated on the interview schedule beside the questions that elicited them. Further elaborations of this finding are noted throughout the discussion as data are presented for each of the selected topics of inquiry.

Age Identification and Aging

Pursuit of realism was found to underlie findings on age identification and aging. This is illustrated by the comments obtained when asking respondents, "Do you consider yourself middle-aged, advanced in years, old, or very old *(anciano)*?" In selecting responses, participants frequently qualified their choices with observations such as the following:

With this old body, what can I say, *realistically* [emphasis added] speaking?

What were you expecting me to choose with these old bones? I cannot fantasize about my years but must face *reality* [emphasis added].

What do these wrinkles tell you? Well, I'm old and must be *realistic* [emphasis added] about it.

Being *realistic* [emphasis added] about my white hair and wrinkles is my last luxury.

A count was obtained for all respondents who qualified their answers on age identification by some reference to realism; 83 of the women in the study relied on the use of a realistic qualifier in responding to this questionnaire item. The count was then broken down by subgroups. Findings indicate that Cubans and Mexicans were more likely to rely on the use of a realistic qualifier (88 percent and 86 percent, respectively) than were Puerto Ricans (77 percent). However, percentages remained high for all three groups with no significant differences among them (table 11.2).

Direct responses to the question on age identification ranged from 61 percent of the participants who chose "advanced in years," to 23 percent who chose "old," to 16 percent who chose "very old." In spite of some participants being in their mid- or late 50s, no respondent chose to identify herself as middle-aged. Thus, it is suggested that the pursuit of realism significantly affects self-reported age identification, whereby being realistic about one's age becomes a normatively prescribed and desirable behavior that requires defining oneself as being over middle age during the later years of life. The strength of this normative orientation, however, is not confined to age identification but is indicated in other dimensions of the aging experience as well.

Pursuit of realism was also apparent in responses to open-ended questions on the meaning of aging. Again, through the use of content analysis, responses to

11.2
Percentage Distribution for Age Identification Using a Realistic Qualifier

Item	%
Reliance on a realistic qualifier by group	
Mexicans (N = 41)	86
Puerto Ricans (N = 27)	77
Cubans (N = 33)	88
All groups (N = 101)	85
Meaning of age	
Direct reference to realism	66[a]
Indirect reference to realism	38[a]
Age identification	
Middle aged	0
Advanced in years/elderly	61
Old	23
Very old	16

[a]Some respondents were counted twice, based on type of response.

these questions indicated that, in elaborating on the meaning of age, the words *realist, realism,* or *reality* were employed a total of seventy-five times by sixty-six of the women studied (table 11.2).

A second category of responses was established in order to group together statements indirectly relating to realism when referring to the aging experience; these statements comprise those which did not contain a direct form of the term but nonetheless embodied a clear reference to realism. Examples of statements in this category include the following:

One has to be reasonable [allusion to realism] when it comes to aging; there is nothing that can be done to stop growing old.

Aging has meant a more down-to-earth [allusion to realism] understanding about life. You can't be fooled by life anymore; it is painstakingly clear.

Look at my face; what does it [allusion to reality] tell you about life and aging?

Statements that did not contain indirect references to realism and were not unanimously selected as such by the panel were dropped from the analysis. A count was then obtained for this second category of responses, revealing a total of forty-one statements by thirty-eight of the women studied containing an indirect reference to realism. It should be noted that in some cases the same respondents were counted twice, based on the type of response given (table 11.2).

Gender-Linked Sanctions

Although, according to the participants, the pursuit of realism as a desirable orientation is held by both men and women, the findings indicate that, as viewed by women, stronger negative sanctions are applied to those women who deviate from established age norms. Respondents indicated—and field work observations support—their opinion that members of the same age group, particularly women, are the ones more likely to punish transgressors and by doing so regulate the enforcement of age norms.

Eighty-two percent of the women expressed disapproval of other older women who did not "behave according to their age." This attitude usually applied to two groups of women: (1) women who insisted on a grooming pattern indicative of younger females (e.g., too much makeup, flashy clothes, bright hair colors and/or extravagant hairstyles); (2) women who violated normative patterns of sex-appropriate behavior in old age (e.g., especially by flirting, courting, or dating). The latter of these normative patterns demands further elaboration.

Sex-Appropriate Behavior

It should be indicated that two different dimensions of sex-appropriate behavior were observed among the older women studied, and norms that regulate the appropriateness of this behavior may be distinguished along these two dimensions. The first corresponds to self-acting behavior, and the second includes referring to the sexual behavior of others. Self-acting behavior is regulated by a clearly defined norm that finds inappropriate any type of public display of sexually relevant behavior for older persons. Informal sanctions are severe, and this is the type of behavior alluded to in the previous paragraph concerning women who did not "behave according to their age."

The second dimension, however, is much more complex and requires special attention. Norms that apply to this dimension may be separated into three different categories: (1) norms that regulate how much and what is talked about in public about the sexual behavior of others (appropriateness in wording is important); (2) norms that permit allusions to self-acting behavior for wives in a group setting; and (3) norms that regulate how much of one's past sexual experience is shared with others.

Older women respond differently to the first set of norms, and, accordingly, two social types may be drawn from which rise two distinct patterns of behavior. The first type is the "active speaker" and the second type is the "active listener." These social types have been developed as formal abstractions to encapsulate the everyday experiences of these older women within their social milieu. As such, they represent the generalized behaviors of older women in the study in relation to other people, their knowledge, and their activities.

Older women who find themselves in the role of active speakers are usually perceived by the rest as being somewhat deviant. They are deliberately blunt when speaking about the sexual behavior of others, particularly young adults. However, it must be pointed out that "speakers" are not deviants in the sense that those who engage in sexual behavior are as defined by the group; that is, "speakers" are not ostracized, stigmatized, or spoken about pejoratively. On the contrary, they are warmly received and are welcome guests in social gatherings, for they are the ones who with their "spicy" comments add a certain flavor to the group.

The "listener" role has been classified as "active" because the role playing involved in it is not as passive as the word *listener* implies. Older women who play the role of active listeners not only encourage speakers to engage in that topic of conversation but, are also responsible for bringing the speaker back in line with accepted group norms if she should transgress too far from the established guidelines of permissible descriptions and/or vocabulary. Thus, "active listeners" play a dual role, for not only do they provide an audience for the speaker but they also become informal group agents of social control.

It is acceptable for older women to talk about sexual behavior, especially in reference to young adults, but it is uncommon and infrequently acceptable to simply talk about sex. Sex as a general topic of conversation is frowned upon, but in reference to concrete cases it becomes a legitimate subject. In general, norms strongly discourage blunt language, detailed descriptions, and/or outright character defamation but tend to allow speakers to indulge in insinuating comments and remarks. The greatest variation among the observed groups was found with regard to the latter, for each had established its own parameters of "propriety." The provocativeness or subtlety of the insinuation depended upon these accepted group parameters.

Wives are allowed to make references to self-acting sexual behavior regardless of their age, but clearly established age norms regulate what is perceived and labeled as a self-acting sex role. Again, insinuations, especially if subtle, are acceptable, but if they become too blunt the older wife is likely to be defined as ridiculous and laughed at by the group. In this manner the group enforces its definition of acceptable or permissible behavior. Direct references to self-acting sexual behavior are usually defined as being in poor taste and thus strongly discouraged by group norms. Indirect references of this type after the sixth decade of life include only those within marriage and exclude possible extramarital affairs, which might have been permissible during the young adult and middle years of a woman's life. Direct references are usually allowed only if they are humorous, as, for example, in a joke.

Age and gender appear to constrain significantly how much of one's past sexual behavior is shared with others, but each criterion affects a different dimension of the interaction process. Age sets the parameters of how much is shared, whereas gender determines what is shared. Nevertheless, both exerted powerful constraints on this topic of conversation among the women studied. For them, age determined the degree of particularity or generality employed in the narration; that is, it was generally agreed by the respondents that in old age, the details of a past love affair became irrelevant. Yet, although a general consensus appeared to exist among the women studied on the relevance and validity of this statement, field work observations only partially confirmed its empirical validity as indicated by everyday behavior. The women talked only in broad, general statements about the details of a romance, carefully avoiding direct sexual connotations (e.g., kissing or caressing), but they carefully described for their women friends all other details, even if minor, relevant to the love affair. Favorites among these were the frequency with which a certain suitor sent flowers or letters and/or showered them with other gifts. Thus, the women took pleasure in recollecting their past experiences along these lines:

Oh, what a loyal and dedicated suitor he was; would you believe me if I were to tell you that for ten years he sent me flowers on my birthday and on the anniversary of the day we met?

While he was in the service, he would write me a letter every other day; I once counted all the letters that he had written me, 546 letters in total!

He was so afraid about talking to my father that he came to the doorsteps twenty-five times but would not knock at the door.

Gender, in general, influenced the context of the conversation while age determined the content. In line with what has been written about traditional female socialization, emphasis was placed on the romantic aspects of the love affair and/or the handsomeness of a given suitor. Actual sexual behavior was rarely, if ever, discussed, nor was the physical prowess of the suitor. On the contrary, the details of the surroundings were stressed rather than sexual behavior as such (e.g., "It was such a huge ballroom crowded with people, and yet he found me").

It is important to note that the content of sex-related conversations was severely constrained by the gender socialization relevant to the time period in which the women were raised. Thus, when talking about the men in their lives, they were not referred to as "lovers" but as "suitors" (the typical word used in Spanish was *enamorado)*, and no explicit reference was made to sexual behavior. Indeed, striking differences were found between men and women on the normative guidelines that determined the appropriateness of sex-related conversations (Bastida, 1984).

Among the three subpopulations of women studied, Puerto Rican women exhibited the least constraint in sharing past experiences and were the ones least likely to severely sanction any type of verbal transgression. Although class difference may appear to be a plausible explanation for this, the empirical findings do not indicate class, as indicated by income, education, and occupation, as a significant background variable. A better insight is gained by isolating occupation from education and income, and then measuring occupation as a categorical rather than an ordinal variable; that is, although occupational variation did not appear significant, a dichotomy of having or not having worked outside the home proved much more fruitful to the analysis.

Among the three subpopulations studied, Puerto Ricans, in general, had the largest proportion of women with a history of labor force participation. Not only had they been more active in the labor force ($N = 22$), but they also had the longest records ($\bar{X} = 21$ years) of participation. Given data limitations, it is possible only to infer that for these Puerto Rican women work outside the home provided greater exposure to other normative subsystems. This exposure, it is suggested, broadened their tolerance level so that what may have been regarded as inappropriate behavior earlier in their lives no longer provoked a negative sanction. No significant variations were found for either Mexican or Cuban women who had been less active in the labor force.

CONCLUSIONS

The findings of this study are consistent with the assumption that core cultural elements of the collective identity system are found among the three subpopulations of women studied. Although variations were found among older Puerto Rican women in reference to the propriety of sex-appropriate behavior, these amounted to differences in degree rather than to radical cultural discontinuities. Of significance to the results presented here and to the broader gerontological literature are the salience and persistence of the "pursuit of realism" as a most desirable and approved core cultural orientation. These findings indicate that there is an overriding norm of "pursuit of realism" regarding the later decades of life, whereby women consistently maintain that they have to be realistic about their age and related aspects of their aging experience.

The pursuit of realism, it is suggested, is a major dimension underlying all aspects of these women's lives, and as such it is empirically manifested in topics as diverse as health, remarriage, death, and life satisfaction. Thus, researchers who delve into the topic of Hispanic aging in any situation would do well to account for this normative orientation in explaining their results. In particular, special efforts should be made to address this topic in cross-ethnic research, for this cultural orientation may have an important confounding effect on cross-tabular data analysis. This cultural orientation may lead to partial misconceptions on the part of researchers when explaining the possible low scores obtained by older Hispanics in scales measuring optimism, subjective health, and life satisfaction.

It is noteworthy, on one hand, that age norms operate like other types of norms insofar as there is a binding, culturally shared agreement on sanctions that reward conformers or punish transgressors. In other words, general consensus exists among these women as to behavior that is described as appropriate and desirable for their age and sex. On the other hand, respondents uniformly attributed greater stricture to age norms that apply to women than to men. This difference was reflected in their comments when responding to items on age-appropriate behavior.

The findings of this study are also of interest when viewed within the context of comparative adult socialization. Although cross-ethnic data of this type must be interpreted with caution since observed differences may reflect historical changes in values, attitudes, and situational experiences as much as changes that accompany age itself, the findings seem congruent with Neugarten's results and theory of adult socialization in general. That is, as Neugarten (1965) observes, personal belief in the relevance and validity of social norms appears to increase for these women upon reaching the fifth decade of life. This is explicitly apparent in the data as women reflected on the system of social sanctions that operates with regard to age and gender appropriateness.

In conclusion, the present study is not readily generalizable since it is based on a nonrandomized population. Nevertheless, the findings support the interpretation that age and gender norms are salient over a wide variety of behaviors and corroborate the view that it is possible to generate valuable insights into adult socialization and aging from a comparative perspective.

REFERENCES

Bastida, E. (1984). Reconstructing the social world at sixty: Older Cubans in the United States. *The Gerontologist, 24* (5) 465–470.

Neugarten, B., Moore, J., & Lowe, J. (1965). Age norms, age constraints, and adult socialization. *The American Journal of Sociology, 70,* 710–717.

Newton Cota-Robles, R. (1980). Issues in research and service delivery among Mexican-American elderly: A concise statement with recommendations. *The Gerontologist, 20,* 208–213.

Spicer, H. (1971). Persistent cultural systems: A comparative study of identity systems that can adapt to constraining environments. *Science, 174,* 785–800.

12

THE ETHNOGRAPHY OF HISPANIC AGING

Jose Cuellar

INTRODUCTION

In 1974, when I was well into the second year of my ethnographic study of aging in the predominantly Mexican East Los Angeles area, I presented a paper entitled "Ethnographic Methods: Studying Aging in an Urban Mexican-American Community" at the annual meeting of the Gerontological Society. I prepared the paper with the conviction that ethnography can contribute significantly to an understanding of the nature of growing and being old among Mexican-Americans and that ethnographic methodology can provide qualitative and quantitative comparative data about the meaning of later life and aging for older Hispanics.

That paper also addressed an additional concern: the serious doubts about the value of ethnographic studies for an understanding of Mexican-American aging raised earlier by several respected critical thinkers (Moore, 1971; Torres-Gil, 1972), who specifically cautioned readers against accepting ethnographies that were badly dated, overromanticized, or geographically limited, or that ignored the growing social class diversity among older Hispanics or rested their conclusions on idealized normative statements about what *should* be rather than what actually prevails. The result of this criticism was a general suspicion and distrust of ethnographies and ethnographers among gerontologists, advocates, providers of services, and others.

I tried to deal with these concerns in my 1974 paper by giving a brief description of each basic ethnographic technique, discussing some of its main potentials and limitations, and providing some examples from my research of the type of data that each technique yields. My assumption was that most non-anthropologists probably needed to be familiarized with the ethnographic method and convinced of its utility before they would accept its methodological approach. I also hoped that the preliminary data presented illustrated the theoretical potential of ethnographic data for generating and testing hypotheses in social gerontology as well as for developing social policy regarding the aged, particularly the Chicano elderly.

Two years later, the Rand Corporation published a critical review of the literature on minority aging (Bell et al., 1976) that was highly critical of the "strong ethnographic flavor" of the literature on aging Mexican-Americans. Their generally overstated criticism was that the ethnographic perspective tried to find the sources of deficits in service utilization and economic development "*within* Mexican-American society and culture" (p. 16). They emphasized questioning of the basic ideas that: (1) Mexican-American culture represented the principal impediment facing Mexican-Americans; and (2) Mexican-Americans may be pictured accurately by reference to the traditional culture. This led Bell et al. (1976) to the following erroneous conclusions: (1) the result of the ethnographic perspective is a distortion of the relative importance of various cultural characteristics; and (2) the ethnographic perspective tends to define Mexican-Americans by reference to the culture of the poor. The researchers' assessment of the negative influence of ethnography on the gerontological study of Mexican-Americans has severely inhibited the development of Hispanic aging ethnography and is overblown because at the time there were fewer than five ethnographic reports with reference to aging.

Therefore, my purpose here remains basically the same as that of my 1974 paper, except that my target is somewhat broader. Instead of being restricted to Mexican-Americans, the discussion deals with an ethnography of aging in a population that encompasses all Spanish-speaking Americans (although this has its own inherent limitations since, at the moment, there are only two ethnographic reports that deal with older Hispanics who are not of Mexican descent).

Also, instead of restricting myself to the use of examples from my own ethnographic research, I make use of recent findings by other ethnographers of Hispanic aging to illustrate the gains and gaps in the ethnography of Hispanic aging. Later in the chapter I summarize the first phase of the Development Research Sequence developed by James P. Spradley as a model approach to designing and implementing a preliminary ethnographic study of Hispanic aging. I include this for two reasons: (1) to help those with little ethnographic research experience to get some idea of how to go about initiating a short-term ethnographic study, and (2) to propose one replicable approach for the collection of basic ethnographic data that can be compared in the future. Of course, I cannot emphasize enough that the reader who decides to follow this approach seriously should study the ethnographic texts of Spradley (1979, 1980) as well as other specific discussions of the applications of ethnographic techniques to the study of aging and old age (e.g., Fry & Keith, 1980) in order to be better prepared to complete the work.

MAJOR THEMES IN ETHNOGRAPHIC RESEARCH

Since one of the major characteristics of the aging segment of the Hispanic population is its tremendous heterogeneity and variation in cultural traditions, the present challenge of Hispanic aging research is to gather data that are comparable across sexes, geographic regions, historical periods, local ethnic communities, and socioeconomic classes, and yet remain valid within the specific ethnic Hispanic community studied, be it Mexican, Puerto Rican, Cuban, Central American, or South American. This methodological need for external comparability and internal validity requires that we strive even more to ground our basic techniques and standardized measures primarily in the Hispanic aging reality rather than adopt and modify those created for the study of aging among the dominant majority. In this respect, ethnography remains the most promising methodology for bridging the gap between external comparability and internal validity.

When one analyzes the critical gerontological literature on Hispanic aging, at least three persistent themes are immediately evident. One is an emphatic underscoring of the diversity of cultural experiences found among the heterogeneous population of older Hispanics in the United States and the need for methodological techniques that help us to examine and explain the variety of patterns found. Another persistent theme is the widely recognized need for the kinds of culturally sensitive data that personalized ethnographic methods can produce. The third—and somewhat contradictory—theme is the continued (albeit somewhat diminished) critical questioning of the validity, reliability, and utility of ethnographic data for understanding contemporary Hispanic aging.

Nonetheless, even a cursory review of the literature suggests that some significant gains have been made in the ethnography of Hispanic aging since 1974, when the only ethnographic reports of Hispanic aging in the United States were those of Lewis (1965) on Puerto Rican aging in New York and Clark and Mendelson (1969) and on Mexican-American aging in San Francisco. At this writing, there are at least twenty studies that report ethnographic findings on Hispanic aging, covering a range of important topics and concerns. At the very least, we can conclude that the ethnography of Hispanic aging is developing, though slowly, but is still in need of both better definition and direction.

Despite recent gains, one fact remains: the present empirical base for theoretical and hypothetical generalizations about Hispanic aging will continue to be seriously inadequate unless we move to expand the ethnographic data base. My analysis of the kinds of ethnographic information most needed and the basic strategies available for obtaining that information among aging Hispanics is intended as both an impetus and a guide for future ethnographies of Hispanic aging.

HISPANIC AGING ETHNOGRAPHY

The ethnography of Hispanic aging is defined here as a systematic approach to the collection of empirical, qualitative, and comparative data for the study of growing old and being elderly among Hispanics. Its fundamental aim is to understand the perspectives of the older persons and groups under study and to discover the ways in which they understand their aging realities.

Indeed, the most important argument in favor of increasing the use of the ethnographic approach is its promise of insights into perspectives of older Hispanics. This is particularly important since the first critical assessments of gerontological studies of Mexican-Americans (Moore, 1971; Torres-Gil, 1972) emphasize the fact that most of the early research failed to consider the older Hispanics' point of view, consistently reflecting instead the situation as defined by Anglo researchers. Indeed, of the various methodologies available, only the ethnographic approach really provides us with the information to represent the older Hispanics' "definition of situation" in a culturally consistent manner and to recommend policies and programs capable of producing solutions consistent with the environment as defined by older Hispanics.

Korte (1979, pp. 105–114) recently presented a convincing argument for making interpretive approaches to the study of Mexican-American elderly the first step toward any theoretical developments that attempt to describe their perceptions of their history and their doings, feelings, and state of mind that affect their specific attitudes toward their own social environments. The three interpretive approaches that Korte (1979, pp. 106–108) suggests are: the oral history approach (documenting of verbatim accounts, opinions, and interpretations of people who witnessed or participated in events of interest) for understanding the influence of collective history on the emotions and experiences of generational cohorts; the "symbolic interaction" approach, which attempts to discover the relationship between symbols, the interactions, and the individuals who generate those symbols (see Denzin, 1972); and the "ethnomethodology" approach, which Korte (1979, p. 109) assesses as having an appeal primarily resting on the possibility of exploring and describing the heterogeneity of various perspectives of aging Mexican-Americans from an "internal view." This, to paraphrase Korte, will move the study of Hispanic aging closer to the examination of everyday life from an "insider's" perspective, showing aging Hispanics in interaction with others over time and away from the outdated ahistorical and stagnant conceptions of older Hispanics as a statistical category conceived by "outsiders."

My own analysis of this necessary shift from "outsider" research to "insider" ethnography of Hispanic aging has focused on the issues involved, but my main concern has been with the nature of the research paradigm (Cuellar,

1979). My analysis of the gerontological literature of Hispanic aging suggests the presence of at least four dimensions that characterize recent research. Each dimension consists of processes, perceptions, and elements that stem from the same base and are related in their effects on the perspectives adopted and the actions taken.

The first is a *critical* dimension that centers on the rigorous analysis and critique of dominant perspectives and institutions that affect Hispanic aging and older persons. This follows in the tradition established by the work of Moore, Torres-Gil, and others. The second is a *holistic* dimension that involves multi-method approaches and multilevel analyses, including the historical, that range from the intersubjective to the institutional, from the local and idiosyncratic to the international and universal. The third is the *community action* dimension, with its emphasis on the generation of research findings and activities that are of use to those who establish policies and plan and implement benefits and service programs designed to increase the well-being of aging Hispanics, par-ticularly those in greatest need. The fourth dimension of the Hispanic aging research paradigm is the *reflexive* one, which introduces analytical introspection into the research process and the critical review of the basic assumptions and biases involved, particularly those related to ethnocentrism and chauvinism—that is, those that highlight the values and virtues of the Hispanic aging popu-lation, ignoring its faults and depreciating the values and virtues of others. This ongoing process of analytical introspection also permits the critical interfacing of personal biography with community history in order to identify significant problems. It is this reflexive dimension that fundamentally links Hispanic aging to the ''insider'' orientation.

ETHNOGRAPHY FROM THE INSIDER PERSPECTIVE

An insider is a member of a specified collectivity (in this case, the aging Hispanic population) who occupies a position in its structure (shares responsi-bilities and rights, privileges, and duties in relationship to other members). Specifically, an insider is an older (as opposed to younger) Hispanic. The in-sider orientation can be summarized as follows: the insider, by virtue of social location, has access to certain information or data not readily accessible to outsiders. The implication is that insiders have structurally imposed potential to develop their familiarity with privileged information into theoretical knowl-edge about Hispanic aging experiences.

Elsewhere I have raised several important methodological questions concern-ing the insider's approach to the study of Hispanic aging (Cuellar, 1979, p. 72). Two of the more important ones are: (1) How does the insider's privileged access to the familiarity with certain information (and not other) affect both the quality and quantity of data collected; and (2) How do insider biases affect the selection of research problems and subsequent interpretation of findings? The answers to these questions need to be addressed more fully. As a start in that direction, we shall identify four of the more salient biases and limitations of the insider's approach (fear, clarity, power, and fatigue) and discuss some ways to combat them.

CAVEATS IN THE INSIDER APPROACH

Insider fear generally stems from anxiety about the unknown. Inaction caused by fears that research will have a negative instead of a positive effect is one of the biggest barriers that insiders face. In order to combat it, the insider researcher must work on developing self-confidence, sound judgment, and creative action.

Clarity is a unique insider's limitation. It stems from the insider's privileged access to information and causes some insiders to assume that they already know the answers to empirical questions and to ignore the need for data collection and analysis. This limitation, unfortunately, often causes insiders to over-speculate or generalize on the basis of personal reflection rather than systematic research. One effective way to deal with the problems of insider clarity is to make a commitment to a disciplined research agenda.

Power can be a very real limitation to insider researchers who can keep their fear and clarity in check. Knowledge is power, and the more accurate knowledge that a researcher acquires, the more power, control over resources, and influence he or she has. The basic problem has to do with the concern that, at some point, the insider researcher's primary focus may shift away from the acquisition of knowledge to the acquisition of power for its own sake. One way to avoid the seduction of power is to maintain a clear focus on the primary reasons for the acquisition of knowledge in order to improve the life conditions of aging Hispanics.

Fatigue is a constant enemy of the insider researchers. There are few insider researchers in Hispanic aging but a great deal of work to be done; many are overextended and overcommitted in vain attempts to satisfy the demands. As a result, insider researchers often exhibit an almost permanent sense of weariness, a constant desire to rest or take a break. One way to combat insider fatigue is to adopt a frugal attitude—engaging in no frivolous actions, acting deliberately at all times, and wasting little energy on low-priority concerns.

We can draw a number of methodological implications for the ethnography of Hispanic aging from this. Insider researchers must pay more attention to both idiosyncratic and sociocultural contexts of Hispanic aging, take the opportunity to examine the experiential milieu in which older Hispanics interact instead of simply collecting their recalled information, and try to link empirical observations with information gathered by interviews in an effort to establish the correlates of Hispanic aging. The introduction of insider researchers into the process is a step closer to an inside view of the aging process in the Hispanic situation because the Hispanic researcher may be in a better position to experience and record critical data on the problems and needs of seniors and *ancianos*.

As Reynolds and Farberow (1973) noted, under ideal conditions the researcher and the data provider should be the same person. Thus, the insider is privy to intimate perceptions and social realities. This means that the insider's methodological training should include ways of observing and recording both internal and external events. It also means that, by reflection or introspection, the insider researcher can prepare beforehand for the tasks of obtaining information on the aging of others.

Next to the ideal insiders (older Hispanics as researchers) are the insider researchers who adopt elderly identities and immerse themselves in a social milieu in which they are themselves viewed as aging Hispanics. Although no such research has been reported, given the success of similar attempts in other contexts, it is likely that this approach could be used advantageously. The basic methodological technique would be to record all experiences in daily journals, with supplemental data gathered using other techniques. This should happen soon in that there are already a number of insiders of Hispanic heritage who are conducting ethnographic research on Hispanic aging.

The following discussion is a summary of the more important and recent ethnographic studies of Hispanic aging, presented in order to illustrate salient gains and gaps in research as well as the utility of some specific ethnographic strategies for collecting data on the various foci of Hispanic aging. A summary of one of the more systematic approaches to ethnography, Spradley's "Developmental Research Sequence" (DRS), is outlined later in this chapter. The goal is to generate a number of specific questions to be raised and issues to be addressed in order to establish a comparative ethnographic data base for understanding the meaning of aging and old age among Hispanics in the United States from one generation to the next.

The ethnographic strategy outlined below will help us to discover the appropriate questions to ask and measures to develop for the study of aging and old age in the different Hispanic American cultural traditions. This approach should help us to generate the more qualitative and comparative data needed for adequate generalizations about the processes and experiences of Hispanic aging. It is my hope that this work will excite and stimulate more thought and ethnographic studies that will seek out the finer nuances in meaning of Hispanic aging and old age. In a real sense, this is a guide for exploring, to some extent, the little known and often ignored dimensions of Hispanic aging. It is also an introduction to the ethnography of Hispanic aging for those who have never had the opportunity to engage in ethnography. Spradley's DRS ethnographic strategy is emphasized because of its simple elegance and its friendliness to first-time users.

GAINS AND GAPS IN THE ETHNOGRAPHY OF
HISPANIC AGING

Hispanic aging has at least five research foci, which roughly correspond to the five dimensions of human life: the sociological, the ecological, the psychological, and culturological, and the biological. Each dimension is characterized by at least two processes that stem from a similar base and are related in their effects on the nature of individuals or groups. The biological dimension includes the physiological processes of regeneration and degeneration as well as specific sex and age differences. The sociological dimension includes the societal processes or social organization and stratification and the roles and statuses of individuals and groups involved. The ecological dimension includes the processes of environmental adaptation and modification as well as the economic production and distribution of goods and services, the specific concerns centered on housing, transportation, income, and food. The psychological dimension includes the mental processes of cognition and conscientization, emotions and experiences, personalities and identities, perceptions, feelings, attitudes, beliefs, and values. The culturological dimension includes the symbolic and expressive processes of communication and creation, symbols and rituals, language, arts, and crafts. The ethnography of Hispanic aging must eventually take all five of these dimensions or foci into consideration during data collection, analysis, and explanation.

Sociological Dimension

The social organization and stratification of older Hispanics in society have received the greatest amount of ethnographic research attention. Essential considerations are the roles (rights and responsibilities) that older Hispanics exercise in their wider kinship networks, their extended and nuclear families and households, and their voluntary associations (see Cuellar, 1978). Valle (1982) has outlined a number of specific social network mapping techniques that appear especially well-suited for dealing with these issues among older Latinos.

Sanchez-Ayendez (1983) recently reported the results of an eighteen-month ethnographic study conducted using in-depth interviews and participant observation to obtain data on the sociocultural dimensions of support systems as an intervening factor in adaptation to old age and to ethnicity. The study focused specifically on the process of aging among older Puerto Rican women living in subsidized housing in a New England city. Sanchez-Ayendez suggests that there are cultural rules underlying the exchange that occurs within a support system. All factors—the type of support given or received, the way it is offered, the individuals involved, and the occasion—are understood within the context of the meaning that interpersonal relationships have for people. According to Sanchez-Ayendez (1983), ''The way a group's cultural tradition defines and interprets relationships is a factor that influences how a person uses his/her networks in order to secure the support he/she needs in old age'' (p. 9).

Lewis (1966) was among the first to demonstrate that the intensive study of the life of even a single extended family can tell us something about older Hispanics: their physiological conditions, their social relations, their environments and economics, their emotions and experiences, and their communication and creativity in the wider society in which they live. The pioneering case study of the Mexican-American family of a seventy-one-year-old grandmother named Beatriz Chavez living in the San Francisco Mission District by Clark and Mendelson (1969) is the earliest available illustration of this technique's value for understanding Hispanic aging.

Perhaps the most important methodological innovation of Lewis (1965) is the approach that presents individuals and incidents from multiple points of view, combining biographies with daily events and activities. The biographies provide a subjective view of each individual older person, while the observations provide accounts of actual daily behaviors. Lewis (1964, p. xxv) underscored how these two types of data supplement each other. For our purposes, this is best illustrated by Velez-Ibanez's (1978) study of youth and aging in four urban Mexican families in central Mexico. His study basically attempted to decipher the crucial differences in adaptation of two sets of families to the same basic urban environment. His findings indicate that the families could be divided into "historic" and "ahistoric" categories, with the following crucial indicators differentiating the "historic" families: (1) the physical presence of an elderly member who has prestigious roles fulfilled within the household; (2) the older member's possession of a private domain of resources, skills, or personality characteristics that command the attention of others; and (3) the older member's ability to draw reinforcement from other social relations outside the immediate family circle (Velez-Ibanez, 1978, p. 154).

Ecological/Culturological Dimensions

In *Bonds of Mutual Trust,* Velez-Ibanez (1983) examines the rotating credit association (RCA), an important cultural invention of Mexicans in both Mexico and the United States. *Bonds of Mutual Trust* provides some interesting ethnographic data about the cultural systems of the socioeconomic networks of older Mexicans. Some of Velez-Ibanez's more important findings are as follows.

Although he found *tandas* (RCAs) among networks of both elderly retired bourgeois males and females and among working-class or marginal sector elderly, he noted that there were some significant differences between classes. One has to do with the factor of age. Working-class or marginal sector elderly who participate in RCAs generally join age-heterogeneous ones, unlike the elderly bourgeois who join age-homogeneous *tandas*. According to Velez-Ibanez (1983, p. 119), one consequence of this for the working-class and marginal elderly is that interdependent relations between age groups are maintained, helping to preserve a sense of continuity throughout the life cycle. RCAs are anchored in recreational activities among the networks of retired elderly bourgeois men and women in Mexico City. For all elderly involved:

The *tanda* provides material proof of the durable reciprocity of present and past relationships. *Tandas* commit those at the end of the life cycle to the future by placing in the distance the obligation to reciprocate by contributions. While the uncertainty of the future is made real by the deaths of those around them, their investment in the future, masked as an obligation, contradicts that uncertainty. (p. 119)

The ecocultural dimension focuses attention on the modification and adaptation of the environment to self and vice versa by older persons, on the one hand, and the relationship of older Hispanics to the means of production and distribution of goods and services on the other.

In his 1972 thesis, Torres-Gil clearly highlighted the need for a better understanding of the way older Hispanics define their own environments by critically analyzing Carp's ("outsider") research and proposing an alternative ("insider") interpretation of the way older Mexican-Americans culturally view their environments. Much more information is needed on how older Hispanics in both rural and urban settings come to terms with their environments by adapting to some aspects and modifying others.

Psychological Dimension

The ethnographic study of the psychological dimension centers on two processes: cognition and conscientization. The work of Korte on interpretive research approaches is particularly important for understanding the way in which historical events are integrated and interpreted by older Hispanics of different generations. On the one hand, this is an effort to address the issue first raised by Moore and others regarding the need to account for differences among members of different generations with different historical experiences. On the other hand, Korte's ethnographic work allows us to appreciate how a rather loosely and vaguely defined symbol, such as the notation of *mortificaciones,* can be used to discover what is unique about each empirical instance of the concept as well as what is common across many different settings (Korte, 1979, p. 111). Thus, Korte (1979) is able to raise questions like, "Is the concept of mortification applicable in interactional settings, and can it be described as 'situated' in interaction?" (p. 111).

Korte has also clearly delineated a theoretical rationale for the study of language use among older Hispanics, one that takes us beyond the important practical concern of effectively communicating with predominantly Spanish-speaking persons in an English-dominant society. He argues that answers to our questions concerning the "social and lingual conduct" of older Hispanics can be found in what C. Wright Mills (1981, pp. 474–477) once called "rationalized acts" or motives that serve as justification for past, present, or future acts. He advocates the study of "vocabularies of motives" (the process of naming anticipated consequences of our actions) such as *"falta de animo* or complaints about *mortificacion"* as a means of learning more about the meaning of such concepts for our interpretations of "morale" or "well-being" among older Hispanics (Korte, 1979, p. 112).

Biological Dimension

The biological dimension has received little ethnographic attention. The variations in the symbolic significance attached to the most basic of human characteristics of sex, age, and physiological status among aging Hispanics must be researched in greater depth. Little is known about the way aging and old age are defined and understood among Hispanics, about the sexual and sensual needs of older Hispanics, about the similarities and differences among different groups of males and females, and about the cultural links to degenerative and death processes. We need more descriptions, based on observations and in-depth interviews, that can help us to interpret the reproduction and degeneration of older Hispanics from one generation to the next in their proper context. In addition, more information on the nutritional conditions and needs of older Hispanics is needed. Ethnographic techniques are particularly helpful in identification and analysis of categories, kinds, and amounts of food eaten by older Hispanics.

Achor (1978) recently tried to convey a sense of contemporary Hispanic aging by providing an ethnographic composition drawn from the lives of several older persons based on research in a Dallas, Texas barrio. Her intent was to provide a life-cycle framework for the description of the barrio's daily life and the details of its population's aging experiences.

An old man trudges the barrio on foot selling fresh produce. An older woman is known for her tamales. Another elderly woman is an accomplished seamstress who makes folk dancing costumes for a children's group. These economic transactions afford elderly barrio residents a way to supplement their often meager incomes in addition to providing them with opportunities for face-to-face interaction with others in the neighborhood. Many live with their married children and remain a vital part of the family circle for as long as they live. Even those who live alone can count on frequent visitors and solicitude when problems arise.

The aged are usually treated with respect and deference at private family gatherings or public barrio functions. Some older barrio residents remain active and alert well into their eighties. Some older barrio men lend a sense of continuity by telling tales, playing musical instruments, and singing at fiestas. Others perform valued family functions, such as tending small gardens and repairing broken items around the house. When an older person becomes ill and requires extended care, it will usually be provided by a younger family member, typically without regard for the severe financial and emotional strains on the family that this may cause, in order to avoid placing the older person in a nursing home (Achor, 1978, p. 81).

A METHODOLOGICAL GUIDE TO THE
ETHNOGRAPHY OF HISPANIC AGING

The general purpose of any ethnography of Hispanic aging is to examine the nature of aging and old age among members of one or more Hispanic communities in the United States. The broad goal is to generate more detailed descriptions and precise analyses of both the salient aging characteristics of Hispanics and the factors related to their conditions and circumstances in old age, as well as to discover the cultural patterns and themes that give life meaning for older Hispanics.

Consistent with the holistic dimension, any ethnographic effort should accumulate data on as many dimensions of Hispanic aging as possible, with a sensitivity to the diversity, plurality, and heterogeneity found among the various ethnic traditions (Mexican, Puerto Rican, Cuban, Central American, and South American) of elderly Hispanics in the United States. Similarly, as ethnographies of Hispanic aging should have a diachronic dimension; that is, they should include the collection of both individual biographies and oral histories of the various Hispanic ethnic communities, on the assumption that Hispanic aging can be understood only in light of the particular historical events that frame the experiences of older Hispanics.

Generally, the ethnographic analyses of Hispanic aging are influenced by the assumptions and premises of the "symbolic interaction" approach: (1) people and things (objects, places, spaces, acts, activities, events, times, goals, and feelings) mean something to aging Hispanics, and these meanings affect the behaviors, beliefs, values, and attitudes of aging Hispanics; (2) the elderly Hispanics' meanings of things are created through their social interaction with significant others; and (3) elderly Hispanics' meanings are modified through collective interpretation.

The ethnography of Hispanic aging can be designed in three phases. The first phase involves identifying, locating, and touring the settings where elderly Hispanics can be found; observing older Hispanics in a variety of social situations; participating in events that involve older Hispanics in primary or secondary roles; taking photographs of persons, events, and activities; learning older Hispanics' special language (especially their vocabulary of motives); asking descriptive questions; and listening and making written and taped records of their answers, comments, discussions, and conversations. The second phase consists of making domain, taxonomic, and componential analyses; asking structured and contrast questions; taking cultural inventories; and discovering cultural patterns and themes. The third phases involves actually writing the ethnographic report.

Ethnographic case studies should include an examination of the ways in which older Hispanics describe their places, persons, objects, languages, and behaviors as the bases for cultural inferences about Hispanic aging in the United States. The ultimate goal of all ethnography of Hispanic aging, of course, is to provide adequate descriptions of Hispanic aging that can be evaluated by both "insiders" and "outsiders" who might use the ethnographies as guides for appropriately considering the experiences of older Hispanics in the United States and providing for their unmet needs.

THE DEVELOPMENTAL RESEARCH SEQUENCE (DRS) METHOD

The DRS method grew out of Spradley's attempt to develop a more systematic approach to ethnographic field work. His DRS method is rooted in the basic assumption that some tasks are best accomplished before others when doing such field work. The result is a well-defined series of twelve steps that are designed to guide an ethnographic investigation from beginning to end. Spradley further breaks down each of the major steps into more manageable tasks. The outline below is a summary of Spradleys' DRS method, specifically adapted for the study of Hispanic aging. The objective is to provide a basis for the collection of comparable data on Hispanic aging for future analyses.

Step 1: Locate key older Hispanics, social setting, and cultural scenes.

1.1. Make a list of at least fifty social situations, scenes, and settings where older Hispanics can be found and of fifty key older Hispanics who may be observed and interviewed.

1.2. Identify the five or six best key older Hispanics and settings in terms of both the theoretical issues of concern and the established requirements and criteria for situation and informant selection: (a) simplicity, (b) accessibility, (c) unobtrusiveness, (d) permissibleness, (e) frequently recurring activities.

Step 2: Do participant observation.

2.1 Make a reconnaissance trip to one or more social settings of aging Hispanics under consideration for more in-depth ethnographic study and make your final selection.

2.2. Do participant observation for at least thirty minutes in at least two unfamiliar settings of aging Hispanics.

2.3. Record some field notes and identify all problems encountered in assuming the role of ethnographic participant observer among older Hispanics.

2.4. Write out several different research project explanations to be used with key older Hispanics identified during the first step.

2.5. Conduct an informal interview with one or more key aging Hispanics.

2.6. Transcribe interview and expand field note accounts.

Step 3: Establish the ethnographic record.

3.1. Set up a field work notebook/file with sections for (a) condensed accounts, (b) expanded accounts, (c) journal, (d) analysis and interpretation, (e) photographs, and (f) tape transcriptions.

3.2. Conduct a period or two of participant observation among aging Hispanics and record your experiences.

3.3. Select one section of expanded field notes and, using concrete language, expand it into several sections.

Step 4: Make descriptive observations and ask descriptive questions.

4.1. Write out a series of grand-tour, mini-tour, example, experience, and native language questions to help guide observations and interviews. Base these on earlier field notes.

4.2. With the above questions in mind, conduct a period of participant observation of a scene or situation involving aging Hispanics in which both grand-tour and mini-tour observations are made.

4.3. Conduct and record an ethnographic interview with a key older Hispanic, using descriptive questions.

4.4. Transcribe the recorded interview.

4.5. Expand the condensed field notes taken during observations.

Step 5: Conduct a domain analysis.

5.1. Conduct a thorough domain analysis: (a) select single semantic relationships; (b) prepare a domain analysis worksheet; (c) select sample field note entries; (d) search for possible cover terms and included terms that fit the semantic relationship; (e) repeat the search for domains, using a different semantic relationship; (f) make a list of all identified domains.

5.2. Make a summary of all domains identified through analysis and review for possible domains for further research.

5.3. Conduct a period of participant observation among aging Hispanics in which additional descriptive observations are made.

5.4 Conduct an ethnographic interview with a key older Hispanic using primarily descriptive questions, but introduce several structural questions to further explore domains.

5.5. Transcribe ethnographic interview.

5.6. Expand condensed account of participant observation.

Step 6: Make focused observations and ask structural questions.

6.1. Enlarge list of cultural domains by making use of the general cultural domains: (a) list the domains tentatively selected for focused observation; (b) write out the structural questions to ask during observations and interviews, and prepare explanations for these questions; (c) identify observation posts that give the best opportunity to make focused observations; (d) identify activities in which aging Hispanics might help to carry out focused observations.

6.2. Using enlarged list, select a tentative ethnographic focus of one or more cultural domains.

6.3. Conduct a focused observation in the field after making careful plans for that observation.

6.4 Conduct an ethnographic interview using structural questions to verify terms already collected and to collect terms for new domains (alternate with descriptive questions).

6.5. Expand condensed account of focused participant observation.

6.6. Transcribe ethnographic interview.

Step 7: Conduct a taxonomic analysis.

7.1. Conduct a taxonomic analysis on one or more domains: (a) select a domain for taxonomic analysis; (b) look for similarities based on the same semantic relationship; (c) look for additional included terms; (d) search for larger, more inclusive domains that might be included as a subset of the domain being analyzed; (e) construct a tentative taxonomy; (f) make focused observations to check out the analysis; (g) construct complete taxonomy.

Step 8: Make selected observations.

8.1. Make a list of aging Hispanics to be formally or informally interviewed.

8.2. Select one or more domains and ask contrast questions to discover dimensions of contrast. Review field notes to answer these questions as needed.

8.3. Conduct a period of field investigation in which selective observations are added to the other two types of observations.

8.4. Expand field notes from condensed accounts of field investigation.

Step 9: Make a componential analysis.

9.1. Make a componential analysis of one or more domains: (a) select domain for analysis; (b) inventory all contrasts previously discovered; (c) prepare a paradigm worksheet; (d) identify dimensions of contrast that have binary values; (e) combine closely related dimensions of contrast into a large one that has multiple values; (f) prepare contrast questions from missing values attributes; (g) conduct selective observations to discover missing information; (h) prepare completed paradigm.

9.2. Conduct a period of participant observation, making use of all three types of observations: descriptive, focused, and selective.

9.3. Expand field notes from condensed accounts.

9.4. Conduct an ethnographic interview in which descriptive, structural, and contrast questions are used.

9.5. Transcribe ethnographic interview.

9.6. Review field notes and search for contrasts that distinguish folk terms in one or more contrast assets already identified.

Step 10: Discover cultural themes.

10.1. Identify as many cultural themes as possible: (a) become immersed in ambience and data; (b) make a componential analysis of cover terms for domains; (c) search for a larger domain that includes the cultural scene; (d) search for similarities among dimensions of contrast; (e) identify organizing domains; (f) make a schematic diagram of the cultural scene; (g) search for universal themes in social conflict, cultural contradictions, informal means of social control, management of interpersonal relationships, acquiring and maintaining status, and solving problems; (h) write a summary overview of the cultural scene.

Step 11: Take cultural inventory.

11.1. Review field notes and take cultural inventory: (a) make list of cultural domains; (b) make list of analyzed domains; (c) collect sketch maps of Hispanic aging settings; (d) make list of Hispanic aging themes; (e) inventory examples; (f) identify organizing domains; (g) make an index or table of contents; (h) inventory miscellaneous data; (i) list additional research possibilities for the future.

Step 12: Write ethnographic report.

REFERENCES

Achor, S. (1978). *Mexican-Americans in a Dallas barrio*. Tucson: University of Arizona Press.

Bell, D., Kasschau, P., & Zellman, E. (1976). *Delivering services to elderly members of minority groups: A review of the literature*. Santa Monica, CA: Rand.

Bengtson, V. L., Cuellar, J. B., & Ragan, P. K. (1978). Stratum contrasts and similarities in attitudes toward death. *Journal of Gerontology, 32,* 76–88.

Clark, M., & Mendelson, M. (1969). Mexican-American aged in San Francisco: A case description. *The Gerontologist, 9,* 90–95.

Cuellar, J. B. (1974, October). Ethnographic methods: Studying aging in an urban Mexican-American community. Paper presented at the 27th Annual Scientific Meeting of the Gerontological Society, Portland, OR.

———. (1978). El senior citizens club: The older Mexican-American in the voluntary association. In B. Myerhoff & A. Simic (Eds.), *Life's career—aging: Cultural variations on growing old* (pp. 207–230). Beverly Hills: Sage.

————. (1979). Insiders and outsiders in minority aging. In E. P. Stanford (Ed.), *Minority aging research: Old issues, new approaches*. (pp. 67–77). San Diego: Campanile Press.

Denzin, N. K. (1972). The research art. In J. Manis & B. N. Meltzer (Eds.), *Symbolic interaction: A reader in social psychology* (2nd ed.) (pp. 76–91). Boston: Allyn & Bacon.

Fry, C. L., & Keith, J. (Eds.) (1980). *New methods for old age research*. Chicago: Center for Urban Policy, Loyola University of Chicago.

Ichheiser, G. (1972). Blind to the obvious. In J. N. Henslins (Ed.), *Down-to-earth sociology* (pp. 3–7). New York: Free Press.

Korte, A. (1979). Interpretive research approaches and the Mexicano elders. In E. P. Stanford (Ed.), *Minority aging research: Old issues, new approaches* (pp. 105–114). San Diego: Campanile Press.

Lewis, O. (1966). *La vida: A Puerto Rican family in the culture of poverty—San Juan and New York*. New York: Vintage Books.

Mills, C. W. (1981). Situation actions and vocabularies of motive. In G. P. Stone & H. Farberman (Eds.), *Social psychology through symbolic interaction* (2nd edition pp. 325–332). Waltham, MA: Xerox College Publishing.

Moore, J. (1971). Mexican-Americans. *The Gerontologist, 11,* 30–35.

Reynolds, D. K., & Farberow, N. L. (1975, April). Experiential research: An inside perspective on suicide and social systems. Paper presented at the annual meeting of the American Institute of Suicidology, Houston.

Sanchez-Ayendez, M. (1983, November). Puerto Rican elderly women: Informal support systems and cultural values. Paper presented at the 36th Annual Scientific Meeting of the Gerontological Society of America, San Francisco.

Spradley, J. P. (1979). *The ethnographic interview.* New York: Holt, Rinehart & Winston.

————. (1980). *Participant observation.* New York: Holt, Rinehart & Winston.

Torres-Gil, F. (1972). Los ancianos de la raza: A beginning framework for research, analysis, and policy. Unpublished master's thesis, Florence Heller Graduate School for Advanced Studies in Social Welfare, Brandeis University, Waltham, MA.

Valle, R. (1982). Social mapping techniques: A preliminary guide for locating and linking to natural networks. In R. Valle & W. Vega (Eds.), *Natural support systems: Mental health promotion perspectives* (pp. 113–122). Sacramento: State of California Department of Mental Health.

Valle, R., & Martinez, C. (1980). Natural networks of elderly Latinos of Mexican heritage: Implications for mental health. M. Miranda & R. Ruiz (Eds), *Chicano aging and mental health* (pp. 76–117). Washington, DC: National Institute of Mental Health.

Valle, R., & Mendoza, L. (1978). *The elder Latino.* San Diego: Campanile Press.

Velez-Ibanez, C. (1978). Youth and aging in central Mexico: One day in the life of four families of migrants. In B. Myerhoff & A. Simic (Eds.), *Life's career—aging: Cultural variations on growing old* (pp. 107–162). Beverly Hills: Sage.

————. (1983). *Bonds of mutual trust: The cultural systems of rotating credit associations among urban Mexicans and Chicanos.* New Brunswick, NJ: Rutgers University Press.

Zepeda, M. (1979). Las abuelitas. *Agenda: A Journal of Hispanic Issues, 9*(6), 10–13.

13

EL CICLO DE LA VIDA Y MUERTE: AN ANALYSIS OF DEATH AND DYING IN A SELECTED HISPANIC ENCLAVE

Roselyn Rael and Alvin O. Korte

The darkness of the sepulchre is but a strengthening couch for the glorious sun, and the obscuring of the night but serves to reveal the brilliance of the stars. . . .
    Netzahualcoyotl, Aztec King of Mexico, (1431–1472)

INTRODUCTION

Anyone reviewing the literature on death, bereavement, and adjustment to loss will quickly discover that little analysis of the Hispanic experience exists on these vital questions. Instead, one must reprocess relevant social science myths. Minority scholars, particularly Mexican-Americans, have had to initially de-mythologize certain points of view before redirecting, rethinking, and expanding scholarship efforts. The paramount work of Romano (1968) attacked the concept of traditional culture, the view that Mexican-Americans are a homogeneous mass, and other fictional images. Only in recent years have some Mexican-American scholars in the field begun to study the nature of their own institutions as socially constructed entities.

ORIGINS OF THE CULT OF DEATH

Moore argues that American culture, in virtue of its orientation to the dominance of nature and the environment, perceives death as the ultimate human weakness. Hence, resentment and denial of death are pervasive. In contrast

Mexico has a fanatic obsession with death, a "death culture." Although Moore grants that her generalizations can be neither confirmed nor denied, she speculates that, for Mexican-Americans, "death will be an issue in a deprived segment of a society in which denial and rejection of death in the larger system are associated with a drive toward power and mastery" (1970, p. 275).

Romanell (1969, p. 22), on the other hand, makes some clearcut distinctions between the North American's pragmatic sense of life and the Hispano-Americano's existential sense of life.[1] North American pragmatism, Romanell contends, is dominance- and achievement-oriented, while the Hispano-Americano's orientations are couched in a tragic sense of life that assigns him the "job of conquering himself."

The origins of *el culto de la muerte,* or the cult of death, have been investigated by various social scientists, writers, and observers of Mexican culture. Wolfe (1959), writing about the Mexican creation myths, explores numerous Aztecan concepts of worlds created and consumed in recurrent cataclysms. According to Aztecan myth, each of the successive worlds was dominated by its own *sol,* or sun. The fifth sun, *El Quinto Sol,* was to be maintained in the heavens by continuous warfare and human sacrifice. Léon-Portilla (1966, p. 17), elaborating on this same theme, recognizes that "into this world, where gods create and destroy, had men been born under the threat of death and of a cataclysm which might put an end to the present age. . . ."

Broadman (1976) further traces the infiltration of Aztec and Spanish Catholic thought into the Mexican "cult of death." In analyzing the embellishments of this cult in Mexican myths and literature, she notes that death and sacrifice were significant religious elements. The Mexican, she contends, can trace his obsession with death back to ancient Aztecan myths.

The death motif in Mexico was artistically and thematically portrayed in the art of Posada, Orozco, and Siquieros, as well as in the celebration of the Day of the Dead, bullfights, and revolution (Robinson, 1963). Some have been repulsed by the "macabre" nature of this art (Moore, 1970); others, such as Brenner (1967) and Paz (1961) have offered penetrating insights that go beyond a romanticized gloss.

Brenner (1967, p. 15), for example, proposes that "ever recurrent in Mexican thought is this concern for the sheer facts of life. Life shifting from one form to another, all still the same; . . . movement defined by stops; life endlessly becoming darkness; and . . . plants and people of necessity dying, at a definite fixed point, to be reborn. Hence, the constant consideration of death. . . ."

Paz (1961) expresses similar sentiments when speaking of the fiesta,

where society is dissolved, is drowned, insofar as it is an organism ruled according to certain laws and principles. . . . Everything is united: good and evil, day and night, the sacred and the profane. Everything merges, loses shape and individuality, and returns to the primordial mass. The fiesta is a cosmic experiment, an experiment in disorder reuniting contradictory elements and principles in order to bring about a renaissance of life. Ritual death promotes rebirth. (p. 52)

Thus, the fiesta represents the quality of life and death and explains why there are both rejoicing and sorrow. Death, for the ancient Mexicans was not the natural end but a resurgence of life. "Death was not the natural end of life but one phase of an infinite cycle." Thus, "life, death, and resurrection were stages of a cosmic process which repeated itself continuously. Life had no higher function than to flow into death, its opposite and complement; and death, in turn, was not an end in itself: man fed the insatiable hunger of life with his death" (Paz, 1961, p. 54).

New Mexico has also had its folk traditions of *bultos* (bloodied saints), its *retablos* (painstakingly carved images of Christ agonized on the cross), its Penitente Order, and its Holy Week rituals. But this is not to say that a "death cult" has also existed in New Mexico. Although the question regarding the existence of a "cult of death" in New Mexico can perhaps never be clearly decided, it can be argued that New Mexico has rich cultural-historical rituals and ceremonies serving as socially constructed modalities to deal with death. Death is felt communally and has its nexus within the family system.

By presenting a cultural-historical background and an analysis of the cultural meanings developed by northern New Mexicans, our purpose is an attempt at what Moore (1970, p. 271) has called a "cultural analysis." One must also recognize that the modernizing forces of the dominant culture have made inroads into the Hispanic culture in northern New Mexico. Some New Mexicans are no doubt familiar with what is described in the following pages; others have no doubt accepted the American way of death with its sanitized and impersonal attributes.

No attempt is made to analyze the psychoanalytic perspective that has so greatly influenced the way in which grief and mourning are considered in the literature and is the background framework in mental health in the dominant culture. Instead, our focus is on the "community of mourners," communal support systems as they once existed and are still extant in some parts of New Mexico. By focusing on systems in one area, others may consider regional diversity in funerary practices or further clarify the nature of such diversity by noting similarities.

A CULTURAL-HISTORICAL PERSPECTIVE ON DEATH

Special regional histories and diversity of geographical areas make generalizations about Mexican-Americans hazardous. Thus, anecdotal data for one region must be weighed carefully when evaluated elsewhere. Similarly, low income may be as much a contributor to behavior as specific cultural influences.

Based on these caveats, an attempt is made in this chapter to confine remarks to the varied facets of a naturalistic view of life and death and the funeral process in a particular region—rural northern New Mexico. The "data" consist of participation and observation, anecdotal content, and interviews collected in several northern counties. The discussion seeks to illustrate and explore the broader questions of attitudes toward life and death, familial and communal influences, and the changes wrought by modernization. In some cases, traditional practices are still extant in small towns, cities, and rural areas. Some of the description is essentially historical, with comparison to current practices in a later section. New Mexico represents a continuum from urban, metropolitan Albuquerque to more traditional areas in the further northern mountain reaches of the Rio Grande drainage basin. New Mexico can be considered a natural laboratory from which to view change.

La Noticia

In most northern New Mexican villages, when a person was known to be terminally ill, both men and women would gather at the patient's home and conduct *visperas,* or prayer vigils, in front of a makeshift altar. The altar was constructed by the immediate family and close relatives and *visperas* were then conducted nightly. In some instances, male or female *rezadores,* or prayer groups, known for their piety and familiarity with the litanies and prayers, were asked to lead the vigils (Lucia Herrera, personal communication, March 23, 1983).

De Córdova (1972), writing about the village of Córdova, says that, when death was near, preparations for the wake and funeral were made:

Upon the arrival of death Maria Antonia, the clapperless bell of the old church, is tolled. This is done by striking it at spaced intervals with a stone. Its clear tones carry their message to all within hearing. On the first stroke, doors and windows are thrown open, and the person tolling the bell is a central figure for perhaps the first time in his life as he makes known to the upturned faces the identity of the newly-dead. (p. 28).

Children would sometimes be sent to the *capilla,* the village church, to find out who had died. News of the death was then transmitted throughout the village by word of mouth (Lucia Herrera, personal communication, March 23, 1983).

Atencio (1983) notes that "mutual aid societies, *sociedades de mutua protección,* . . . were basically burial societies that provided social support to their members at all times . . ." (p. 33). Given the poverty in these villages in the 1930s and 1940s, many funeral tasks had to be performed by village and family members, such as preparing food, building the coffin, and marking and digging the grave.

The home of the deceased became the scene of much activity. Women were typically assigned the task of cleansing and preparing the corpse for burial. Part of the preparation of the body included, for example, tying strips of white muslin around the face in order to prevent the jaw from dropping (Lucia Herrera, personal communication, March 23, 1983). Coins or small pebbles were used to keep the corpse's eyes closed (de Córdova, 1972). This process closely parallels the Jewish preparation of corpses:

When death is finally established, the eyes and mouth are gently closed by the eldest son or the nearest relative. The arms and hands are extended alongside the body; the lower jaw is closed and bound before rigor mortis sets in. The body is placed on the floor, feet towards the door, and is covered with a sheet. A lighted candle is placed close to the head of the body. In the house of the dead it is customary to turn all mirrors to the wall or cover them. A dead body should not be left alone. It must be guarded constantly . . . until the funeral. . . . The dead . . . must not be left either defenseless or unattended (*Encyclopedia Judaica,* 1971, p. 1426).

After the body was cleansed and prepared, it was placed on a slab and covered with a white muslin sheet, where it remained until the coffin was prepared by the village *carpinteros* [carpenters]. Once constructed, the coffin was lined with black and white muslin. The body was placed inside the coffin and removed to the largest room in the house, where it was placed in a central location. The men set up the *tarimas,* or wooden benches, in preparation for the *velorio,* or wake. The women prepared votive candles which were placed all around the coffin, also in preparation for the *velorio* (Lucia Herrera, personal communication, March 23, 1983).

The bells were tolled a second time, summoning all able-bodied men to gather for *la sacada de la sepultura,* or the digging of the grave. An overseer or *mayordomo* was elected from the group to supervise and complete the task. Every male who owned a pick and shovel brought it along. Teams of horses were hitched and driven in a caravan to the *campo santo,* the local cemetery. The men typically brought hard liquor with them and drank it as they worked and exchanged anecdotes, reminiscences, jokes, and stories about the deceased (Lucia Herrera, personal communication, March 23, 1983). Ovens were heated, wood was chopped, and a sheep or calf was slaughtered by local *carniceros,* or butchers. Neighborhood women prepared bread and large kettles of stew and chili with the fresh meat (de Córdova, 1972).

In the home, mirrors were either covered or turned to face the wall; vanity was not to be tolerated during this period of *luto,* or mourning. Shortly before the start of the *velorio,* people arrived in family groups. Upon approaching the coffin, they knelt beside it, offering *sudarios,* or prayers for the dead (de Córdova, 1972; Weigel, 1976). A bowl was placed nearby to receive contributions from those who were able to make them (Brown, 1937). As Medina so elegantly states, "You didn't take death out of the house; you integrated it with the living" (Antonio Medina, personal communication, December 22, 1983).

El Velorio

Lucero-White (1945) differentiated between two kinds of *velorios,* those for the *santos,* or saints, and those for *difuntos,* or dead. The *velorio,* as she pointed out, meant to watch over, to guard, and "to dedicate oneself to something during the hours destined for sleep and relaxation." The *velorio,* then, was a watching over, a night-long vigil or wake (Lucero-White, 1945, p. 255).

Sturdy *tarimas* lined the walls of the central room. Separate *tarimas* were placed near the front of the coffin for use by the *rezadores.* The *dolientes* (*doliente* conveys the meaning of hurt or *dolor,* or being in pain), or family of the bereaved, were seated in a central or accessible place, sometimes off the main room (de Córdova, 1972), where friends, neighbors, or villagers could convey *el pesame,* condolences, to them. *"Siento mucho su pesar"* ("I'm sorry for your loss") was—and still is—said to each of the *dolientes.*

De Córdova (1972) says that, as families arrived in groups, they passed to an inner room where the bereaved family was seated to receive neighbors and friends.

The women would burst into loud wails while the men stood by self-consciously. When the wailing dies down, there are murmured expressions of sympathy, after which the menfolk leave the room and join those watching the body. . . . Outside in the patio, several bonfires have been lit for warmth and light (de Córdova, 1972, p. 49).

In summer *velorios* were held "in the open yard, candles and lanterns lighting the procession and the yard" (Jaramillo, 1941, p. 75).

The *velorio de difuntos,* according to Lucero-White (1945), was undergoing changes even in the early 1940s. She observed, "People still sit up all night with their dead and recite prayers, but they are loath to sing chants, believing them to be offensive to their English-speaking neighbors. Many of the chants . . . belong to the repertory of the Penitentes, an institution frowned upon by the Americans" (p. 255). These chants, known as *alabados,* still exist, and occasionally a family requests the singing of these sorrowful lamentations during the rosaries.

In his study of *alabados,* Valdez notes that there are three distinct types: (1) *passiones,* or chants of consolation, which he associates with mournful Lenten services; (2) *canticos,* or hymns; and (3) *alabanzas,* praises of the deeds of particular saints. The *alabado* reminds the bereaved and those in attendance of the finitude of this life and the needed preparation for the continued journey from it (Facundo Valdez, personal communication, December 29, 1983).

Lucero-White (1945) says that the one who received no rest was the *rezador,* who sang until dawn. Lucero-White and Jaramillo (1941) contend that supper was served at about midnight, whereas de Córdova (1972) states that the rosary was said at midnight. In any event, much food was available for guests and all those who maintained the long vigil.

Insofar as traditional practices were concerned, no one, including children and *inocentes,* was excluded from either the *velorio* or the funeral itself. Inocentes, or mentally retarded individuals, one informant notes, were included in all activities so they could learn the process of cleansing their hearts of envy, spite, and wicked thoughts (Lucia Herrera, personal communication, March 23, 1983).

El Entierro

Interment, or *entierrio,* means the return of the body to the earth, *la tierra.* This fact is recognized in the folk philosophy of *"Adios Acompañamiento":*

De la tierra fui formado

La tierra me ha producido

La tierra me a sustenado

Y a la terra estoy rendido

The *entierro,* like the *velorio,* was considered to be an opportunity to exercise *el ultimo acompañamiento,* a normative obligation to accompany the deceased, as well as the bereaved family. People traveled long distances to attend the *velorio* and the funeral mass or join the funeral dirge as a means of fulfilling this obligation.

Some have noted that, when a funeral is held, all attend it, even if they had met the deceased only once (Moore, 1970). In their study of El Cerrito, Leonard and Loomis (1942) observe that the network of relations extended into neighboring states.

In the absence of hearses, teams of horses were specifically trained to lead funeral processions. During the funeral procession to the local *campos santo,* the horses were draped with black shawls *(mantillas).* The wagons were lined up in specific order: the first wagon carried the coffin; the second one transported the *rezadores;* the third one transported the immediate family; the rest transported the extended family and friends of the bereaved or the deceased (Lucia Herrera, personal communication, March 23, 1983).

Although local clergy often visited the bereaved family, they typically did not participate in the *velorio* or the burial itself (Lucia Herrera, personal communication, March 23, 1983). Lucero-White (1936) notes that "if priests were not available, the funeral mass was dispensed with. The chants at the interment would be lead by the *rezadores.*" It should also be noted that, if the deceased were a member of the *penitente* brotherhood, the *hermandad* (brotherhood) would provide the *alabados* [chants] and prayers at the *velorio* and the interment (de Córdova, 1972; Jaramillo, 1942; Lucero-White, 1945); this is still practiced today.

After the funeral caravan arrived at the *campo santo,* the *rezadores* gathered around the *sepultura,* or grave, and recited *sudarios* and sang the *alabados de passiones.* These particular chants essentially offered the consolation that, "since Jesus suffered and ascended into heaven, they too [the deceased] must suffer in order to obtain salvation" (Aranda, 1885). The chants *"El Ultimo Acom-*

pañamiento" and *"Adios Acompañamiento"* traced the significant stages of the life, growth, and development of the deceased.

After these rituals were completed, the immediate family members were given an opportunity to view the body for the last time before it was lowered into earth. The family and all those in attendance then tossed handfuls of earth on top of the coffin after it was placed in the grave as a final *despedida* (farewell).

Luto

Luto not only refers to the black clothing worn by the person in mourning, but also denotes the period of bereavement and the individual's personal pain, grief, and affliction caused by another's death (*Enciclopedia universal ilustrada,* 1931, p. 881).

Traditionally, the surviving spouse would *guardar el luto,* that is, observe a period of mourning, for a year. During this time, mirrors were turned to the wall, no music was played, and dances and other festivities were disallowed. The surviving spouse wore black clothing all year.

A mass was conducted on the eighth day of mourning *(la misa de ochos dias).* This mass was announced by sending out black-bordered cards to relatives and friends of the deceased. At the end of the year, another mass was celebrated, *la misa de el cabo de año,* the anniversary mass, signifying the end of the year of bereavement (Jaramillo, 1941).

AN OVERVIEW

Death has traditionally been a family and communal affair borne by everyone in these small communities. It is striking to note that the community and family members still have many opportunities not only to offer their *despedidas* but also to observe normative expectations, such as the *acompañamiento* at various points from the *velorio* to the funeral.[2] Jaramillo (1941) notes that, even after the funeral, people called to offer sympathy to the bereaved for weeks. Communal support is still evidenced by the partaking and giving of food, frequent visitation of the terminally or critically ill, and attendance at wakes and funerals.

In many regionally based medical hospitals serving rural areas, it is not uncommon to see entire families keeping vigils over an older person who is terminally ill. La Sociedad de San José, a mutual aid organization currently marking its centennial celebration, provides *enfermeros* (male nurses) to care for such patients. These individuals are empowered to designate several family members to watch over the dying individual (Vigil, 1984).

Daily visits to a sick person are a form of *despedida,* acknowledging what that person has meant to others during his life, as well as dealing with the delicate matters of life and death. *Vigilar al enfermo,* providing round-the-clock vigils in hospital settings, is considered to be a way in which all parties concerned accept death as the final act of living. Thus, its reality has already been acknowledged and accepted, and the severity of the shock is then minimized.

Many termini in the *luto* process offer opportunities to the community to give condolences, material support, or physical and spiritual presence. Those who are not physically present may offer masses for the repose of the soul of the deceased individual. Interestingly, as in the past, Hispanos in northern New Mexico offer anniversary masses. Since church calendars are often crowded, several decedents are usually "remembered" at one mass. Some people publish a semipoetic memorial in local newspapers as an annual remembrance. One person purchased such a notice for someone who had died thirty-six years previously, and a local priest mentioned a person giving a stipend for a mass for someone who had died forty-two years previously.

In addition to *la misa de el cabo de año,* novenas, and special pilgrimages to *santuarios* (sanctuaries of worship), northern New Mexicans typically place wreaths or small wooden crosses alongside roads or at sites where accidental deaths have occurred. These wreaths or crosses serve as reminders that passersby should offer a *sudario* for that person. These locations are commonly referred to as *descansos,* or resting places (Lucia Herrera, personal communication, March 23, 1983; Weigel, 1976).

A funeral brings community and family members together to mourn and suffer. Some families have been known to postpone the funeral for a day or two so that a close relative can attend. It is a time for family reintegration and solidarity (Moore, 1970). Cousins and other relatives who do not know each other perhaps meet for the first time. Coming together for the various facets of the funeral also means that familial and communal bonds are strengthened.

The eulogy in northern New Mexico is more than a recounting of the deceased's good attributes. It is a way for the family to *dar las gracias,* give special thanks. As Medina has succinctly stated, *dar las gracias* involves a formal acknowledgment on the part of the family to the community *por el acompañamiento* (the accompaniment), to those who led the religious services at the *velorio,* and to those who so freely gave of themselves during this critical period. Medina further states, *"Las gracias son a Dios por una vida, por una alma que se revelo adelante de nosotros como una encarnación"* ["Thanks are given to God for a life, for a soul that was made manifest among us as an incarnation."] (Antonio Medina, personal communication, December 22, 1983; also see de Córdova, 1972). The eulogy, then, is a means by which to thank the community for its support and care, to thank the family for having "loaned" the deceased's life to the community, and to give thanks for one's own life. Medina also proposes that the eulogy is not only a time for giving thanks but a time for healing and expiation. Recognizing the healing process as fragile and tender, Medina contends that, when a child is born, the community rejoices; when an individual dies, others experience their own death (Antonio Medina, personal communication, December 22, 1983). Life and death are communal experiences, and are not to be treated lightly.

LOS CICLOS DE VIDA Y MUERTE

Death as an eschatological issue reflects the meanings that a culture imparts to the duality of life and death. Berdyaev (1960) notes: "The fact of death alone gives true depth to the question as to the meaning of life. Life in this world has meaning just because there is death; if there were no death in our world, life would be meaningless. The meaning is bound up with the end" (p. 249).

Northern New Mexicans have developed a framework of meanings as an attempt to make sense of the duality of life and death. These folk precepts are not denominational but reflect a natural philosophy rich in its own insights and meanings.

In his lifelong quest to find answers to the question of death, Ernest Becker (1973, 1975) summed up this age-old dilemma: What man fears is not so much extinction as extinction *with insignificance*. Life has to count for something— if not for oneself, then at least in a larger scheme of things. In *Escape from Evil* (1975), Becker turns the question into a religious one:

As Otto Rank put it, all religion springs, in the last analysis, not so much from . . . "fear of natural death as of final destruction." But it is the culture itself that embodies the transcendence of death in some form or another, whether it appears religious or not. It is very important for students of man to be clear about this: culture itself is sacred since it is the "religion" that ensures in some way the perpetuation of its members. (p. 4)

One of the fundamental existential ideas present in Mexican-American thought is the cyclical nature of life and death, *el ciclo de vida y muerte*. The New Mexican Hispanic sees the birth and death of nature, the changes of seasons, and incorporates them into his daily thoughts. It is perhaps a recognition of the cycle of change to acknowledge that where there is life, there is death: *"Dentro de la vida hay muerte y dentro de la muerte hay vida"* ("Within life there is death and within death there is life.") (Antonio Medina, personal communication, December 22, 1983). In effect, this dictum confronts us with a recognition of the change from one cosmic form to another. Life is eternal. Death changes life's form. *No es mas que cruzar la raya* ("It is nothing more than crossing that line [from life to death].") (Carmelita Romero, personal communication, December 28, 1983).

Death is not seen as a finality but as a transformation of life. Life itself is to be seen as a gift from God, the source of His creation. It is, in essence, an acceptance that an individual's life is "on loan" and must be surrendered to nature. *Somos prestados* ("We are on loan"). One way in which being *prestado,* "on loan," is reflected is at the moment of a person's death. *"Dios no lo presto"* means that this cosmic form embodied in a physical being, this energy, was on loan to us (Antonio Medina, personal communication, December 22, 1983).

Children's lives are to be seen in the same way. *La vida es prestada* means that their lives are loaned and can be reclaimed. Similarly, upon an elderly person's death, mourners offer consolences, reminding the children of the bereaved family, *"Se los presto por tantos y tantos años"*; in effect, God loaned the person for so many years.

Hispanics do not hide from death. They live with it and embrace it (Paz, 1961). But to know death is to recognize its presence among us. Medina, speculating about the Hispanic way of death, prefaces his remarks by noting that some persons inoculate themselves against death by embracing materialism. "The more insulated I am in materialism, the less conscious I become about death walking with me every step of the way" (Antonio Medina, personal communication, December 22, 1983). Paz (1961) also observes that "The cult of life, if it is truly profound and total, is also the cult of death, because the two are inseparable. A civilization that denies death ends by denying life" (p. 60). It is the acceptance of death that makes the Hispano of northern New Mexico "the knight of faith." Following Kierkegaard, Becker notes that the knight of faith

is the man who lives in faith, who has given over the meaning of life to his Creator, and who lives centered on the energies of his Maker. He accepts whatever happens in this visible dimension without complaint, lives his life as a duty, faces his death without a qualm. No pettiness is so petty that it threatens his meanings; no task is too frightening to be beyond his courage. He is fully in the world on its terms and wholly beyond the world on his trust in the invisible dimension. (Becker, 1973, pp. 257–258)

Attesting to these values is what one wise "knight" imparted as he described his situation: *"Hay nomás que llegar al punto donde todo lo que queda es la voluntad de Dios"* ("The important idea is to reach a point in life where all that remains is to do God's will.") (Mano Moises Romero, personal communication, December 28, 1983).

The meaning of suffering has always concerned existential thinkers. In Mexican-American thought, suffering is not seen as an end in itself, but is regarded as a way to solve and conquer the problem of death. *"No hay mas remedio que sufrir lo que Dios manda"* ("There is no other remedy than to suffer what God has ordained.") (Mano Moises Romero, personal communication, December 28, 1983).

Berdyaev (1960, p. 250) contends that the meaning of death "is never revealed in an endless time; it is to be found in eternity. But there is an abyss between life in time and life in eternity, and it can only be bridged by death and the horror of final severance." Death must be suffered. *La ultima mortifi-cación,* the last mortification, then, is suffering one's own death. An elderly northern New Mexican recently concluded, *"El remedio de la muerte es suf-rir"* ("For death there is no other remedy but to suffer it.") (Mano Moises Romero, personal communication, December 28, 1983).

One must live to die, and one must die to live. Humanness, physical exis-tence, and life are bound to nature. Experiences with death and dying signify a change from one cosmic form to another—form and matter, flesh and blood, return to the earth to become another cosmic form.

The Hispano becomes part of the *celebración,* the celebration of life and death, from the day of birth. Groping for meanings becomes tied and absorbed into cultural environment and ultimately becomes a part of the "religion" of the culture. By becoming totally immersed in this "religion" of the culture, the individual accepts the universal, absolute, and unchallengeable beliefs and values of his community. Many of the themes recurrent in the Hispanic value system become forms by which loss, restitution, and expiation are carried out.

The Hispano cannot operate in a vacuum and must be supported and assisted by the community in the quest for answers to the countless "why's" of exis-tence and suffering. The individual is cognizant at the onset of life that "life is at the start a chaos in which one is lost" (Becker, 1973, p. 47). Hispanos need the community as much as it needs them to celebrate the agonies of life and death. The community, then, becomes the primary point of reference that allows the individual to share in both the mundane and significant celebrations of life and death. It is, however, the individual who paves the way for these collective celebrations via the immediate family. After individuals have tied into the community, they become part of the pulsating life in it; they become the loci of the collective power that celebrates the existential search for the meaning of life and death.

The paradoxes of life and death are contemplated by the community as a whole. The fears and anxieties of losing control and command of oneself are assuaged and dealt with at the community level. Hispanos do not fear life or death because they perhaps intuitively know that they are not alone in their fears. Individual strengths and weaknesses are absorbed by the community, thereby creating an intimacy with the cosmic forces and processes of life and death.

The community affirms the locus of the self, even in the face of death. The fact that Hispanos are *consciente de la muerte,* conscious of death, provides the necessary elements for a free and enlightened acceptance of it. This en-lightenment leads the way to a cosmic understanding and enrichment of com-munal celebrations of both life and death.

For Hispanics, life is a continual celebration that culminates the celebration of death. The celebration of life is *una celebración de agonia,* a celebration of agony, that turns the harshness of death into a gentler sorrow of laying to rest one's own kin. Death then is directly and inwardly eternal; it is the celebration of one's own imminent passing from one cosmic form to another. Death in this sense is experienced not as a wish but as a desire to attain immortality. Death experienced in a communal sense creates a spirit of unity, of deity, and of diversity. In order to experience a good death, one must be conscious of death walking at one's side. As Medina concludes, *"Si uno vive la vida consciente de la muerte y conoce que la muerte es su compañero, entonces tiene uno un sentido que la vida es muy rica"* ("If one is conscious of death and recognizes that death is one's constant companion, then one has a rich sense of life.") (Antonio Medina, personal communication, December 22, 1983.

NOTES

1. Romanell's "Hispano-Americano" refers to all of Latin America. In this chapter, "Hispanic" refers to northern New Mexicans' use of "Hispano" or "Hispanic" as a self-referencing label.

2. This is part of the more generalized leave-taking, or *despedida,* so important in the daily interpersonal behaviors of Mexican-Americans.

REFERENCES

Aranda, C. (1885). Exercise of the good death. *The penitente papers.* Las Vegas, NM: Imprenta de la Revista Catolica.

Atencio, T. (1983). Ideology in social work: The perspectives of Chicanos. In G. Gibson (Ed.), *Our kingdom stands on brittle glass* (pp. 23–29). Silver Spring, MD: NASW Publications.

Becker, E. (1973). *The denial of death.* New York: Free Press.

———.(1975). *Escape from evil.* New York: Free Press.

Berdyaev, N. (1960). *The destiny of man.* New York: Harper & Row.

Brenner, A. (1967). *Idols behind altars.* New York: Biblo & Tanner.

Broadman, B. L. C. (1976). *The Mexican cult of death in myth and literature.* Gainesville: University Presses of Florida.

Brown, L. (1937, August 9). The wake. Unpublished manuscript. New Mexico Writer's Project.

de Córdova, L. (1972). *Echos of the flute.* Santa Fe, NM: Ancient City Press.

Encyclopaedia Judaica. (1971). Jerusalem: Keter Publishing House.

Enciclopedia universal ilustrada. (1931). Madrid: Espasa-Calpe, S.A.

Jaramillo, C. (1941). *Shadows of the past.* Sante Fe, NM: Ancient City Press.

León-Portilla, M. (1966). Pre-Hispanic thought. In M. de la Cueva et al., *Major trends in Mexican philosophy* (pp. 2–58). Notre Dame, IN: University of Notre Dame Press.

Leonard, O., & Loomis, C. P. (1938). *Culture of a contemporary rural community: El Cerrito, New Mexico.* Washington, DC: U.S. Department of Agriculture.

Lucero-White, A. (1936, August 8). El velorio. Unpublished manuscript. New Mexico Writer's Project.

———.(1945). Wakes for the dead and the saints. *El Palacio, 52* (12), 255–258.

Moore, J. (1970). The death culture of Mexico and Mexican-Americans. *Omega, 1,* 271–291.

Paz, O. (1961). *The labyrinth of solitude*. New York: Grove Press.

Robinson, C. (1963). *With the ears of strangers*. Tucson: University of Arizona Press.

Romanell, P. (1969). *Making of the Mexican mind: A study in recent Mexican thought*. Notre Dame, IN: University of Notre Dame Press.

Romano, O. (1968). The anthropology and sociology of the Mexican-Americans: The distortion of Mexican history. *El Grito, 2* (1), 13–26.

Vigil, M. E. (1984, February 10). Sociedad de San Jose prepares for centennial celebration. Unpublished manuscript. Las Vegas, NM: New Mexico Highlands University.

Weigel, M. (1976). *Brothers of light, brothers of blood: The penitentes of the southwest*. Albuquerque: University of New Mexico Press.

Wolfe, E. (1959). *Sons of the shaking earth*. Chicago: University of Chicago Press.

14

CABLE TELEVISION, TELECOMMUNICATIONS, AND U.S. HISPANIC ELDERLY

Roberto Anson

INTRODUCTION

In less than fifty years since its creation, television has changed how we see ourselves. The explosion in the cable communications field offers the potential for increased opportunities for programming and for interactive services directed toward the needs of older Americans in entertainment, news, and information. Tapping this area and properly serving the needs of Hispanic and minority elders represent a major challenge. The power of the visual media is in their ability to dramatize and to simplify. We have all benefited from and been hurt by this double-edged sword. Minorities, the elderly, the poor, the handicapped, women, and other underserved segments of the population have historically been victimized by both the print and the electronic media.

CHALLENGES

Will the Hispanic elderly benefit from cable television, or will they, for the most part, be excluded from this information and entertainment medium because of cost and other reasons? Will our grasp exceed our reach? Do we have the knowledge, finances, resources, and power base needed to mobilize our community? Are we only to complain about the many problems facing our minority community, or will we begin the difficult process of mastering the required skills and accumulating the needed resources to convert our hopes into reality? The answers to these and other questions depend on the individual and collective response of the Hispanic community to developments in the field of cable and telecommunications.

Key questions are the following:

1. Will older Americans living on fixed incomes, the poor, and the minority elderly be able to afford cable services?

2. What is being done about underwriting the cost to the public and to older persons whose incomes are limited?

3. What options are open to the indigent and to low-income minority elders in terms of this new communications technology?

4. How can the elderly and the non-English-speaking aged become literate about cable television and its related technology.

5. How can the potential for abusing the privacy of consumers be minimized or eliminated?

Most of us want the benefits of cable, but few of us welcome the work needed to reap such advantages. The famous Spanish artist Francisco Goya once drew a picture of an ancient tottering along under the burden of years with the accompanying caption, "I'm still learning." We must seriously ask ourselves and our community whether we are still actively learning about new developments in the fields of cable television and telecommunications, and whether we are systematically exploring how to apply all of these technological innovations to benefit the minority community. If we are, we should share our experiences with others. If we are not, we should accept the challenge before the door is closed even further.

ADVANTAGES OF CABLE TELEVISION

Cable has three technical advantages over broadcast television: (1) it offers an increased number of channels; (2) it can "narrowcast" to audiences in distinct geographic areas and thus better target specific audiences; and (3) it potentially includes two-way communication. Cable functions as a medium between media. It resembles the telephone system more than broadcast television in that it operates by wire rather than signal, goes from point to point, and can be two-way interactive.

Cable and its technology create new opportunities for solving problems confronting older persons, such as lack of transportation, inadequate and costly health care services, vulnerability to crime, isolation from society, inadequate income, and lack of access to information. The use of a two-way communication system could help administrative agencies provide governmental services to the public.

GROWTH OF CABLE TELEVISION

Prior to the 1970s, cable largely served remote rural areas. The 1970s and 1980s witnessed the penetration of cable into millions of American households as well as a revolution in communications that has increased the number and variety of services available through this technology. The percentage of households with cable over a twenty-year span highlights the dramatic growth of this field: 1970—7.6 percent, 1980—20 percent, 1985—46 percent, 1990 (projection)—58 percent or more. In addition, 31 percent of the country's more than 80 million homes with television received cable services as of January 1982, representing a 45 percent increase from 1980. Cable is a $5 billion industry.

According to *Television Digest,* between 1970 and 1983 the number of cable systems increased from 2490 to 5600, and the number of subscribers for basic cable services increased from 4.5 to 25 million. The average national monthly fee paid by cable subscribers for basic or first tier level services in 1982 was about $8.50.

Cable has greatly affected the share of prime-time viewership. In 1979, the networks' share of prime-time viewers was 90 percent. An industry survey shows that this share has been nibbled down to 79 percent, and it is estimated that only 60 percent will remain by 1990. The lack of a commonly shared news and entertainment base can be expected to have both positive and negative consequences.

Cable subscribers are younger and more affluent than the general population. The capital intensive nature of the cable industry and the intense competition among companies for lucrative franchises have created a field with big winners and even bigger losers. Cable bids are being filed at a time when the national franchising process is slowing and bit cable companies are trying to scale back on their promises, having discovered that the elaborate systems they agreed to build are not economically feasible to construct or operate. All of these facts will affect the minority community in the cable process.

ISSUES AND PROBLEMS

Published articles concerning cable television and the Hispanic elderly prior to 1984 are almost nonexistent, and the priority given to this area of telecommunications by Hispanic organizations at the local, regional, and national levels has been acutely limited.

Understanding the growth of cable television and the Hispanic elderly requires detailed knowledge of development in three separate fields: mass media and communications, minorities, and the elderly. The fabric of developments in these fields must be carefully woven together without substituting one for the other in order to better understand the present circumstances, to develop the skills needed to fine-tune the picture, and to develop a strategy that will accelerate progress.

Although Hispanic elderly are heavy viewers of television—largely Spanish-language television—cable can offer benefits to Hispanic elders. The major problem is that most cable subscribers are younger and more affluent, while most Hispanic elderly are poor. Few data are available on Hispanic viewership of cable. In addition, in most cases Hispanics have not become active in the cable franchising process, which largely determines the rate charges and the services offered. Because cities and communities are rapidly being wired nationwide, failure of the Hispanic and minority community to actively participate in all phases of the cable process will relegate them to being consumers and purchasers of service with little or no voice in this field. For example, effective involvement in the franchising process can make the difference between convincing cable companies to include a Spanish-language channel in their basic service instead of including it in the more expensive levels.

Historically, there have been many obstacles to participation by minorities in cable and other media. Most prominent among these are lack of experience in management and operations, which results in a disadvantage in competing with established corporations and in attracting investment capital for small businesses. These were cited repeatedly in congressional hearings held in late 1981 on small business, minority enterprise, and the cable television industry. Other problems range from lack of specialized training and skills to inconveniently located work sites.

Until now, cable companies' efforts to involve Hispanics and other minorities have been slow and halting. Few efforts to involve them in ownership, in employment, or in programming have occurred. Indeed, with the industry free of most regulatory controls—including the ones that promoted affirmative action in broadcasting—its responsiveness to minorities may lessen even further. Minorities are becoming conscious of "electronic redlining"—selective wiring that can deprive large sections of a community of the important services promised by cable.

Armando Rendon, past president of the Washington, D.C. based Hispanic Public Affairs Association (HPAA), identifies a key dilemma facing Hispanics:

Media's inability or reluctance to fine tune the picture it conveys of America adversely has affected Hispanic America, the second largest and fastest growing minority group in the country. Hispanic Americans understand, manifest the classic chicken-egg dilemma they face: which comes first, image or reality?

HISPANICS IN CABLE

A major problem is the scarcity of Hispanics in all phases of cable. The area in which the absence of Hispanics is most noticeable is ownership of cable companies. As of 1983, there were only five Hispanic-owned cable firms: Buena

Vista Cable Vision (Los Angeles, California); Eatonville Cable (Sumner, Washington); Mercure Telecommunications, Inc., (Albuquerque, New Mexico); Southwest Cable (Espanola, New Mexico), and Tele-Vu, Inc. (Grants, New Mexico).

Hispanic media organizations have only recently begun to include workshops on cable television as part of their conference agendas. An important example was the first National Hispanic Media Conference held in San Diego in December 1982. Participants on the panel on cable included Alicia Maldonado, program director for the Fresno, California cable firm; Jess Margarito, director of programming and information services at the Valley Cable Television company in Los Angeles; and Concepcion Lara, western regional manager of Galavision in Los Angeles. Other examples of Hispanics with leadership and expertise in cable include Antonio Ruiz, executive director of the District of Columbia Cable-Design Commission; Awilda Ramos, co-chair of Boston's Commission on Cable Television; Pedro Morales, a member of the Montgomery County (Maryland) Cable Communications Advisory Committee; and Roberto Anson, chair of the Cable TV Committee for the Montgomery County (Maryland) Commission on Aging.

The absence of a single resource directory listing Hispanics by state and region who are involved in cable along with their areas of specialty limits the potential for networking, information sharing, unity, and progress. This is a greatly needed project.

Employment figures released by the FCC for 1982 show that Hispanics represented 4.6 percent of the total broadcast work force of over 159,000 persons, an increase of only 1/10 of 1 percent from 1981. Yet, total employment for stations having 5 or more employees reflected a gain of nearly 5000 employees, or 3.2 percent over 1981 data. Both blacks and Hispanics in telecommunications are employed mostly as professionals and technicians, not as officials, managers, or sales workers. This is unfortunate since managers and officials in the industry are usually recruited from the ranks of salespeople and marketers. In the cable industry, slightly more than 2000 of the over 40,000 employed are Hispanics—about 5.3 percent—with few in sales or management.

MEDIA GROUPS

In the early 1970s, Chicano activists formed media action groups such as the Mexican-American Anti-Defamation Committee and the Chicano Media Coalition, which later evolved into the National Latino Media Coalition in the mid-1970s and then disbanded in 1979. Since 1981, there has been a dramatic proliferation of local, state, and national media organizations formed by Hispanic professionals.

One of the oldest and largest of these Hispanic media agencies is the California Chicago News Media Association (CCNMA), based in Los Angeles at the University of Southern California Journalism Department. Founded in 1972 as a focal point for Hispanic journalists, the CCNMA has recently served as a catalyst in motivating and assisting the creation of Hispanic groups in electronic and nonprint media.

The National Association of Spanish Broadcasters (NASB) in Washington, DC began operation in 1979, and the Spanish Radio Broadcasters of America (SRBA) based in Albuquerque, New Mexico was founded in 1980. Both are examples of recent organizational developments in broadcasting. The Hispanic Telecommunications Network in San Antonio, Texas, operated by the Roman Catholic Church, offers innovative and useful television programming for Hispanics in the Southwest.

An effective group active in minority media policy is the Bilingual-Bicultural Telecommunications Council, Inc. (Bi-Tel). As a multi-ethnic group organized to combine the skills of academicians, researchers, and practitioners in telecommunications, it is one of the few Hispanic organizations committed to promoting a national Hispanic media policy.

A professional association with a large urban base, Latinos in Communications (LinC), has actively pursued increased job opportunities and attention to Hispanic interests in New York City. During 1983, more than fifty Latinos working at Chicago area television stations formed Hispanics in Television (HIT) to promote progress in employment, programming, and policy-related areas. An important activist group is Minorities in Cable (MIC), a nonprofit organization based in New York City. Founded in 1980 to serve as a national forum, information resource, and recruitment service for the cable industry, it now has in excess of fifteen chapters nationwide. MIC is composed of executive, entrepreneur, public interest, and community groups and academics whose goal is to promote minority interest in cable.

TELEVISION AND HISPANICS

Television services for Hispanics can be grouped into three broad categories: (1) Spanish-language television, (2) English-language commercial television, and (3) cable television programming aimed at Hispanics in Spanish, English, or bilingual format. Although Spanish television has become a more than $50 million per year business, its future is not guaranteed.

No television stations are wholly owned by U.S. Hispanic interests. Majority ownership of the Spanish International Network (SIN) is non-Hispanic. As of early 1982, there were twelve Spanish language television stations in the United States as well as a Spanish station in Houston in the developmental stage. Of the twelve stations, ten are affiliates of SIN. Spanish-language stations operate in New York (WNJU-TV, WXTV), Los Angeles (KBSC-TV, MKEX-TV), San Antonio (KWEX-TV), Miami (WLTV), San Francisco (KDTV), Chicago (WCIU-TV), Phoenix (KTVW-TV), Fresno (KFTV), Corpus Christi (KORO-TV), and Sacramento-Stockton (KLOC-TV). The two independent Spanish stations operating in the United States are WNJU-TV in New York City and KBSC-TV in Los Angeles. Both are owned by the Oak Broadcasting System.

The single most important force in Spanish-language television in the United States is SIN. In 1979, *Advertising Age,* an industry publication, proclaimed the initiation of the biggest shake-up in communications since the introduction of television: the age of satellite communications. Those sweeping changes in the industry had already taken place in 1961, with the launching of Spanish-language KWEX-TV in San Antonio. This was SIN's first station. As the first commercial broadcaster to move to full satellite networking, SIN has grown to represent today a network of over one hundred affiliates. In addition, SIN's network programming signal was also carried by over a hundred cable systems and translators (low-power repeater stations) as of early 1982. SIN, also known as the National Spanish Television Network, provides programming and serves as sales representative for ten of the U.S. Spanish stations. Most of SIN's affiliates are satellite-interconnected and transmit Spanish programming twenty-four hours a day, seven days a week.

Spanish language television in the United States owes its fundamental existence to the revolutionary advances in electronic media technology and its actual development to the aggressive use of this new technology to create the satellite-connected network of SIN, Inc. The future impact of SIN is hopeful.

Another breakthrough in U.S. Hispanic television was the emergence in 1979 of GalaVision, the Spanish-language version of Home Box Office. GalaVision has been described as one of the hottest growth industries in the 1980s, and the service is yet another result of space-age technology. GalaVision is a premium pay television service in Spanish available to cable television subscribers. For an extra cost of about $7.00 to $9.50 per month, Hispanics and interested others with access to a cable hookup can view GalaVision's movies, *novelas,* variety shows, and sports specials.

U.S. Hispanics display a strong preference for Spanish-language over English-language television. Spanish stations consistently draw the largest Hispanic audience among the television stations in the market. *Novelas* make up about one-third of Spanish television's total broadcast time. The most distinctive aspect of Spanish television is the immense importance of the *novela* format, whose audience is primarily female. As with Spanish radio, a sense of loyalty to Spanish television also exists, except that viewers are loyal to specific programs rather than to specific stations.

Most of Spanish television's programming produced within the United States is limited to local news programs, public affairs presentations, talk shows, and an occasional series or special. The majority of Spanish-language television programming aired in the United States is produced in Latin American countries, with Mexico dominating the market.

HISPANIC ELDERLY AND TELEVISION

Important considerations are, first, that most Hispanic elderly do not speak English and thus are dependent on Spanish-language media and, second, that watching television is perhaps one of the most prevalent activities among Hispanic elders. In a nationwide HOPR survey (1982), when respondents were asked what they usually did for relaxation and entertainment, the most frequent response (44 percent) was "watch television." Little, however, is known about the effect that television has had on Hispanic elders, and the differential viewing habits among Puerto Rican, Cuban, Mexican-American, and other Latin American elderly are also not known. Further research is needed in this area, and it is hoped that educational institutions, and foundations, and funding sources will give the field of Hispanic telecommunications much higher priority.

A 1979 Gallup survey reveals that, of Hispanics 50 years of age and older, 59 percent watch Spanish television daily; up to 1 hour is viewed by 16 percent, 1 to 3 hours by 25 percent, and over 3 hours by 14 percent of the Hispanics surveyed in this age group. Older Hispanics are more likely to watch Spanish television than are younger Hispanics. Less affluent Hispanics also view a greater amount of Spanish television than do higher income Hispanics. In general, Hispanic women watch Spanish television more frequently and for longer periods of time than do Hispanic men.

PUBLIC ACCESS

Public Access cable television represents one of the most important opportunities for Hispanic elders and their communities to develop locally based programming that reflects their language, culture, and community concerns. Failure to fully utilize this resource could create a major obstacle to visibility and to minority-oriented programming.

The term public access means that television is run by and for the people, showing programs made by community members. Public Access allows local residents to produce and star in their own television programs. This, however, does not guarantee that large numbers of people will be watching. Public Access channels on cable television were mandated in 1972 by the FCC. The FCC required cable companies to provide public, government, and educational access in the form of an open channel, equipment, and space for use by the general public and community organizations. Public Access television operates on the premise that every individual has the right to mass media access and to an equal voice in community affairs. Thus, minority groups, the aged, and other segments of the population have a greater chance of representation and visibility.

The Hispanic community should give close attention to several important areas in access and make sure that provisions for them are part of the franchise agreement. These areas are: (1) staffing, (2) facilities, (3) equipment, (4) channels, and (5) programming. Cities often ask for one access center per fifty thousand residents. All access should be available to the public, free of charge, on a first-come, first-served basis. This includes access to all facilities, equipment, and channel time.

Many problems must be overcome to make effective use of this resource. A persistent problem is limited amount of portable equipment made available by cable companies and the frequent necessity of repair for hardware. Volunteers and participants should be prepared for a sizeable investment of time because this is a labor- and time-intensive operation. Also, a shortage of editing equipment can effectively undermine the enthusiasm and ability of community groups to produce a final product.

THE ELDERLY AND TELEVISION

The history of the "old-old" in America encompasses the total growth of the mass media, roughly in segments of twenty years. The two decades from 1900 to 1920 were periods involving "talking or listening to talk." The period from 1920 to 1940 witnessed the spread of radio and motion pictures. The 1940s and 1950s were the backdrop to the most widespread of all modes of communication up to that moment in human history—the development and acceptance of television. The 1960s and 1970s brought such refinements as color television.

Television researchers have historically given considerable attention to the viewing habits of children and adolescents but have only occasionally been concerned with those of adults. Even more neglected, until the past decade, were the habits of persons age 65 and over. This state of affairs is incongruous for several reasons. Older people watch more television than any other age group, although older people are infrequently seen on television itself. When they do appear on television, they are often portrayed negatively.

As a source of social models, television is often thought to exert the most powerful influence of all of the mass media. The National Council on Aging (NCOA) takes the position that television is the means by which elimination of ageist stereotyping must occur. Research reveals that television is the single most important source of information for most people.

The general sensory decline that often occurs in conjunction with the aging process is also responsible for increased dependence on television. Reading may be restricted by failing eyesight, and hearing impairment may limit the use of radio. Television, because it provides auditory and visual information simultaneously, allows an older person to fill in perceptual gaps.

The most recent and comprehensive analysis of the image of aging on television to date is the study by Gerbner and his associates. This investigation included a content analysis of prime-time programs for the years 1969 through 1978. Examples of key facts underscored in several studies on aging and television include the following:

1. For the elderly, television viewing clearly ranks as the single most common leisure activity.

2. Program types most consistently viewed are news, documentaries, and public affairs.

3. Much of the subject matter in prime-time programming is action, violence, romance, and comedy. When the elderly appear in these programs, they are often portrayed as either victims or villains.

4. Both the functions of viewing and the viewing habits of the elderly appear to vary with activity level, health status, and degree of losses that often accompany the aging process. Viewing is clearly more indiscriminate for the more isolated and widowed populations than for those who are still married and socially mobile.

What role does television play in the lives of the elderly? The following statements typify common views on this topic:

1. Television provides safe, nonthreatening companionship. Also, some older people "form" fairly intense friendships with television characters.

2. Personal and mediated communication patterns are inversely related over the life-span.

3. A major effect of television is that it offers a convenient way for marking off time.

CASE EXAMPLES

In Reading, Pennsylvania, older people, with some technical assistance, are producing live, two-way cable programs on topics ranging from their mayor to their money. This author visited the system managed by the nonprofit Berks Community Television organization and was impressed with the diversity of programming and the popularity of the cable system, which encouraged inter-generational content. The project was initially funded by the National Science Foundation and administered by New York University's Alternative Media Center (AMC) to evaluate the effect of interactive cable television on the delivery of social services to the elderly. With about $80,000 worth of equipment, AMC combined Reading's existing cable system with hookups for home viewers, portable video equipment, and a complete remote origination unit.

Reading's success in creating authentic "people television" can largely be attributed to its two-way capability and its simple format. The system works because it uses television to involve, not to isolate. The Reading cable system is probably the most successful and the best known in the nation. The extensive cooperation of local officials and of community and service delivery organizations also has contributed significantly to the acceptance and use of the system and, ultimately, to its overall success. However, the Reading example, as well as others, cannot be automatically duplicated or transferred to other systems.

In California, older adults found an outlet for their creative energies through PACE (Public Access Cable Television by and for Elders). This project, no longer in operation, involved older people producing programs for cable television in San Diego, which has a population of over 200,000 persons age 60 and over. PACE programming was cable-cast four hours weekly over the local Public Access channel. Also, a thirteen-week half-hour series aired on Sunday afternoons and reached about 250,000 subscribing households. For those not served by cable, the San Diego State University Center on Aging showed PACE and other senior-oriented video programs countywide at remote viewing rooms in senior centers, libraries, and housing complexes.

The area agency on aging in San Jose, California has produced its own programming with portable equipment for viewing over the local access channel, finding this to be an effective and low-cost outreach tool. It is hoped that other area agencies on aging across the nation will make full use of the community access channels in their efforts to provide information, services, and entertainment to seniors.

The Video Museum Program for the Elderly was formed in the early 1980s as a result of the combined cooperation of a local museum (the Kenosha Public Museum of Kenosha, Wisconsin), an area agency on aging, and other community groups and foundation sources. This innovative project serves as an outreach program that brings museum exhibits and displays to nursing homes, senior centers, nutrition sites, and senior citizen group meetings through a color video media system. A similar video museum project for the Mexican-American, Cuban, Puerto Rican and other Latin American cultures would serve as a source of stimulation and pride to Latinos in the community for young and old alike. The videotapes could also be aired over the community access channels of local cable systems.

TRENDS

The past is not always a predictable guide to the future because of unexpected and rapid developments in technology. The probability and the preferability of any given trend or forecast can be determined only by technological, economic, and consumer forces. The following trends, therefore, are more suggestive than predictive.

1. The number of cable systems carrying Spanish-language programming will continue to grow steadily in the 1980s and will escalate measurably during the 1990s.

2. Spanish-language syndicated television programs will become a regular fixture of the media and will serve as a vehicle for launching the careers of promising stars.

3. Bilingual programs will probably become the most popular format for both television and cable television programming aimed at the U.S. Hispanic community.

4. Cultural age stereotypes and the media are likely to change as the elderly population grows in number and as it evolves into a better educated, more vigorous, and more financially secure group.

5. Television will have an even greater impact on the future aged than on those who are currently elderly (they were not raised with it as an early environmental influence).

6. A new kind of ghetto—engendered by the absence of security and fire alarm systems and isolated by a lack of information from data banks, catalogues, and newspapers—is likely to emerge in the future.

7. The emergence of two-way cable television interface with computers may become the most revolutionary development for the aged and for society at large by the end of this century.

8. Program distribution options made possible by the expansion of cable, direct broadcast satellite (DBS), multipoint distribution service (MDS), and satellite master antenna service (SMATV) may offer profitable opportunities for minority-oriented programming.

SOLUTIONS

The complexity of the cable industry and the numerous problems facing Hispanic elders and other minorities requires a multifaceted approach to participation in cable systems. Opportunities exist in the areas of ownership, employment, management, contracting, construction, and programming, to name only a few. Hispanics might advocate that companies do 20 to 25 percent of their purchasing with minority owned or controlled businesses. The Hispanic community could also urge cable companies to create a contract compliance office with staff trained to locate minority vendors and to help Hispanic and other minority vendors to get started in cable-related fields.

Local origination (LO) programming is programming originated locally by the cable operator. This area of programming is of critical importance to the Hispanic community because it provides opportunities for Hispanic independent producers to serve their communities by joint venturing with cable companies to produce relevant programming. LO might provide opportunities for locally produced Hispanic programming to be distributed on a regional and national level.

Cable television expert Kathy Coster, formerly with the National Cable TV Information Center in Arlington, Virginia, and now producing video programs on aging-related topics for the Maryland Library Video Network in Woodland Maryland, under the sponsorship of the library system, suggested the following action for those wishing to influence programming for local access channels: (1) form a local advisory committee to identify issues, ideas, and resources for local programming; (2) take this information to both the cable company awarded the cable franchise and the nonprofit cable community corporation (or some similar entity if it exists) and work with them on programming; and (3) recruit volunteers to be trained in operating the equipment, in script writing, and in program development.

Videotapes have already been produced in communities throughout the nation on topics related to the Hispanic elderly. The problem is that there is no single agency or clearinghouse where copies can be kept to be loaned, rented, or sold to other cable systems, community access centers, or interested local groups for viewing over their cable systems. Why reinvent the wheel when a videotape may already exist on a certain topic? This knowledge and the availability of the tape might then allow groups to make effective use of their limited time and resources to produce original videotapes on topics or issues that have not yet been covered. A consortium of aging, educational, and cable organizations might develop a proposal and seek funding for this and other projects. Preparing a national directory of Hispanics in cable would be another valuable project that could aid progress.

A promising area for study is the comparison of media representations of aging across cultures. One could conceivably develop an index of the status of the aging in various cultures by examining how elderly characters are portrayed in the contemporary literature of different nations. A comparison of how elders are treated in various Latin American countries and how Hispanic elderly in the United States are treated and how this treatment has changed over time would represent a valuable research project. Educators and gerontologists need to encourage and persuade undergraduate and graduate students to undertake studies, surveys, and research relating to the Hispanic elderly and television. Universities should sponsor forums, seminars, and conferences on Hispanics and telecommunications. The growth of careers in the field of telcommunications makes this a practical and logical possibility for both individuals and institutions.

A fourfold strategy is proposed to maximize the use of existing resources. This multistrategy approach includes: (1) use of tapes that are already produced and that allow for insertion of local information (one to five minutes of local data); (2) use of existing videotapes that are loaned, rented, or purchased from other jurisdictions; (3) production of original programming for viewing over access channels; and (4) use of original or existing programming that can be presented to seniors on a videocassette recorder for viewing at senior centers, nutrition sites, senior housing centers, or meetings and conferences. These tapes may or may not be aired over access channels. This ensures the greatest possible use of the videotape and seeks to reach different members of the Hispanic elderly community.

The 1981 White House Conference on Aging's report featured some recommendations worthy of careful consideration:

1. Those engaged in funding and administering programs for the elderly should examine telecommunications technology as a tool for providing information and services.

2. A clearinghouse should be established for information on telecommunications technology so that older persons can petition for access to new services at affordable rates.

3. Older persons and their advocates should become involved in the franchising process.

4. Public and private sources of funding should provide financing for the education and training of older persons in the skills needed to make effective use of cable television.

5. Public and private agencies should encourage providers of cable systems to link senior centers to nursing homes, adult day care centers, and apartment complexes for older persons and facilitate social interaction among older persons through this technology.

6. Studies need to be conducted to determine the impact, if any, of this new technology on those older persons who do and do not subscribe.

Perhaps the greatest hope for improving the image of Hispanic elders on television lies with Hispanic youth and the encouragement of intergenerational projects. This approach is recommended because about 40 percent of the Hispanic population is under 20 years of age. In addition, cable television's audience is largely youth- and adult-oriented. In addition, subscribers are usually well educated and have incomes that can accommodate the monthly fees charged by cable systems. As early as junior and senior high school, youth could be involved in media projects that involve both themselves and the elderly.

CONCLUSION

The problems are many, but so are the benefits. The consequences of failing to swiftly plan and act can only serve to deny the Hispanic elderly and their communities the progress and services they need. Cable television offers many opportunities for information, news, and entertainment. Developing the strategies and skills needed to convert these opportunities into reality should become one of the objectives of all organizations serving the minority elderly and the Hispanic community.

CABLE TELEVISION INFORMATION RESOURCES
Hispanic-Owned Cable Companies

Buena Vista Cable TV
2036 Lemoyne Street
Los Angeles, California 90026
213/668-1330

Eatonville Cable
18423 Old Buckley Highway
Sumner, Washington 98390
206/863-0425

Mercure Telecommunications, Inc.
7320 4th Street, N.W.; P.O. Box 10160
Albuquerque, New Mexico 10160
505/897-7797

Southwest Cable
P.O. Box 3680
Espanola, New Mexico 87533
505/753-7304

Tele-Vu, Inc.
216 N. Second Street
Grants, New Mexico 87202
505/287-9451

Cable Organizations

Cable Television Information Center (CTIC)
1800 N. Kent Street, Suite 1007
Arlington, Virginia 22209
703/528-6846

Minorities in Cable (MIC)
c/o United Church of Christ
Office of Communications
105 Madison Avenue
New York, New York 10016
212/683-5656

National Cable Television Association (NCTA)
Human Resources Department
1725 Massachusetts Avenue, N.W.
Washington, D.C. 20036
202/775-3550

National Federation of Local Community Programmers (NFLCP)
906 Pennsylvania Avenue, S.E.
Washington, D.C. 20003
202/544-7272

Women in Cable (WIC)
2033 M Street, N.W., Suite 703
Washington, D.C. 20036
202/296-7245

National Hispanic Cable

GalaVision
Same address as SIN

Spanish International Network TV (SIN)
250 Park Avenue, Suite 700
New York, New York 10017
212/953-7507

Spanish Universal Network
2990 Richmond Avenue, Suite 140
Houston, Texas 77098
713/522-2013

REFERENCES

American Jewish Committee. (1977, December 8). Conference report on images of old age in the American media. New York: American Jewish Committee.

Anson, R. (1982, November). Special issue on communications. *Noticias*. Ogden, UT: National Hispanic Council on Aging.

Astor, G. (1975, May). *Minorities and the media*. New York: Ford Foundation.

Black, N. (1981, October 19). Minorities face problems in cable TV. *Washington Post*, p. 15.

Chairen, P., & Sandler, M. W. (1983). *Changing channels*. Reading, MA: Addison-Wesley.

Coster, K. (1983). Unpublished workshop outline.

Coster K., & Webb, B. (1978). *Gray and growing: A manual of video program packages for the older adult*. Baltimore, MD: Baltimore County Public Library.

Guernica, A., & Kasperuk, I. (1982). *Reaching the Hispanic effectively: The media, the market, the methods*. New York: McGraw-Hill.

Gupta, U. (1981, October). Cable TV: Electronic redlining. *Black Enterprise*, 87–94.

Kubey, R. W. (1980). Television and aging: Past, present, and future. *The Gerontologist, 20*

Marron, T. (1980). Cable television programs for the older adult. Unpublished paper, University of Maryland, College Park.

Minorities in media. (1983, September 23). *U.S.A. Today*, p. 8.

National Federation of Local Community Programmers. (1982). Special issue on women and minorities in community television. *Community Television Review*.

Quigley, J. (1982, November). Special report on minority participation in cable. *CTIC Cable Report, 3*.

Report of the Technical Committee on Creating an Age-Integrated Society: Implications for the Media; 1981 White House Conference on Aging. (1980). Washington, DC: U.S. Government Printing Office.

Saxon, A. (1981). Minority marketing in the 80s—electronic media: Television. *Forum, 3*, 22.

U.S. Commission on Civil Rights. (1978, February). *Window dressing on the set— women and minorities in television: A report*. Washington, DC: Author.

U.S. House of Representatives. (1977, September 8). Age stereotyping and television. Hearing before the Select Committee on Aging, 95th Congress. Washington, DC: U.S. Government Printing Office.

Western Gerontological Society. (1978). Special issue on television and aging. *Generations*.

REFERENCES

Achor, S. (1978). *Mexican Americans in a Dallas barrio*. Tucson: University of Arizona Press.

Aguirre, B. E., & Bigelow, A. (1983). The aged in Hispanic groups: A review. *International Journal of Aging and Human Development, 17*(3), 177–201.

Ailinger, R. L. (1985). Beliefs about treatment of hypertension among Hispanic older persons. *Topics in Clinical Nursing, 7*(3), 26–31.

Anson, R. (1980). Hispanics in the United States: Yesterday, today, and tomorrow. *The Futurist, 14* (4), 25–32.

Applewhite, S. R. (1981). Disadvantaged elderly. In N. Ernst, & H. R. Glazer-Waldman (Eds.), *The aged patient: A sourcebook for the allied health professions* (pp. 65–83). Chicago: Year Book Medical.

Bastida, E. (1978). Family structure and intergenerational exchange of the Hispanic American elderly. *The Gerontologist, 18*(5), 48.

———. (1979). Family integration in later life among Hispanic Americans. *Journal of Minority Aging, 4*, 42–49.

———. (1984). The elderly of Hispanic origin: Population characteristics for 1980. *Mid-American Review of Sociology, 9*(1), 41–47.

———.(1984). Reconstructing the social world at 60: Older Cubans in the United States. *The Gerontologist, 24*(5), 465–470.

Becerra, R. M. (1983). The Mexican-American: Aging in a changing culture. In McNeely, R. L. & Colen, J. *Aging in minority groups*. Beverly Hills, CA: Sage.

Becerra, R. M., & Shaw, D. (1984). *The Hispanic elderly: A research reference guide*. Lanham, MD: University Press of America.

Berger, P. S. (1983). The economic well-being of elderly Hispanics. *Journal of Minority Aging, 8*(1–2), 367–46.

Carrasquillo-Morales, H. A. (1982). Perceived social reciprocity and self-esteem among elderly barrio antillean Hispanics and their familial informal networks (Doctoral dissertation, Syracuse University, 1982). *Dissertation Abstracts International, 43 (7-A),* 2463.

Colen J. N., & Soto, D. (1979). *Service delivery to aged minorities: Techniques of successful programs.* Sacramento: California State University, School of Social Work.

Crawford, J. K. (1982). Correlates of chronic illness among older Hispanics. *Society for the Study of Social Problems* 1844.

Cuellar, J. B. (1978). El senior citizen's club: The older Mexican-American in the voluntary association. In B. G. Myerhoff & A. Simic (Eds.), *Life's career aging* (pp. 207–209). Beverly Hills: Sage.

Cuellar, J., & Week, J. (1980). *Minority elderly Americans: The assessment of needs and equitable receipt of payable benefits as a prototype in Area Agencies on Aging* (Final Report). San Diego: Allied Home Health Association.

de Anda, D. (1984). Informal support networks of Hispanic mothers: A comparison across age groups. *Journal of Social Service Research, 7*(3), 89–105.

Dean, C. (1984). Problems encountered by the aged Mexican-American in health care and hospitalization. *Kansas Nurse, 59*(1), 8–10.

Delgado, M. (1982). Ethnic and cultural variations in the care of the aged. Hispanic elderly and natural support systems: A special focus on Puerto Ricans. *Journal of Geriatric Psychiatry, 15*(2), 239–255.

Delgado, M., & Finley, G. E. (1978). The Spanish-speaking elderly: A bibliography. *The Gerontologist, 18*(4), 387–394.

Delgado, M., & Humm-Delgado, D. (1982). Natural support systems: Source of strength in Hispanic communities. *Social Work, 27,* 83–89.

Donaldson, E., & Martinez, E. (1980). The Hispanic elderly of East Harlem. *Aging,* 302–306.

Eribes, R. A., & Bradley, R. M. (1978). Underutilization of nursing home facilities by Mexican-American elderly in the southwest. *The Gerontologist, 18*(4), 363–371.

Fairchild, T. J., & Applewhite, S. R. (1982). Demographics of the minority aged. In American Association of Homes for the Aging (Eds.), *Aging, race and culture: Issues in long-term care* (pp. 15–22). Washington DC: American Association of Homes for the Aging.

Finley, G. D., & Delgado, M. (1979). Formal education and intellectual functioning in the immigrant Cuban elderly. *Experimental Aging Research, 5*(2), 149–154.

Franklin, G. S., & Kaufman, K. S. (1982). Group psychotherapy for elderly female Hispanic outpatients. *Hospital & Community Psychiatry, 33*(5), 385–387.

Freire, P. (1970). *Pedagogy of the oppressed.* New York: Seabury.

Garcia, A. (1981). Factors affecting the economic status of elderly Chicanos. *Journal of Sociology and Social Welfare, 8*(3), 529–537.

———. (1982). Work and retirement of the economic status of elderly Chicanos. In N. J. Osgood (Ed.), *Life after work: Retirement, leisure, recreation, and the elderly.* New York: Praeger.

———. (1984). Life satisfaction of elderly Mexican Americans. *Journal of Minority Aging, 9*(1–2), 30–38.

Gibson, G. (1983). *Our kingdom stands of brittle glass.* Silver Spring, MD: National Association of Social Workers.

Gonzalez, del Valle, A. (1982). Group therapy with aged Latino women: A pilot project and study. *Clinical Gerontologist, 1*(1), 51–58.

Gratton, B. (1987). Familism among the Black and Mexican-American elderly: Myth or reality. *Journal of Aging Studies, 1*(1), 19–32.

Greene, V. L., & Mohanah, D. J. (1984). Comparative utilization of community based long-term care services by Hispanic and Anglo elderly in a case management system. *Journal of Gerontology, 39*(6), 730–735.

Guttmann, D. (1980). *Perspectives on equitable share in public benefits by minority elderly* (Executive Summary). Washington, DC: Catholic University of America.

Holmes, D., Teresi, J., & Holmes, M. (1981). Differences among blacks, Hispanic and whites in knowledge about and attitudes toward long-term care services. New York: Community Research Application.

Kalish, R. A., & Reynolds, D. K. (1977). The role of age in death attitudes. *Death Education, 1*(2), 205–230.

Lacayo, C. G. (1980–1981). *Hispanic support systems and the chronically ill older Hispanic.* Los Angeles: Asociación Nacional pro Personas Mayores.

———. (1980). *A national study to assess the service needs of the Hispanic elderly.* Los Angeles: Asociación Nacional pro Personas Mayores.

———. (1984). Hispanics. In E. B. Palmore (Ed.), *Handbook on the aged in the United States* (pp. 253–267). Westport, CT: Greenwood Press.

———. (Ed.), & Vasquez, C. (Comp.). (1981). *A research, bibliography, and resource guide on the Hispanic elderly.* Los Angeles: Asociación Nacional pro Personas Mayores.

Lockery, S. A. (1982). Ethclass as a predictor of selected service patterns of black, Hispanic and white elderly (Doctoral dissertation University of Southern California, June, 1982). Dissertation Affiliation.

Lopez, A. W., et al. (1984). Health needs of the Hispanic elderly. *Journal of the American Geriatrics Society, 32*(3), 191–198.

Lopez-Aigueres, W., Kemp, B., Staples, F., et al. (1984). Use of health care services by older Hispanics. *Journal of American Geriatric Sociology, 32*(6), 435–440.

Maldonado, D., Jr. (1975). The Chicano aged. *Social work, 20*(3), 213–216.

———. (1975). Ethnic self identity and self understanding. *Social Casework, 56* (10), 618–622.

———. (1979). Aging in the Chicano context. In D. E. Gelfand & A. J. Kutzik (Eds.), *Ethnicity and aging: Theory, research and policy* (pp. 175–183). New York Springer.

———. (1985). The Hispanic elderly: A socio-historical framework for public policy. *Journal of Applied Gerontology, 4*(1), 18–27.

Maldonado, D., Jr., & Applewhite, S. L. (Eds). (1985). *Cross-cultural social work practice in aging: A Hispanic perspective.* Arlington: University of Texas at Arlington, Graduate School of Social Work.

Maldonado, D., Jr., & McNeil, J. (Eds). (1982) *Service strategies in aging: Coping with the times.* Arlington: University of Texas at Arlington, Graduate School of Social Work.

Manuel, R. C. (1980). Leadership factors in service delivery and minority elderly utilization. *Journal of Minority Aging.*

Markides, K. S. (1980). Ethnic differences in age identification: A study of older Mexican Americans and Anglos. *Social Science Quarterly, 60*(4), 659-666.

Markides, K. S., Boldt, J. S., & Ray, L. A. (1986). Sources of helping and intergenerational solidarity: A three-generations study of Mexican Americans. *Journal of Gerontology, 40:* 390–392.

Markides, K. S., Hoppe, S. K., Marin, H. W., et al. (1983). Sample representatives in a three-generation study of Mexican Americans. *Journal of Marriage and the Family, 45*(4), 911–916.

Markides, K. S., & Krause, J. (1985). Intergenerational solidarity and psychological well-being among older Mexican Americans: A three-generations study. *Journal of Gerontology, 40*(3), 390–392.

Markides, K. S., & Vernon, S. W. (1984). Aging, sex-role orientation, and adjustment: A three-generations study of Mexican-Americans. *Journal of Gerontology, 39*(5), 586–591.

Martinez, M. A. (1980). Los ancianos: Attitude of Mexican Americans regarding support of the elderly (Doctoral dissertation, Brandeis, February 1980), Dissertation Affiliation.

Martinez, M. Z. (1979). Family policy for Mexican-Americans and their aged. *Urban and Social Change Review, 12*(2), 16–19.

McNeely, R. L., & Colen, J. L. (1983). *Aging in minority groups.* Beverly Hills, CA: Sage.

Mendoza, L. (1981). Los servidores: Caretakers among the Hispanic elderly. *Generation, 5*(3), 24–25.

Mindel, C. H. (1980) Extended familism among urban Mexican Americans, Anglos, and Blacks. *Hispanic Journal of Behavioral Sciences, 2,* 21–34.

Miranda, M., & Ruiz, R. A., (Eds.) (1981). *Chicano aging and mental health.* Rockville, MD: U.S. Department of Health and Human Services, Public Health Service, Alcohol, Drug Abuse, and Mental Health Administration, National Institute of Mental Health.

Mirande, A. (1977). The Chicano family: A reanalysis of conflicting views: *Journal of Marriage and the Family, 39*(4), 747–756.

———. (1980). Familism and participation in government work-training programs among Chicano aged. *Hispanic Journal of Behavioral Sciences, 2*(4), 355–373.

Montiel, M. (1978). *Hispanic families: Critical issues for policy and programs in human services.* Washington, DC: National Coalition of Hispanic Mental Health and Human Services Organizations.

Newton, F. C. R. (1980). Issues in research and services delivery among Mexican American elderly: A concise statement with recommendations. *The Gerontologist, 20*(2), 208–213.

Perez, A. M. (1981, April). *Boston's Hispanic older workers: A status report with recommendation for training and employment programs.* Boston: Economic and Employment Policy Administration of Boston, Hispanic Office of Planning and Evaluation.

Rathbone, M. E., & Hashimi, J. (1982). The Hispanic elderly: Cuban, Puerto Rican, and Mexican. In E. Rathbone McCuan & J. Hashimi (Eds.), *Isolated elders: Health and social intervention* (pp. 141–175). Rockville, MD: Aspen Systems.

Salcido, R. M. (1979). Problems of the Mexican-American elderly in an urban setting. *Social Casework, 60*(10), 609–615.

Sanchez, A. L. (1983). Salud popular: An ethnographic study of the lay health beliefs and health seeking behaviors of Hispanic elderly. (Doctoral dissertation, University of Washington, 1983) *Dissertation Abstracts International, 44(4-A),* 1142.

Santisteban, D., & Szapocznik, J. (1981). Adaptation of the multidimensional functional assessment questionnaire for use with Hispanic elders. *Hispanic Journal of Behavioral Sciences, 3*(3), 301–308.

Sotomayor, M. (1973, May) *The role of the aged in a colonized situation: An orientation for Mexican American community workers in the field of aging,* Topeka: Institute on Aging.

————. (1975). Social change and the Spanish speaking elderly. *La Luz, 4* (4), 15–16.

Starrett, R. A., & Decker, J. T. (1984). The utilization of discretionary services by the Hispanic elderly: A causal analysis. *California Sociologist, 7*(2), 159–180.

Starrett, R. A., Mindel, C. H., & Wright, R. (1983). Influence of support systems on the use of social services by the Hispanic elderly. *Social Work Research and Abstracts, 19*(4), 35–40.

Stephens, R. C., Oser, G. T., & Blau, Z. S. (1980). To be aged, Hispanic, and female—The triple risk. In M. B. Melville, (Ed.), *Twice a minority, Mexican-American women* (pp. 249–258) St. Louis: C. V. Mosby.

Szapocznik, J., Lasaga, J., Perry, P., & Solomon, J. R. (1979). Outreach in the delivery of mental health services to Hispanic elders. *Hispanic Journal of Behavioral Sciences, 1,* 21–40.

Szapocznik, J., Santisteban, D., Kurtines, W. M., Hervis, O. E., & Spencer, F. (1982). Life enhancement counseling: A psychosocial model of services for Hispanic elders. In E. E. Jones & S. J. Korchin (Eds.), *Minority mental health.* New York: Praeger.

Torres-Gil, F. (1982). *Politics of aging Among elder Hispanics.* Washington, DC: University Press of America.

Torres-Gil, F., & Becerra, R. S. (1977). The political behavior of the Mexican-American elderly. *The Gerontologist, 17*(5), 391–404.

Torres-Gil, F., & Negm, M. (1980). Policy issues concerning the Hispanic elderly. *Aging, 2–5,* 305–306.

Torres-Gil, F. (1986). An examination of factors affecting future cohorts of elderly Hispanics. *The Gerontologist, 26*(2), 140–146.

U.S. Department of Health, Education, and Welfare, Administration on Aging. (1980) The decade of the Hispanic. *Aging, March-April* (305–306).

Valle, R. & Mendoza, L. (1978). *The elder Latino.* San Diego: Campanile Press.

Weeks, J. R., & Cuellar, J. B. (1981). The role of family members in the helping networks of older people. *The Gerontologist 21*(4), 388–394.

Wright, R., Jr. (Ed.). (1980). *Black/Chicano elderly: Service delivery within a cultural context.* Arlington: University of Texas at Arlington, Graduate School of Social Work.

Wright, R., Jr., Saleebey, D., Watts, T. D., & Lecca, P. J. (1983). *Transcultural perspectives in the human services: Organizational issues and trends.* Springfield, IL: Charles C. Thomas.

INDEX

CONTRIBUTORS

ROBERTO ANSON, Commissioner, Montgomery County, Commission on Aging, Bethesda, Maryland

STEVEN R. APPLEWHITE, Assistant Professor, School of Social Work, Arizona State University, Tempe, Arizona

ELENA BASTIDA, Associate Professor, Department of Sociology, Wichita State University, Wichita, Kansas

JEANNINE COREIL, Assistant Professor, Department of Preventive Medicine and Community Health, The University of Texas Medical Branch, Galveston, Texas

JOSE CUELLAR, Senior Ethnogerontologist, Stanford Geriatric Center, Stanford School of Medicine, Stanford University

JOHN M. DALEY, Professor, School of Social Work, Arizona State University, Tempe, Arizona

DANIEL T. GALLEGO, Associate Professor, Sociology Department, Weber State College, Ogden, Utah

ALEJANDRO GARCIA, Professor, School of Social Work, Syracuse University, Syracuse, New York

ALVIN O. KORTE, Professor, Department of Social Work, New Mexico Highlands University, Las Vegas, New Mexico

DAVID MALDONADO, Associate Professor, Perkins School of Theology, Southern Methodist University, Dallas, Texas

KYRIAKOS MARKIDES, Associate Professor, Department of Preventive Medicine and Community Health, The University of Texas Medical Branch, Galveston, Texas

JUAN PAZ, Visting Assistant Professor, School of Social Work, Arizona State University, Tempe, Arizona

ROSELYN RAEL, Associate Professor, Department of Social Work, New Mexico Highlands University, Las Vegas, New Mexico

MELBA SÁNCHEZ-AYÉNDEZ, Associate Professor, Graduate School of Public Health, Medical Science Campus, University of Puerto Rico, Río Piedras, Puerto Rico

MARTA SOTOMAYOR, Executive Director and C.E.O., National Hispanic Council on Aging, Washington, D.C.

FERNANDO TORRES-GIL, Assistant Professor, Ethel Percy Andrus Gerontology Center, University of Southern California, Los Angeles, California

MARGARITA C. TREVIÑO, Director of Research and Development, Baylor Health Care System, BaylorFast, Dallas, Texas

About the Editor

STEVEN R. APPLEWHITE is an Assistant Professor in the School of Social Work at Arizona State University, Tempe. He is the author of *Genetic Screening and Counseling: A Multidisciplinary Perspective* as well as book chapters and monographs on the Hispanic elderly.